Theoretical Approaches to Turkish Foreign Policy

This volume, with contributions from well-respected experts on Turkey, examines how well different theories and frameworks in international relations explain various aspects of contemporary Turkish foreign policy (TFP).

Exploring the value of both structural (neorealist) and ideational (constructivist) approaches, this book's theory-informed case studies on the features of TFP including Neo-Ottomanism; the role of religion; and Turkey's relations with the European Union, the Middle East, Russia, and the United States provide an analytical perspective on developments that have captured the attention of both academics and policymakers. More importantly, this collection examines the shift in Turkey's foreign policy stance from Western and secular (non-sectarian) to Islamist, Turkist, Neo-Ottomanist, and Eurasianist orientations.

With Turkey assuming importance across a number of regions and issues, this book will be a great resource for academics, researchers, and advanced students of Middle East Studies, and Politics and International Relations. This book was originally published as a special issue of the journal *Turkish Studies*.

Paul Kubicek is Professor of Political Science and Director of International Studies at Oakland University, USA. He has published widely on Russian and Turkish politics and has taught at Koç University, Boğaziçi University, and Antalya Bilim University in Turkey. He is the editor of the journal *Turkish Studies*.

Theoretical Approaches to Turkish Foreign Policy

Edited by
Paul Kubicek

LONDON AND NEW YORK

First published 2024
by Routledge
4 Park Square, Milton Park, Abingdon, Oxon, OX14 4RN

and by Routledge
605 Third Avenue, New York, NY 10158

Routledge is an imprint of the Taylor & Francis Group, an informa business

Introduction, Chapters 1–3 and 5–8 © 2024 Taylor & Francis
Chapter 4 © 2022 Hakkı Taş. Originally published as Open Access.

With the exception of Chapter 4, no part of this book may be reprinted or reproduced or utilised in any form or by any electronic, mechanical, or other means, now known or hereafter invented, including photocopying and recording, or in any information storage or retrieval system, without permission in writing from the publishers. For details on the rights for Chapter 4, please see the chapter's Open Access footnote.

Trademark notice: Product or corporate names may be trademarks or registered trademarks, and are used only for identification and explanation without intent to infringe.

British Library Cataloguing-in-Publication Data
A catalogue record for this book is available from the British Library

ISBN13: 978-1-032-41345-7 (hbk)
ISBN13: 978-1-032-41346-4 (pbk)
ISBN13: 978-1-003-35764-3 (ebk)

DOI: 10.4324/9781003357643

Typeset in Minion Pro
by codeMantra

Publisher's Note
The publisher accepts responsibility for any inconsistencies that may have arisen during the conversion of this book from journal articles to book chapters, namely the inclusion of journal terminology.

Disclaimer
Every effort has been made to contact copyright holders for their permission to reprint material in this book. The publishers would be grateful to hear from any copyright holder who is not here acknowledged and will undertake to rectify any errors or omissions in future editions of this book.

Contents

Citation Information   vii
Notes on Contributors   ix

Introduction: Contrasting theoretical approaches to Turkish foreign policy   1
Paul Kubicek

1. The motives behind the AKP's foreign policy: neo-Ottomanism and strategic autonomy   15
M. Hakan Yavuz

2. Populism, victimhood and Turkish foreign policy under AKP rule   37
Mehmet Arısan

3. The transnational politics of religion: Turkey's Diyanet, Islamic communities and beyond   57
Ahmet Erdi Öztürk and Bahar Baser

4. Erdoğan and the Muslim Brotherhood: an outside-in approach to Turkish foreign policy in the Middle East   78
Hakkı Taş

5. An examination of the underlying dynamics of Turkey-European Union relations through the lenses of international relations theory   99
Oya Dursun-Özkanca

6. Constructing a realistic explanation of Turkish – US relations   121
Lenore Martin

7. Structural dynamics, pragmatism, and shared grievances: explaining Russian-Turkish relations   140
Paul Kubicek

8 Between escalation and détente: Greek-Turkish relations in the aftermath of the Eastern Mediterranean crisis 158
Ioannis N. Grigoriadis

Index 177

Citation Information

The chapters in this book were originally published in the journal *Turkish Studies*, volume 23, issue 5 (2022). When citing this material, please use the original page numbering for each article, as follows:

Introduction
Contrasting theoretical approaches to Turkish foreign policy
Paul Kubicek
Turkish Studies, volume 23, issue 5 (2022) pp. 645–658

Chapter 1
The motives behind the AKP's foreign policy: neo-Ottomanism and strategic autonomy
M. Hakan Yavuz
Turkish Studies, volume 23, issue 5 (2022) pp. 659–680

Chapter 2
Populism, victimhood and Turkish foreign policy under AKP rule
Mehmet Arısan
Turkish Studies, volume 23, issue 5 (2022) pp. 681–700

Chapter 3
The transnational politics of religion: Turkey's Diyanet, Islamic communities and beyond
Ahmet Erdi Öztürk and Bahar Baser
Turkish Studies, volume 23, issue 5 (2022) pp. 701–721

Chapter 4
Erdoğan and the Muslim Brotherhood: an outside-in approach to Turkish foreign policy in the Middle East
Hakkı Taş
Turkish Studies, volume 23, issue 5 (2022) pp. 722–742

Chapter 5
An examination of the underlying dynamics of Turkey-European Union relations through the lenses of international relations theory
Oya Dursun-Özkanca
Turkish Studies, volume 23, issue 5 (2022) pp. 743–764

Chapter 6
Constructing a realistic explanation of Turkish – US relations
Lenore Martin
Turkish Studies, volume 23, issue 5 (2022) pp. 765–783

Chapter 7
Structural dynamics, pragmatism, and shared grievances: explaining Russian-Turkish relations
Paul Kubicek
Turkish Studies, volume 23, issue 5 (2022) pp. 784–801

Chapter 8
Between escalation and détente: Greek-Turkish relations in the aftermath of the Eastern Mediterranean crisis
Ioannis N. Grigoriadis
Turkish Studies, volume 23, issue 5 (2022) pp. 802–820

For any permission-related enquiries please visit:
http://www.tandfonline.com/page/help/permissions

Notes on Contributors

Mehmet Arısan is Associate Professor at Istanbul University, Faculty of Political Sciences, Department of Political Science and International Relations, Turkey. He has published book chapters and articles on Turkish political transformation, modernity, and emergence of national identity. His current research interests are political discourse analysis, formation of political subjectivities, and turkish political modernization.

Bahar Baser is Associate Professor of Politics at Durham University, UK. She is also Associate Research Fellow at the Security Institute for Governance and Leadership in Africa (SIGLA) at Stellenbosch University, South Africa. Her research interests include ethno-national conflicts and political violence, conflict resolution, third-party mediation, migration, and diaspora studies.

Oya Dursun-Özkanca is Professor of Political Science and Endowed Chair of International Studies at Elizabethtown College, USA. She is the author of *Turkey–West Relations: The Politics of Intra-alliance Opposition* (2019) and *The Nexus Between Security Sector Reform/Governance and Sustainable Development Goal-16: An Examination of Conceptual Linkages and Policy Recommendations* (2021).

Ioannis N. Grigoriadis is Associate Professor and Jean Monnet Chair of European Studies at the Department of Political Science and Public Administration at Bilkent University, Ankara, Turkey. He is also Senior Fellow and Head of the Program on Turkey at the Hellenic Foundation for European and Foreign Policy (ELIAMEP). His research interests include late Ottoman and Republican Turkish politics and history with a focus on nationalism and democratization.

Paul Kubicek is Professor of Political Science and Director of International Studies at Oakland University, USA. He has published widely on Russian and Turkish politics and has taught at Koç University, Boğaziçi University, and Antalya Bilim University in Turkey. He is the editor of the journal *Turkish Studies*.

Lenore Martin is Professor at the Department of Political Science and International Studies at Emmanuel College, Boston, USA, and Associate of both the Weatherhead Center for International Affairs and the Center for Middle Eastern Studies at Harvard University, USA. She co-chairs the Middle East Seminar at Harvard. She has written books and numerous articles analyzing national security in the Gulf, the larger Middle East, and Turkey.

Ahmet Erdi Öztürk is Associate Professor of Politics and International Relations at London Metropolitan University, UK. He is also Marie Sklodowska-Curie Fellow at Coventry University, UK, and German Institute for Global and Area Studies (GIGA), Hamburg, Germany. He is the author of *Religion, Identity and Power: Turkey and the Balkans in the Twenty-First Century* (2021) and co-editor of *Authoritarian Politics in Turkey* (2017); *Ruin or Resilience? The Future of the Gulen Movement in Transnational Political Exile* (2018); and *Islam, Populism and Regime Change in Turkey* (2019).

Hakkı Taş is Research Fellow at the German Institute for Global and Area Studies (GIGA), Hamburg, Germany. His research interests include populism, political Islam, and identity politics, with a special focus on Turkey and Egypt. His research has been funded by several institutions, including the Swedish Institute, Alexander von Humboldt Foundation, and Gerda Henkel Foundation.

M. Hakan Yavuz is Professor of Political Science at the University of Utah, Salt Lake City, USA. He has published widely on the collapse of the Ottoman Empire, Islamic movements, and Turkish politics.

INTRODUCTION

Contrasting theoretical approaches to Turkish foreign policy

Paul Kubicek

ABSTRACT
This article introduces a Special Issue dedicated to applying international relations theories to Turkish foreign policy. More specifically, it contrasts structural or neo-realist approaches with ideational or constructivist ones, suggests general strengths and shortcomings in each, and briefly suggests how both might apply to TFP. It also introduces the eight substantive articles in the Special Issue.

Turkish foreign policy (TFP) has become a significant topic of interest, evidenced by frequent media coverage, a myriad of policy papers, and numerous more rigorous academic studies. This can be partially explained by Turkey's centrality on a number of pressing regional and global issues, as well as Turkey's foreign policy activism and its status as a 'rising' or 'emerging' power. Most accounts of contemporary TFP also remark on its apparent shift away from its longstanding focus on the West towards one that is both more oriented toward the Middle East and Eurasia and more devoted to advancing a more nationalist, sectarian, or even neo-Ottoman or neo-imperial agenda.[1] This shift cannot be simply explained by or dated to the rise of the Justice and Development Party (*Adalet ve Kalkınma Partisi*, AKP) in 2002, as there have been notable changes in TFP in the two decades of AKP rule. In particular, an early focus on 'Zero Problems with Neighbors,' which featured a push for European Union (EU) membership, multidirectional and multilateral diplomacy, conflict mediation efforts, emphasis on trade and economic policy, democracy promotion, and soft power[2], has given way, certainly by 2015/2016, to a foreign policy that is, in many respects, more aggressive, unilateral, often openly anti-Western and revisionist, and centered on hard power, strategic autonomy, and security concerns.[3] Examples include Turkey's actions in Syria, Libya, the Eastern

Mediterranean, and the Caucuses, establishment of military bases in the Middle East and Africa, closer ties with Russia, and anti-Western rhetoric from its leaders.

While even casual observers of TFP can all agree that something *is* different about many of its most recent manifestations, there is no consensus about what is behind this shift. This special issue of *Turkish Studies* aims to fill this gap, dedicating itself to a theory-informed analysis of recent developments in TFP. More specifically, it examines which one of two[4] major perspectives in international relations theory—neo-realism or constructivism, or, put differently, structural or ideational perspectives—better explains some of the most important policies and policy shifts under the AKP. Collectively, it presents several empirically-rich papers that develop and test hypotheses and expectations arising from these theories. Whereas each contributor may be more comfortable with or more inclined to emphasize one perspective over the other, we aim to have a balance of perspectives in our analysis of contemporary TFP. If the overall conclusions—TFP has multiple drivers, both structural and ideational perspectives can give one purchase to understand particular phenomena, and these perspectives are often not mutually exclusive and may present similar expectations —do not present a consensus view favoring one paradigm over the other, it is nonetheless our hope that this project will contribute to on-going debates and offer some new insights.

More specifically for this special issue, we wish to interrogate Turkey's apparent turn away from its longstanding Western and secular (non-sectarian) orientation in foreign policy, what one might label a 'Kemalist' approach, to one that finds more room for other identities or geopolitical orientations (e.g. Islamist, Turkist, Neo-Ottomanist, Eurasianist). While such a framing would seemingly privilege the constructivist position insofar as these other foreign policy approaches appear are based on identities that openly challenge the Kemalist or more traditional orientation, we also wish to take into consideration the underlying factors and context that have given more prominence to these new voices and perspectives, including changes in the international or regional power structures, that might open up new possibilities for Turkey. For example, an analysis of Turkey's recent engagement with Russia or activism in the Middle East might acknowledge ideational factors such as the rise of a pro-Russian 'Eurasianist' discourse, the emergence of a Neo-Ottoman orientation, or sectarianism/Islamism as helping to drive or shape TFP, but at the same time be aware of changing global and regional dynamics (e.g. power vacuums caused by Western disengagement, Russia's centrality to the conflict in Syria, Turkey's own rising power) that also affect TFP. Sorting out structural and ideational factors may not always be easy, but the aim is to move beyond description and provide a solid analysis of important developments in TFP.

We might also note that this debate over competing theoretical frameworks has larger implications. If neo-realist perspectives offer the most explanatory power, it follows that domestic politics or ideologies of the AKP matter far less, and that what was are actually witnessing in contemporary TFP—as opposed to the justifications that might be proffered for said policies—would occur under any Turkish government. While policymakers cannot immediately transform the international balance of power, they could alter regional power alignments—e.g. Western actors could become more involved in security issues in Turkey's immediate neighborhood and/or work to improve Turkish security—and thereby affect TFP. Conversely, if ideational elements are paramount, we would expect the drivers of change in TFP to be found in the machinations of Turkish politics with the rise of different political actors, identities, and ideologies. In this case, policymakers would want to focus more on the development and implications of different foreign policy approaches or orientations that underlie much of TFP, recognizing that the apparent shift in TFP is not simply situational or a result of cost–benefit calculations but more the result of an identity shift that may have larger implications, particularly with respect to Turkey's future place in Western institutions.

In this introductory framework paper, we will outline the main features of neo-realism and constructivism and tentatively suggest how they might help us understand TFP, both past and present. At the same time, we will suggest how each may have particular limitations or might work hand-in-hand with other frameworks to provide a fuller explanation of particular features of TFP. We will also briefly introduce each article and note its contributions to the larger project.

Neo-realism and Turkish foreign policy

Neo-realism is one of the most well-used paradigms in the study of world politics and foreign policy. Like its forebear, realism, neo-realism focuses on power, recognizing that maintaining and securing power is a chief aim of states under conditions of anarchy and, subsequently, that power capabilities—chiefly defined in military or economic terms—enable or constrain state behavior. Neo-realism's chief insight is that the power distribution in the international system among great powers provides an overarching structure to the system and conditions the behavior of states. Kenneth Waltz, usually credited as the founder of neo-realism, suggested that states 'are free to do any fool thing they care to, but they are likely to be rewarded for behavior that is responsive to structural pressures and be punished for behavior that is not.'[5]

Neo-realism can be viewed, on some level, as a product of the Cold War, as it argued (at least in Waltz's original formulation) for the stabilizing features of bipolarity in producing a balance of power. Over the past several decades, a neo-realist would thus expect profound and potentially destabilizing changes as the Cold War's bipolar system gave way to a (brief) period of American hegemony into the early 2000s which in turn as evolved into a more multipolar environment characterized by American disengagement from some of its previous commitments, the emergence of China as a global power, and the rise of numerous other countries (albeit on a more regional level).[6]

Turkey is a regional or middle power, inherently limited by its power (in)capabilities in some aspects of foreign policy.[7] Simply put, Turkey lacks the means to set unilaterally the regional or global agenda or transform the systemic balance of power, and its foreign policy is thus often reactive and/or predicated on working within particular alliance structures or power arrangements. Nonetheless, neo-realism provides a set of expectations or hypotheses about the behavior of middle powers under various structural conditions. In particular, neo-realism would expect middle powers to be most constrained under conditions of bipolarity, as during the Cold War.[8] Indeed, during that time Turkey was ensconced in the Western bloc, a position that limited its ability to fashion a more independent or activist foreign policy. True, Turkey did not always see eye-to-eye with its fellow Western partners, but with some notable exceptions where Turkey had both high interest and decisive power capabilities (e.g. Cyprus), it more or less followed the lead of the United States, the most powerful Western nation. It recognized that joining with the West was the best means to ensure its own security against a Soviet Union that had, at times, threatened Turkey's sovereignty and interests. In other words, Turkey's Western orientation had a clear *Realpolitik* logic and addressed what Karaosmanoğlu identified as its primary longstanding fears—fear of territorial loss and fear of abandonment.[9] Aydın, likewise adopting a historical perspective, noted that structural factors linked to the Cold War explain the high degree of continuity in TFP.[10]

The end of the Cold War and the collapse of the Soviet Union allowed Turkey to pursue some of its interests in regions (e.g. Central Asia, the Caucuses) that previously had been effectively 'off limits'. However, in the first post-Cold War decade, American hegemony defined much of world politics, and Turkish initiatives, particularly in the post-Soviet space, often received the blessings of Washington, as Turkey and the secular, Western-oriented elements of the 'Turkish model' were seen as a means to advance the larger Western agenda.[11] Furthermore, because Turkey was in no position to challenge US/Western hegemony and faced a more benign security environment, many of its initiatives through the early 2010s had a more 'liberal' cast, focusing on positive-sum economic interactions, democracy promotion (particularly in light of the 'Arab Spring'), international cooperation (e.g. The Alliance of Civilizations initiative), and multilateral institutions such as the EU, UN or G-20. Süsler suggests that much of TFP in the early 2010s corresponded with what a neo-realist might have expected of a 'middle power'[12]

However, it is worth noting that even during this period, Turkey's status as a rising power—evidenced both by its growing economy and increasing confidence and activism in global and regional affairs—made it at times critical of the existing international order, perhaps best evidenced by then-Prime Minister Recep T. Erdoğan's 2013 declaration (later much repeated) that 'the world is bigger than five' (referring to the UN Security Council)[13] and Turkey's interest in being included among the BRICS (Brazil–Russia–India–China–South Africa), which have been pushing for their own greater say in global affairs. Öniş and Kutlay note that because Turkey's status is that of an 'emerging middle power,' as opposed to an 'established' one such as Canada or Australia, it means that it faces a dilemma insofar as it may be 'both critical of the existing liberal order dominated by the established Western powers and, at the same time, have an incentive to be a part of an international order based on liberal norms.'[14] In this sense, one can assess 'revisionist' elements of TFP. Insofar as Turkey seeks to re-align itself or alter existing power structures to allow it to pursue policies more in line with its (perceived) power.[15]

This dilemma has become more apparent over time, as the overall global system and regional dynamics in Turkey's neighborhood have seen profound changes, opening up new opportunities for Turkish policymakers. Oğuzlu dates this shift to the global financial crisis of the late 2000s, which weakened both Western countries and the legitimacy of the Western-created liberal international order.[16] By the 2010s, China's rise was undeniable, and Russia also (re)emerged as an important actor on several global and regional security issues. Both challenged the West. Multipolarity (or post-unipolarity, in Oğuzlu's terms) resulted from balancing against US dominance as well as America's retreat from core elements of its global leadership role under both Presidents Obama and Trump. At the same time, many of Turkey's more diplomatic or soft power initiatives failed, most clearly in the case of Syria. 'Zero problems with neighbors' turned into 'nothing but problems with neighbors'. This included relations with the West—its EU bid stalled, it was blamed for causing the refugee/migrant crisis of 2015/2016, Western countries offered lukewarm (at best) support for President Erdoğan during and after the July 2016 coup attempt, it was subjected to US economic sanctions, and the US provided political and military support for Kurdish groups in Syria that Ankara considered a fundamental threat to its own security. As a result, TFP has been increasingly 'securitized' and Turkey has also embarked upon various 'soft balancing' policies vis-à-vis its erstwhile

Western partners, particularly by cooperating with Russia.[17] Several of these more recent trends will be analysed in papers in this volume.

Although neo-realism can provide parsimonious explanations of international politics, it has limitations. One is that, with some exceptions (e.g. a military build-up or attack), the international environment does not present unambiguous challenges or opportunities. States often confront a menu of possible responses to a given situation. Yes, a neo-realist would suggest that when constraints are fewer, a middle power such as Turkey will have more opportunities to exercise or augment its power, but global or regional power balances by themselves do not suggest the manner or the guise under which a state pursues its objectives. Put somewhat differently, neo-realism may present, at best, only vague hypotheses about a state's foreign policy. Waltz himself concedes that states' actions are not determined by structure, but that structures 'shape and shove.'[18] In other words, the international structure provides context (constraints and/or opportunities) and may act as a necessary but not sufficient element to explain states' behavior. In the case of Turkey, for example, one could imagine that in today's multipolar environment Turkey could theoretically seek greater power and influence by pursuing a range of competing policies in its immediate neighborhood, including those promoting democracy and good governance, cultivating economic relations with its less developed neighbors, bandwagoning with the leading powers to advance its own or multilateral goals, balancing against those same powers to reshape regional dynamics, or even adopting a more unilateral course. It could also rely more (or less) on hard or soft power, although the latter concept would be alien to most working in the neo-realist tradition. Indeed, as is revealed in the articles in this Special Issue, Turkey arguably has pursued all of the above, at various times and with varying degrees of commitment, in the past decade. How much neo-realism, by itself, is able to explain the twists and turns of TFP is unclear.

Perhaps the most common critique against neo-realism is that it purposefully overlooks country-level factors (e.g. regime type, domestic political considerations, leadership) that may shape foreign policy. Indeed, neo-realism notoriously assumes that all states, sharing the same goal to amass power in order to survive under conditions of anarchy, are essentially the same. In Waltz's words, neo-realism 'abstract[s] from every attribute of states except their capabilities.'[19] However, one can easily imagine that foreign policy often may be shaped by domestic or individual-level factors. Neoclassical realism, an amendment of sorts to neo-realism that attempts to blend together structural factors with intervening variables such as domestic political imperatives, ideologies, perceptions, or even leader-specific features, can be employed to remedy some of these lacunae. In this way, it 'accounts for state behavior in a way that a more parsimonious systems-level theory is unable to achieve.'[20] Indeed, several articles in this Special Issue employ to neoclassical realism to supplement a more straightforward neo-realist or structural account. However, whether systemic and domestic variables can be genuinely disentangled and whether this more comprehensive approach can yield well-defined, useful hypotheses (as opposed to *ad hoc* explanations) is not clear.[21]

Constructivism and Turkish foreign policy

Constructivism, which has risen to prominence in international relations theory in the twenty-first century, offers more than just a 'tweak' or amendments to neo-realism. Rather, it stands as comprehensive challenge to structural approaches.[22] Constructivism rests on a number of core claims, most notably that international relations are determined more by identities, shared ideas, and an intersubjective social context than by material forces.[23] Actors develop relations with others through shared norms and practices. Structures by themselves do not have inherent meaning or significance; their meanings are constructed and interpreted by actors, giving them more agency (e.g. Wendt's famous claim that 'anarchy is what states make of it'). States' interests are not *a priori* givens or as simple as seeking survival or maximizing power. Rather, they derive from identity/ideational factors, and as these factors change, interests can change. In contrast to neo-realism, constructivists emphasize the role of culture, which animates identities. Finally, constructivists also, at least implicitly, devote more attention to domestic politics, as who rules matters significantly in constructing or changing a state's identity.

Constructivist approaches have been well-utilized in the study of TFP. For example, Turkey's longstanding orientation toward the West (as well as its relative aloofness for several decades from the Middle East and broader Muslim world) has been explained as a manifestation of the country's Kemalist identity, which equated modernization with Westernization and predicated Turkey's joining of the 'civilized world' with maintaining strong ties with Western countries. In Bozdağlioğlu's words

> Turkey's decision to join the West was not simply motivated by a desire for protection, but rather stands as an integral part of the Turkish modernization project ... .[This] created a Western identity for the state, which determined the course of Turkish foreign policy.[24]

However, as Bagdonas notes, Kemalism also has multiple interpretations and points of emphasis (including, in her view, a 'realist' element prioritizing survival as well as an anti-imperialist outlook that tempered Turkey's identification with the West), thereby providing a 'repertoire' for decision-makers.[25] For example, while Kemalism in many places and circumstances paid respect to multilateralism and international law, it also emphasized the 'Turkishness' of the state and Turkey's concomitant obligation to protect ethnic Turks in Cyprus and the Caucuses.[26] Furthermore, Kemalism was not unchallenged within Turkey, and as other actors (most prominently Islamic-oriented ones) achieved some measure of influence, they impinged upon the prevailing Western identity and orientation in TFP.[27]

This last point has expanded into a veritable cottage industry since the rise of the AKP, as its self-declared goal of constructing a 'New Turkey' represents a challenge to the longstanding identities in both Turkish domestic politics and TFP. The largest strand in this vast (and ever-expanding) literature emphasizes the AKP's Islamic orientation and subsequent turn away from the West and toward the Middle East and broader Muslim world, a development most associated with the reconceptualization of TFP's fundamental tenets by Foreign Minister (2009-2014) (later Prime Minister [2014-2016]) Ahmet Davutoğlu. Davutoğlu emphasized history and geography in identifying both TFP's priorities and strengths, but fundamentally this was a geo-cultural argument, resting on cultural ties (Islam and Ottoman heritage) and the subsequent potential to exercise 'soft power'.[28] What this meant in practice, however, has arguably changed over time. Some writers identified TFP's normative aspects that rested on its (former) status as a 'Muslim democracy' or a moralist discourse (most evident in the initial years of the Syrian conflict) centered in part on Islamic solidarity.[29] Some noted how the (re)imagination of the Ottoman period was invoked in a benign, multicultural manner to foster inter-civilizational dialogue (e.g. the 'Alliance of Civilizations' initiative),[30] whereas others (typically writing more recently) see the rise of Turkey's Islamic identity as empowering nativist authoritarians and legitimizing civilizational competition, eventually reducing any previously affective dimension of relations with the West to transactionalism.[31] Still others view TFP as more of an epiphenomenon, focusing on how debates over and shifts in foreign policy are driven by domestic political disputes, utilized to legitimize a particular domestic agenda or to take the battle over Turkish identity 'outside' into the foreign policy arena [32] It is worth noting as well that whereas 'Islamic' or 'Neo-Ottoman' are the most frequently invoked identities in the AKP era—and contributors in this special issue will explore both—there are other cultural (Eurasianist, pan-Turkist) and political (populist) identities that have been embraced by Turkish political actors and have arguably exercised some influence over TFP.[33]

It is worth mentioning, however, that while constructivist and ideational perspectives offering more contextually-contingent explanations and address some of the problems associated with structural approaches, they are not without their own shortcomings. Often, they de-emphasize critical questions about *why* particular ideas/identities/discourses take hold at a particular time

—to which a neo-realist might retort (to employ Marxist terms) that the constructivist 'super-structure' is merely a reflection of the material (power) base. In this respect, one might argue that constructivism might be more a method or approach than a full-blown causal theory, capable of describing and even analysing processes but harder-pressed to isolate variables and develop testable hypotheses.[34]

Plan of the special issue

This special issue contains both broader, thematic explorations of TFP as well as more focussed studies of TFP directed to different countries and/or regions.

Hakan Yavuz considers the question of neo-Ottomanism, a phenomenon that has received extensive scholarly and popular attention. His far-reaching article places the development of neo-Ottomanism in historical context and documents how it has evolved during the AKP period. While neo-Ottomanism is commonly understood as grounded in ideational or cultural terms, Yavuz notes that it dovetails with a more 'realist' push for strategic autonomy in TFP. In this sense, he finds that neo-Ottomanism also responds to more 'realist' or structural imperatives, thus providing an option for TFP in a dynamic strategic environment. Yavuz, however, remains sceptical that Turkey's movement away from the West on both ideational and strategic grounds will yield many positive outcomes.

Mehmet Arısan's article is the most explicitly constructivist or ideational, as it traces the development and impact of what he identifies as a conservative populist discourse in Turkey. He argues that such a discourse has been politically relevant since the 1950s, employed by Islamic-oriented actors against the secular, Westernized Kemalist establishment. The AKP has taken this discourse to a new level, and in foreign policy it is manifested not only in civilizational discourse regarding Turkey's role in the Islamic world, but also in a sense of victimhood. Arısan suggests this also feeds into conspiracy thinking, particularly in regards to Western countries, which has become more pronounced after the 2016 coup attempt in Turkey.

Erdi Oztürk's and Bahar Baser's article focuses on the role religion plays in TFP, including an analysis of both historical and contemporary cases. They emphasize that the place of religion in TFP is multifaceted, involves both state and non-state actors, and has been more prominent under the AKP. While consideration of religion is far more in line with a constructivist approach that emphasizes culture, history, and identity, they find that the effectiveness of Turkish policy across different regions is affected by several considerations, including power relations between Turkey and the target state or region.

Hakki Taş, in the first of five regional/country-specific case studies, considers TFP in the Middle East, in particular Ankara's relations with various affiliates of the Muslim Brotherhood (MB). Given both the AKP's and the MB's Islamic-oriented approach to politics, one might expect that relations between the two would illustrate a more ideational or constructivist orientation in TFP. Taş, however, argues that what mattered more was how the MB was able, for a time, to help advance Turkey's material interests in the region, and that structural factors (e.g. multipolarity on the regional level) created spaces for Turkey's activism. Notably, as the MB has been weakened and Turkey also found itself in a more challenging environment, it has tried to distance itself from the MB.

Oya Dursun-Özkanca's contribution examines Turkish-EU relations, in particular their deterioration since the 2016 coup attempt. She finds that structural explanations rooted in balancing behavior are persuasive, but she supplements this with aspects of neoclassical realism that consider domestic or state-level factors as intervening variables. She highlights both Turkey's relative power position and its desire to pursue a more autonomous foreign policy as well as how Turkey and the EU have opposing interests on topics such as Cyprus, the Eastern Mediterranean, Syria, and Libya. In the end, she notes that Turkish-EU relations have become far more transactional in nature, as Turkey's pro-Western orientation has given way to a more nationalist-oriented one.

Lenore Martin's article explores Turkish-US relations, focussing on various crisis that have manifested themselves since 2016 and led to increased tensions and suspicions between the two sides. These include US support for the Syrian Kurds and American refusal to extradite Fethullah Gülen, both of which raised ire in Ankara, and Turkish energy exploration in the Eastern Mediterranean and purchase of an air defense system from Russia, both of which have been harshly criticized by the US and other NATO members. She employs both neo-realism and constructivism to examine these phenomena, but she finds both wanting. Instead, she suggests how a more holistic, integrated neoclassical realist approach, which integrates structural factors with domestic-level variables, may offer better explanations of TFP.

Paul Kubicek explores Turkey's relations with Russia, a long-term adversary with whom Turkey has recently established more friendly and cooperative relations despite the two countries being on opposite sides of conflicts in Syria, Libya, and the Caucuses. He finds that structural explanations, rooted in Turkey's own rising power, disengagement by the West in parts of Tureky's neighborhood, and the functional need to cooperate with Russia on vital issues help explain Turkey's apparent turn to Russia. As for ideational factors, he emphasizes the two countries' shared grievances against the West over the oft-mentioned rise of an 'Eurasianist' ideology or bloc in Turkey. He notes, however, that the 2022 war in Ukraine may reconfigure regional and global politics, creating perhaps a more bipolar situation and thus making Turkey 'choose' between Russia and the West.

Finally, Ioannis Grigoriadis investigates Turkish-Greek relations, which he notes (as with relations with US and Europe overall) have become more conflictual in recent years. He suggests that the lack of prospects for Turkish EU membership have worked against reconciliation between these long-time rivals. Furthermore, he notes that both neo-realist (e.g. regional competition in the region and the rise of powers more hostile to Turkey) as well as constructivist explanations (e.g. the development of the 'Blue Homeland' (*Mavi Vatan*) doctrine that envisions Turkey as a maritime power) shed light on how Turkish-Greek relations have evolved.

While the papers, as a whole, do not argue for one approach over the other —some authors see merit in both, some do favor a particular paradigm, and some are keen to point to weaknesses in different theoretical approaches— our hope is that they do illustrate how international relations theories can shed some light on aspects of TFP while at the same time suggesting that some issues remain unresolved or contentious and thus spur future research.

Notes

1. Early works that picked up on this trend include Öniş, 'Multiple faces'; Sözen, 'A Paradigm Shift'; and Başer, 'Shift-of-axis.'
2. Notable contributions that focus on these features of TFP in the late 2000s-early 2010s include Kirişci, 'The transformation': Kacar and Lesage, 'Turkey's Profile'; and Falk and Farer, 'Turkey's New Multilateralism'.
3. Book length works that document these developments include Cagaptay, *Erdogan's Empire* and Candar, *Turkey's Neo-Ottomanist Moment*.
4. A third 'major school,' liberal-internationalism, we would contend, offers much less explanatory power for TFP *circa* 2020 than neo-realism and constructivism, although it can be invoked to explain the aforementioned emphasis on multilateralism, international institutions, and soft power in the early 2010s.
5. Waltz, 'Evaluating Theories,' 915. The *locus classicus* for neo-realism remains Waltz, *Theory of International Politics*.
6. The most prominent articulation of this position, in particular the dangers of the rise of China, is John Mearsheimer. See Mearsheimer, *The Tragedy*.
7. For extended discussion of Turkey's status as a 'middle power,' see Öniş and Kutlay, 'The dynamics'; Dal, *Middle Powers*; and Süsler, 'Turkey: An Emerging Middle Power.'
8. Holbraad, *Middle Powers*.
9. Karaosmanoğlu, 'The Evolution,' 202.
10. Aydın, 'Determinants of Turkish Foreign Policy.'
11. Bal, "Turkish Model".
12. Süsler, 'Turkey: An Emerging Middle Power.'
13. This has even been labeled a 'campaign' and invoked by Erdogan as injustice. See "Dünya 5'ten Büyüktür' kampanya oldu,' *Hürriyet*, September 26, 2014.

14. Öniş and Kutlay, 'The dynamics,'
15. This point is developed at length by Candar, *Turkey's Neo-Ottomanist Moment*.
16. Oğuzlu, 'Turkish Foreign Policy.'
17. Dursun-Özkanca, *Turkey-West Relations*, utilizes elements of neorealism to analyze these developments.
18. Waltz, 'Evaluating Theories,' 915.
19. Waltz, *Theory of International Politics*, 99.
20. Foulon, 'Neoclassical Realist Analyses.'
21. For an explicitly neoclassical realist account of TFP, see Şahin, 'Theorizing the Change.'
22. The title of a seminal constructivist text, Alexander Wendt's, *Social Theory of International Politics*, is a clear rejoinder to Waltz.
23. There are, to be sure, various strands of constructivism and debates over the advantages and limitations of a constructivist approach. In addition to Wendt, see Hopf, 'The Promise'; Checkel, 'The Constructivist Turn'; Bertucci, Hayes, and James, *Constructivism Reconsidered*; and Kubálková et al, *International Relations*.
24. Bozdağlıoğlu, 'Modernity,' p. 71. See also Bozdağlıoğlu, *Turkish Foreign Policy*
25. Bagdonas, 'A Post-Structuralist Approach,' p. 45.
26. Uzer, *Identity and Turkish Foreign Policy*.
27. Bozdağlıoğlu, 'Modernity.'
28. The best-known source is Davutoğlu, *Stratejik Dernlik*,
29. Dal, 'Assessing Turkey's "Normative Power",' and Bagdonas, 'Reading Turkey's Foreign Policy.'
30. Yanık, 'Constructing Turkish 'Exceptionalism'.'
31. Çınar, 'Turkey's "Western" or "Muslim" Identity,' and Bashirov and Yilmaz, 'The Rise of Transactionalism.'
32. Özpek and Yaşar, 'Populism and foreign policy,' Coşkun, Doğan, and Demir, 'Foreign Policy as Legitimation Strategy' and Hintz, *Identity Politics*.
33. Aktürk, 'The Fourth Style of Politics,' and Köstem, 'When Can Idea Entrepreneurs.'
34. Checkel, 'The Constructivist Turn.'

Disclosure statement

No potential conflict of interest was reported by the author(s).

References

Aktürk, Sener. "The Fourth Style of Politics: Eurasianism as a Pro-Russian Rethinking of Turkey's Geopolitical Identity." *Turkish Studies* 16, no. 1 (2015): 54–79.

Aydın, Mustafa. "Determinants of Turkish Foreign Policy: Historical Framework and Traditional Inputs." *Middle Eastern Studies* 35, no. 4 (1999): 152–186.

Bagdonas, Özlem Demirtas. A Post-Structuralist Approach to Ideology and Foreign Policy: Kemalism in the Turkish Foreign Policy Discourse." PhD Dissertation, Central European University, 2008.

Bagdonas, Özlem Demirtas. "Reading Turkey's Foreign Policy on Syria: The AKP's Construction of a Great Power Identity and the Politics of Grandeur." *Turkish Studies* 15, no. 1 (2014): 139–155.

Bal, İdris. ""Turkish Model" and the Turkic Republics." *Perceptions* 3, no. 3 (1998): 105–129.

Başer, Ekrem. "Shift-of-axis in Turkish Foreign Policy: Turkish National Role Conceptions Before and During AKP Rule." *Turkish Studies* 16, no. 3 (2015): 291–309.

Bashirov, Galeb, and Ihsan Yilmaz. "The Rise of Transactionalism in International Relations: Evidence from Turkey's Relations with the European Union." *Australian Journal of International Affairs* 74, no. 2 (2020): 165–184.

Bertucci, Mariano, Jarrod Hayes, and Patrick James. *Constructivism Reconsidered: Past, Present, and Future*. Ann Arbor: University of Michigan Press, 2018.

Bozdağlıoğlu, Yücel. *Turkish Foreign Policy and Turkish Identity: A Constructivist Approach*. New York: Routledge, 2003.

Bozdağlıoğlu, Yücel. "Modernity,: Identity, and Turkey's Foreign Policy." *Insight Turkey* 10, no. 1 (2008): 55–75.

Cagaptay, Soner. *Erdogan's Empire: Turkey and the Politics of the Middle East*. London: IB Tauris, 2020.

Candar, Cengiz. *Turkey's Neo-Ottomanist Moment: A Eurasianist Odyssey*. London: Transnational Press, 2021.

Checkel, Jeffrey. "The Constructive Turn in International Relations Theory." *World Politics* 50, no. 2 (1998): 324–348.

Çınar, Menderes. "Turkey's 'Western' or 'Muslim' Identity and the AKP's Civilizational Discourse." *Turkish Studies* 19, no. 2 (2018): 176–197.

Coşkun, Bezen, Salih Doğan, and Mustafa Demir. "Foreign Policy as Legitimation Strategy for the AKP's Hegemonic Project of the 'New Turkey'." In *Authoritarian Politics in Turkey: Elections, Resistance, and the AKP*, edited by Bahar Başer, and Ahmet Öztürk, 83–98. London: IB Tauris, 2017.

Dal, Emel Parlar. "Assessing Turkey's "Normative" Power in the Middle East and North Africa Region: New Dynamics and Their Limitations." *Turkish Studies* 14, no. 4 (2013): 709–734.

Dal, Emel Parlar. In *Middle Powers in Global Governance: The Rise of Turkey*. Cham Switzerland: Palgrave Macmillan, 2018.

Davutoğlu, Ahmet. *Stratejik Dernlik: Türkiye'nin Uluslararası Konumu*. Istanbul: Küure Yayınları, 2004.

Dursun-Özkanca, Oya. *Turkey-West Relations: The Politics of Intra-Alliance Opposition*. Cambridge: Cambridge University Press, 2019.

Falk, Richard, and Tom Farer. "Turkey's New Multilateralism: A Positive Diplomacy for the Twenty-First Century." *Global Governance: A Review of Multilateralism and International Organizations* 19, no. 3 (2013): 353–376.

Foulon, Michiel. Neoclassical Realist Analyses of Foreign Policy." *Oxford Research Encyclopedia of Politics*, September 2017, accessed April 4, 2002 at tinyurl.com/yckr4pem.

Hintz, Lisel. *Identity Politics Inside Out: National Identity Contestation and Foreign Policy in Turkey*. Oxford: Oxford University Press, 2018.

Holbraad, Carsten. *Middle Powers in International Politics.* London: Macmillan, 1984.
Hopf, Ted. "The Promise of Constructivism in International Relations Theory." *International Security* 23, no. 1 (1998): 171–200.
Kacar, Yusuf, and Dries Lesage. "Turkey's Profile in the G20: Emerging Economy, Middle Power and Bridge-Builder." *Studia Diplomatica* 63, no. 2 (2010): 125–140.
Karaosmanoğlu, Ali. "The Evolution of the National Security Culture and the Military in Turkey." *Journal of International Affairs* 54, no. 1 (2000): 199–216.
Kirişçi, Kemal. "The Transformation of Turkish Foreign Policy: The Rise of the Trading State." *New Perspectives on Turkey* 40 (2009): 29–56.
Köstem, Seçkin. "When Can Idea Entrepreneurs Influence Foreign Policy? Explaining the Rise of the 'Turkic World' in Turkish Foreign Policy." *Foreign Policy Analysis* 13, no. 3 (2017): 722–740.
Kubálková, Vendulka, Nicholas Onuf, and Pail Kowert, eds. *International Relations in a Constructed World.* Armonk NY: ME Sharpe, 1998.
Mearsheimer, John. *The Tragedy of Great Power Politics (Updated Edition).* New York: WW Norton, 2014.
Oğuzlu, H. Tarik. "Turkish Foreign Policy in a Changing World Order." *All Azimuth* 9, no. 1 (2018): 127–136.
Öniş, Ziya. "Mutliple Faces of the 'New' Turkish Foreign Policy: Underlying Dynamics and Critique." *Insight Turkey* 13, no. 1 (2011): 47–65.
Öniş, Ziya, and Mustafa Kutlay. "The Dynamics of Emerging Middle-Power Influence in Regional and Global Governance: The Paradoxical Case of Turkey." *Australian Journal of International Affairs* 71, no. 2 (2017): 164–183.
Özpek, Bilgehan. B., and N. Tanriverdi Yaşar. "Populism and Foreign Policy in Turkey Under the AKP Rule." *Turkish Studies* 19, no. 2 (2018): 198–216.
Şahin, Mehmet. "Theorizing the Change: A Neoclassical Realist Approach to Turkish Foreign Policy." *Contemporary Review of the Middle East* 7, no. 4 (2020): 483–500.
Saraçoğlu, Cenk, and Özhan Demirkol. "Nationalism and Foreign Policy Discourse in Turkey Under the AKP Rule: Geography, History, and National Identity." *British Journal of Middle Eastern Studies* 42, no. 3 (2015): 301–319.
Sezal, Mustafa, and Ihsan Sezal. "Dark Taints on the Looking Glass: Whither 'New Turkey'?" *Turkish Studies* 19, no. 2 (2018): 217–239.
Sözen, Ahmet. "A Paradigm Shift in Turkish Foreign Policy: Transition and Challenges." *Turkish Studies* 11, no. 1 (2010): 103–123.
Süsler, Buğra. "Turkey: An Emerging Middle Power in a Changing World?", LSE Ideas, May 2019, available at http://eprints.lse.ac.uk/107799/1/LSE_IDEAS_Turkey_Middle_Power_May_2019.pdf.
Uzer, Umut. *Identity and Turkish Foreign Policy: The Kemalist Influence in Cyprus and the Caucuses.* London: IB Tauris, 2010.
Waltz, Kenneth. *Theory of International Politics.* Reading MA: Addison-Wesley, 1979.
Waltz, Kenneth. "Evaluating Theories." *American Political Science Review* 91, no. 4 (1997): 913–917.
Wendt, Alexander. *Social Theory of International Politics.* Cambridge: Cambridge University Press, 1999.
Yanık, Lerna. "Constructing Turkish "Exceptionalism": Discourses of Liminality and Hybridity in Post-Cold War Turkish Foreign Policy." *Political Geography* 30, no. 2 (2011): 80–89.

The motives behind the AKP's foreign policy: neo-Ottomanism and strategic autonomy

M. Hakan Yavuz

ABSTRACT
This paper examines the role of ideas and identities in the making of the AKP's foreign policy in Turkey. After briefly examining the institutional and international constraints on Turkish foreign policy before 2002, the discussion turns to the driving factors in three evolutionary stages of AKP's foreign policy. It becomes apparent that a neo-Ottoman worldview and accompanying identity constitute the interpretive framework of the AKP's political elite. The article traces how this worldview became dominant in Turkey's policy making after the government dismantled the country's Kemalist institutions and the AKP consolidated its political power.

Introduction

This article asserts that Turkey's quest for strategic autonomy has been motivated by its unearthing of a neo-Ottoman identity in the pursuit of national needs and interests.[1] To fully understand the factors driving Turkey's foreign and security policies, one must examine the changes in both the domestic and international environments. Thus, neoclassical realism is the most useful approach to decipher the macro- and micro-dynamics of Turkey's foreign policy.[2] This requires scholars and policy makers to shuttle between *inside-out* and *outside-in* perspectives to develop a comprehensive picture of Turkey's foreign policy. The first requires readers to understand the role of individual and group identities and their respective ideologies in the making of foreign policy, along with the dynamic interaction between the state and society.[3] This perspective must be complemented with an outside-in approach, focusing on global and regional factors and their effect on Turkey's domestic and foreign policy. This article focuses on the identity and ideology of the ruling Justice and Development Party (*Adalet ve Kalkınma Partisi*, AKP) to unpack Turkey's recent foreign policy.

The leaders of Islamic-oriented AKP, which has ruled the country since 2002, believe that the West, especially the United States (US), is a fading power and the twenty-first century multipolar system offers more opportunities for Turkey to carve out an autonomous foreign policy path which will better serves its interests. While it still maintains relatively close ties with Western powers, the pro-Islamist elite, whose worldview is profoundly shaped by a neo-Ottoman identity, has jettisoned the old infatuation with the West and cultivated purely transactional and interest-based relations with the US and the European Union (EU), without any shared normative base as a guiding strategic philosophy. This new foreign policy, also labeled as neo-Ottoman, is derived from a new form of Islamo-Ottoman-Turkish nationalism. The case of Turkish foreign policy indicates, however, that the boundary between identity and national interest is intertwined, as the former plays a constitutive role in defining the latter. Islamic-cum-Ottoman identity dominates President Recep T. Erdoğan's sense of national identity and this, in turn, defines the Turkish national interest.[4] Yet, Erdoğan's assertive foreign policy has done more to induce regional countries to align against Turkey than in opening spaces for realizing Turkish national ambitions.

Understanding the hegemonic Islamic (neo-Ottoman) interpretive framework of the AKP elite is crucial to decipher contemporary Turkish foreign policy. This framework is heavily shaped by an Islamized reading of Ottoman history and Islamic civilization. The AKP elite believes that the Erdoğan era ended the hegemony of Kemalist 'native aliens' and brought Islamically-oriented politicians and intellectuals into power.[5] This framework advances several core ideas: the modern-state system in the Middle East is artificial as it was imposed by European imperial powers; Islam is the native vocabulary and way of life of the region; the region's current rulers are puppets of the West and alien to Islamic civilization; and the Muslim Brotherhood and the AKP seek to correct this historical abnormality. The Arab Spring is regarded '[as] just doing that, normalizing Middle East history by bringing to power political parties that truly represented the peoples of the Middle East.'[6] AKP politicians thus expected the Arab Spring to form political solidarity among Muslim countries. However, understanding the worldview of Erdoğan and former Foreign Minister (later Prime Minister) Ahmet Davutoğlu are also crucial in unpacking recent foreign policy moves in Libya, the Karabakh region and Syria, along with the rupture in relations with Egypt and its regional allies.[7] As Erdoğan single-handedly determines the parameters of foreign policy, his sense of history, ideology and identity are critical to understanding the continuity and changes in Turkish foreign policy.

This article will focus on the following questions: what were the defining features of Turkish foreign policy?; how did the new discovery of national identity as Islamic and Ottoman shape AKP's activist and ambitious foreign policy?; what explains the AKP's pro-EU foreign policy in the first years of its rule (2002-210)?; why and how did the AKP move to more Islamized and adventurist foreign policy during the Arab Spring?; and how should we explain the nationalistic and militarized foreign policy since 2015? As far as the role of institutions and ideas in foreign policy are concerned, there are two different periods to consider. From 2002-2007, there were potent, effective institutions in place as the AKP sought to consolidate its legitimacy. During this period, the AKP did not yet bring the whole scope of its Islamized neo-Ottoman identity into the realm of foreign policy making. As the AKP eventually gained control of the state institutions after the 2007 national elections, it did not hesitate to bring its Islamized neo-Ottoman and civilizational identity intentions to the forefront. However, other factors, including security anxieties arising from the issue of Kurdish separatism and Turkish hostility towards the intervention of great powers in its neighborhood underpinned another feature of Turkish foreogn policy: the quest for strategic autonomy.

To reiterate, the AKP's foreign policy went through several stages but it remained identity-based and security-oriented. A neo-Ottoman-Islamic identity is redefining the goals of Turkish foreign policy by imbuing regional issues with aspects of shared Ottoman history and tradition. Turkey's divided self-identity also sits at the center of its foreign policy dualities. By duality, I mean a condition where national identity and interests are domestically contested by rival sectors of the society. This entails two distinct and often opposed civilizational orientations.[8] In 'Clash of Civilizations,' published more than a quarter of a century ago, Samuel Huntington defined Turkey as a 'torn country'.[9] He explained this phrase as signaling Turkey's painful and ongoing difficulties to shift its orientation to another civilizational perspective (Western) while not wanting to see its Islamic roots fully subsumed to Western-inspired thinking. Turkey's Western identity has been repeatedly challenged by new societal and political actors and the search for Turkey's Islamic roots has, in the last few decades, certainly been rejuvenated.[10] The history of modern Turkey can thus be seen as the story of the conflict between two Turkeys —one a secularist and progressive nation (Kemalist) and the other Islamic and conservative (neo-Ottoman). As the AKP, representing the latter, gained control of the state, it also transformed Turkish foreign foreign policy.[11]

Post-national identity: the neo-Ottomanism of the AKP

The debate surrounding neo-Ottomanism highlights the tensions associated with the entangled histories of empire and nation-state in the Turkish context.[12] To unpack neo-Ottomanism, one must examine how competing ideals and memories of the Ottoman Empire persist in guiding the ongoing nation-state project of the Republic of Turkey. Although the Kemalist nation-building project used all means possible to suppress Ottoman heritage, this imperial 'ghost' has haunted the state and society since the empire's collapse in the last century. As Turkey became more secular, which was accompanied by moving closer to the West, the search for its lost soul intensified. The Ottoman past offers a reservoir of experiences, lessons, and opportunities about how to reshape the present and come to terms with the roots of Turkish identity. As Turkey becomes more self-confident and economically prosperous, neo-Ottomanism echoes loudly in every corner of Turkish society's cultural, political, and social spaces. Fundamentally, contemporary Ottoman nostalgia is about rewriting the past to cope with present-day issues. In the process of trying to recapture history through a favorably colored lens, the yearning for past glories fuels a primal desire for autonomy, along with legitimizing claims to regional power status, which many segments of Turkish society view as historically proper.

In the process of reconstituting this neo-Ottoman identity, the Republic's founding philosophy is being reformulated today, and the fragments of the past provide the essential means for this reconstruction.[13] For the conservative AKP elite, Turkey's national identity was something to be rediscovered in the Islamic and Ottoman past in opposition to the Kemalist westernizing reforms, which tried to construct national identity within the contours of the European model. The AKP's geopolitical imagination is heavily informed by its understanding of the Ottoman Empire and this identity underlies its quest for strategic autonomy. Turkey's growing conservative public largely supports this newly imagined 'Ottoman' Turkey and this helps legitimize Turkey's authoritarian turn under the presidential system with Erdoğan at the top. Thus, he has instrumentalized foreign policy to mobilize his domestic constituencies.[14] It is built on 'Making Turkey Great Again' (a Turkish version of the slogan that drew nationalists to Donald Trump in the US), but also reflects his inflated sense of self and power in attempting to redesign the region according to his Ottomanized ideological worldview. Turkey had been projected as the only regional power capable of restoring order and stability. Erdoğan's proactive foreign policy has diverted attention from Turkey's domestic problems while highlighting the status and power of a new Turkey. This, in turn, activates populist neo-Ottoman nationalism while stripping critics of Erdoğan's foreign policy of their legitimacy, at least in the eyes of Erdoğan's most loyal supporters.

Foreign policy in Turkey after 2011 has thus become a constituent component of Erdoğan's Islamo-nationalist project. By identifying the West as an external 'other' or 'foe,' Erdoğan is redefining the nation as Islamo-Ottoman and articulates national interests primarily on that basis. There is a mutually constitutive relationship between the AKP's understanding of national identity and its neo-Ottoman foreign policy. This differentiates his vision of Turkey from the secular-Kemalist vision that had been in place since the early days of the Turkish Republic.

Sociopolitical origins of Turkish foreign policy

To understand Ankara's foreign policy after the end of the Cold War, one should examine the interaction between domestic and international factors. However, a more nuanced understanding requires an inside-out approach by stressing the impact of new political actors and their political identity, which is based on collective memory and new challenges. Neoclassical realism – nuanced with a constructivist emphasis on ideas, memories, and human agency – leads to the most useful avenue in unpacking the factors driving this new post-Cold War foreign policy. Identity and civilizational outlook, along with concerns for security and economic development, are the most critical factors that influence contemporary Turkish foreign policy. But, one must start with the brief general framework of Turkish foreign policy put in place shortly after the Republic of Turkey was established in 1923.

Turkey's pro-Western reforms in concert with the goal of creating a secular nation-state following the European model framed the new republic's foreign policy. The founding fathers, whose personalities and ideological worldviews were shaped by the traumatic demise of the Ottoman state and decades-long wars (1877-1920), had placed their faith in science and Western values. They implemented Westernizing reforms to shape the state and society, commonly known as Kemalism, which became the state ideology. The Kemalist worldview provided an operational map of action for the foreign ministry's bureaucracy. Turkish society, an amalgam of diverse ethnic, religious and ideological groups, was dominated by the homogenous Kemalist state structure.[15]

During the first two decades of the Republic (1920s-1940s), its foreign policy became an extension of its domestic Westernizing reforms. The young Republic wanted to be enveloped securely to realize these 'civilizing' reforms. Due to external threats, Mustafa Kemal Atatürk formed two major alliances during the interwar period. Turkey led the 1934 Balkan Entente against the expansion of Mussolini as well as the 1937 Saadabad Pact to create stability around the country.[16] The founding fathers of the Republic deliberately stayed away from Middle East politics because (1) they wanted to reorient Turkey's domestic culture and institutions toward the West; (2) they did not want a conflict with European colonial powers; and (3) they carried negative memories from the First World War regarding the Arab elite's cooperation with the British against the Ottomans. Because of these perceptions and limited resources, the five defining principles of Turkish foreign policy until World War II were driven by an inward looking policy that focused on domestic transformation; the decision not to pursue a revanchist or irredentist foreign policy; preservation of national security, sovereignty of the state and territorial integrity; improvements in economic conditions; and the close identification with Western institutions and norms to establish long-lasting peace with major powers in Europe.

The cold war and Turkish foreign policy

Turkey remained neutral during World War II to ensure its territorial integrity and preserve sovereignty. During this period, an *outside-in* perspective is more useful to decipher Turkey's foreign policy. When, after the war, the Soviets began to present a clear external threat—demanding, for example, changes to the Soviet-Turkish border, basing rights on the straits, and a revision of the Montreaux Convention[17]—Turkey was in no position, by itself, to resist Soviet aggression. Ankara had no option but to rely on the US, and it eventually joined NATO in 1952. Within the bipolar Cold War conditions, Turkey played the role of buffer state as a barrier to Soviet expansionism, and this, in turn, helped to improve Turkey's image in the US as well as in Western European countries.

When the international system was dominated by two superpowers, Turkey's foreign and security policies were an extension of its ties with NATO and the US. Turkey had no choice but to compromise its foreign policy and embrace strong security ties with the US and follow American wishes. This foreign policy orientation helped Turkey to resist Soviet territorial demands and ideologically to stay connected to the country's Westernization project of Turkey while receiving economic and technological support from the West. Negative outcomes of this Western orientation were the loss of autonomy in foreign policy; dependence on the US in regard to the defense industry; and a further disconnect from its geopolitical space. The conflict over Cyprus and the US support for the Greek Cypriots compelled Ankara to craft step by step a multidimensional foreign policy by developing closer ties with other countries, especially in the Middle East states. However, these new overtures never replaced Turkey's pro-Western orientation.

Post-cold war foreign policy

In the post-Cold War era, more so than external factors, internal factors, especially the shifting dynamic between the state and society, and the formation of new political elite, shaped foreign policy. During this period, Turkey pursued a more independent foreign policy and sought to maximize its interest and minimize instability in its region. Turkish foreign policy evolved in three stages: the period of a more assertive and identity-based foreign policy of Turgut Özal (1983-1993), the period of weak coalition governments (1993-2002), and the AKP period (2002-present). After briefly emphasizing the economic basis of neo-Ottoman thinking during the period of Özal, I will focus on the AKP period.[18]

Changes in the political map were paralleled in the economic and cultural spheres, especially starting with the liberalization policies of Özal, who became prime minister in 1983. With the shift toward an export-oriented economic policy of the 1980s, Anatolian and newly urbanized entrepreneurs in Istanbul, largely Islamic oriented in cultural terms and close to Özal's newly created Motherland Party, challenged the preeminence of state-subsidized large industrialists.[19] The dynamic private sector known popularly as the 'Anatolian tigers' along with emerging new economic centers eroded the economic base of secularism. Segments of the new, mainly Anatolian, bourgeoisie used its wealth to promote an alternative Ottoman-Islamic worldview and identity. Economic diversification led to a parallel effect in Islamic-Ottoman cultural discourse and symbols used to communicate that discourse. Thus, in addition to the increasing political power of the provincial capital, the ideological basis of the Turkish Republic was challenged by privatization in education and the media, as television stations, newspapers, and magazines representing a wide spectrum of views, including Islamic ones, proliferated. Civil society associations, including cultural foundations, trade unions and organizations arising from Sufi networks, steadily used their votes and economic means to influence the political parties of the center-right as well as the religious-right. Moreover, counter-intellectuals, supported by the Anatolian bourgeoisie worked to re-shape a collective memory and identity that more amenable to Islam and the Ottoman past. This new discourse treats Turkey more as a civilization-state that represents the Ottoman Empire/Islam legacy than as a nation-state in the more conventional contemporary terms.[20] This pushed forward the recruitment of religiously oriented party loyalists for high office in the bureaucracy and the police.

These socio-cultural transformations form a crucial background to the rise of the AKP and had an important impact on reformulating Turkey's identity and national interest. They challenged the traditional statist discourse of the Kemalist establishment, whose sensations of siege and doom were exacerbated as their mission to become part of the West was abruptly halted by what was perceived as the determination of the EU to exclude 'Muslim Turkey' while it contemplated the admission of former Warsaw Pact adversaries. At the same time, Turkey's foreign policy became hostage to the domestic insecurity arising from the Kurdish and Islamic challenges to the homogenizing policies of Kemalism. After the end of the Cold War, due to the weak coalition governments and ineffective politicians, the Turkish military filled the vacuum and Turkish foreign policy was shaped by security concerns, especially the Kurdish problem.[21] The army remained in a strong position in the first decade of the post-Cold War period (1990-2002) and worked closely with the Ministry of Foreign Affairs.

AKP's foreign policies (2002-2022)

No party has instrumentalized foreign policy to the extent of the AKP, which has used foreign policy to gain legitimacy, undermine its domestic opponents, mobilize its grassroots base, differentiate itself from previous governments, and transform itself into a marker of its new Islamo-nationalist identity.[22] In this section, the following question is addressed: what are the driving factors of Erdoğan's foreign policy? Under Erdoğan's leadership, Turkish foreign policy has passed through three stages: Europeanization and a market-oriented foreign policy (2002-2010); the Arab Spring and Islamization of foreign policy (2011-2013); and the quest for autonomy and the militarization of foreign policy (2013-present). A major binding element that underlies these three stages is the reconfigured discovered national identity comprising Islamic, Ottoman, and Turkish dimensions. This new identity, as suggested above, is rooted in nostalgia for the Ottoman Empire. Thus, the construction of a neo-Ottoman vision, identity, and project constitute the normative basis of AKP's foreign policy. The AKP's search for a new national identity (Ottoman and Islamic) and its 'new foreign policy vision' (strategic autonomy) has become most visible in the most recent stage.

Duality of foreign policy: European and neo-ottoman?

Erdoğan believes that Turkey is the heir of the caliphate and the Ottoman Empire and should, like the Ottomans, lead the Muslim world as the regional hegemon. Likewise, Davutoğlu refers to the Ottoman past to criticize and delegitimize Kemalist identity and foreign policy as artificial and not in the interest of his imagined entity of an Islamo-Turkish nation. From Davutoğlu's perspective, Ottoman history and its civilizational practices constitute the core identity and daily practices of people in post-Ottoman territories. This past has been reproduced as collective memory and in Davutoğlu's view, it imposes its 'will' on the domestic and foreign policy of Turkey.[23] Many elites of the AKP, including former President Abdullah Gül, argue that Turkey has to do what its history (a romanticized Ottoman past) requires of it. After defining the nation on the basis of its imagined past, the AKP elite has defined its national interest in terms of restoring Turkey's historical greatness and in leading the Muslim word.

This is a clear rupture from the Kemalist conception of national identity and foreign policy vision. Erdoğan and his cohorts challenged traditional Turkish strategic culture (Westernization and the closer ties with the Western institutions) with two new assumptions that Turkey was: (a) a great country with the Ottoman legacy and mission; and (b) a key international player to shape its regions (the Middle East, the Balkans, and the Caucasus). The narrative representing the belief of Turkey as a great country comes from a rose-colored-lens reading of the Ottoman imperial past, which seeks to challenge the successes of the Kemalist Republic by measuring the net results against an idealized portrait of the Ottoman past. This neo-Ottomanist orientation propels a narrative heavily based on exaggerated remembrances of an Islamic Ottoman past and efforts to establish a civilizational foreign policy as if Turkey is the head of the Islamic (Sunni) world. Ibrahim Kalin, Erdoğan's chief foreign policy advisor, insists that the history and culture of Turkey constitute an asset in the national government's desire to become a regional leader.[24] From the writings of Kalin, one can conclude that his imagined nation is constituted by Islamic culture and Ottoman history. He defines the nation in opposition to the Kemalist conception of a secular and Westernized Turkish nation seeking to Europeanize on its own terms. Meanwhile, Davutoğlu insists that the Muslim communities in the Balkans are 'entrusted' to Turkey because of the Ottoman legacy. He argues that the former Ottoman territories carry the Ottoman spirit in their daily practices and their desire to see Turkey as the leader and heir of this imperial glory. Davutoğlu coined the term '*tarihdaş*' (people sharing the same history and imperial space) to reimagine the post-Ottoman ecumene, that consists of those who all shared the Ottoman past and live in post-Ottoman territories. Thus, he argued quite paternalistically that the Republic of Turkey, as the inheritor of the Ottoman past, has a historical responsibility toward its *tarihdaş* and is a natural leader to shepherd them.[25]

The AKP leaders imagine themselves as Ottoman rulers and have sought to project Turkish power into the ex-Ottoman territories, many (but not all) of which are inhabited by Muslims. The AKP leadership also contends that Turkey, as an internationally recognized and respected actor, has the necessary hard and soft capacities to pursue its strategically autonomous foreign and security policy. Davutoğlu seeks to draw the parameters of Turkish foreign policy from his sense of historic mission. He says:

> This situation is nothing but the weight of the element of history as one significant parameter of power making itself felt. Turkey, which has been seen as the inheritor of 700 years of Ottoman history, is still seen as a political

center by the people in its close territorial basin. The Ottoman reminder in Turkey's close territorial basin makes these groups see Turkey as the power to protect them in their original land or as a place of refuge in case of a possible attempt at abolition. This leads Turkey to come face to face with new regional missions oriented by the parameters of history. This is nothing but an expression of the fact that history exceeds the will limited to particular periods and exerts its authority over daily politics.[26]

Ian Lesser argues that Turkey 'remains a place where historical images and geography retain their full force for both policymakers and the public.'[27] Indeed, the shadow of history constitutes the national security culture of Turkey. The collective memories about persecution, deportation, massacres and eventually the partition of Turkey with the 1920 Treaty of Sevres set the framework of Turkish strategic culture, which is shaped by the traumas of the collapse of the Ottoman state. These memories play an important role in the sacralization of Turkey's security culture.[28]

Davutoğlu persistently argues that Turkey is not an ordinary nation-state because of its history, geographic location and culture. Turkey needs to pursue an effective foreign policy, bearing in mind its shared memories and responsibilities. Turkey, for Davutoğlu, is neither a frontier country to contain Russia nor a bridge between the East and West. Instead, it is a central state with a historic mission to provide stability to its neighboring regions. Although many scholars read this new activist foreign policy as a sign of expansionism, the intent was not to dominate the regions but rather redefine the role of Turkey as an inheritor of the Ottoman legacy and provide stability.

It is important to recall that the AKP's worldview was shaped by the Islamist ideology of the National Outlook Movement of Necmettin Erbakan, whose foreign policy vision was based on binaries, such as Islamic versus Western identity, victimizer versus victim, and colonial versus colonized.[29] Erbakan wanted to create an Islamic version of NATO, the EU, and/or UNESCO. Erbakan preferred cooperation and an alliance of Muslim countries under the leadership of Turkey. For Erbakan, the West represented colonialism, racism, and exploitation. He accused the West of being the source restricting development and triggering irreconcilable political problems in the Middle East. Erbakan positioned himself by defining his foes as puppets and sycophants of Western colonialism. He described his foreign policy as '*şahsiyetli dış politika*' (an independent formulation or a foreign policy that reflects the historic mission of Turkey as the heir of the Ottoman Empire). Erbakan, then Prime Minister, was removed from office by the February 28, 1997 'soft' military coup, as the military viewed his Islamism as a threat to the Republic. Erbakan's ouster, however, opened a space for young Islamists, such as Erdoğan and Gül, who would go on to form the AKP, which positioned itself as more European and liberal in orientation.

Europeanization stage (2002-2010)

There are three defining characteristics of this stage: it was activist, ambitious and sought domestic and international legitimacy. The members of the AKP leadership, Erdoğan, Gül, and Bülent Arınç, presented themselves as reformers supporting Turkey's European orientation and accepting the secular nature of the state. They presented the EU membership as a way of differentiating themselves from Erbakan, enhancing their legitimacy in the eyes of the West, undermining the power of the military and the rigid Kemalist establishment, and ending the Kemalist nation-building project in favor of recognizing diverse identities in society. They embraced the EU as an ally to protect the liberal legal and political system in order to prevent the country from banning political parties with an Islamic orientation. EU membership became the orienting compass point for all anti-Kemalist forces such as Islamists, Kurds, and liberals. Erdoğan masterfully exploited EU membership criteria to undermine the power of the secular Kemalist establishment, to expand political space, and to enhance his legitimacy in the eyes of Western powers.

In this period the AKP also sought to diversify Turkey's foreign policy to foster regional integration by stressing economic and cultural factors through the introduction of visa-free travel and numerous free-trade agreements with Middle Eastern countries. Erdoğan shifted from a security-centric domestic and foreign policy to more rule-oriented, liberal, and democratic solutions by stressing zero problems with neighbors. This included refusal to support the US invasion of Iraq in 2003. This shift in policy also involved uncoupling security concerns associated with Kurdish and Islam-based political and cultural claims. Erdoğan's approach to the Kurdish issue in the early 2000s had two goals: to remove the power of the military from the political system and expand its electoral base among the Kurdish voters. With the EU's help, Erdoğan succeeded in marginalizing the military while allying himself with the EU membership process.

Additionally, the regional security environment was also more conducive to accepting these changes in domestic and foreign policies, and the AKP pushed forward numerous initiatives to foster peace and better relations with neighboring states. For example, Erdoğan did not hesitate to display his pro-European inclination by ignoring nationalist forces and pushing for the unification of Cyprus on the terms of the UN-led and EU-supported Annan Plan in 2004.[30] In 2008 Turkey initiated a dialogue with Armenia to open the border and establish diplomatic relations. It also tried to create a free-trade zone with several Middle East countries. Due to these initiatives, Turkey was recognized as a 'Muslim model country' in terms of working and internalizing the Western norms of the international system.[31]

In addition to a pro-Western foreign policy for tactical reasons, there were still aspects of neo-Ottoman identity starting to affect foreign policy. In 2005, Ekmeleddin Ihsanoglu became the secretary-general of the Organization of Islamic Cooperation. Together with Spain, Ankara formed the Alliance of Civilizations in the UN to work toward cooperation and better understanding of diverse civilizations. When Israel launched Operation Cast Lead in Gaza, Erdoğan accused Israel of instigating state-sponsored terrorism against 'innocent Muslims.'[32] Criticism of Israel improved Erdoğan's image in the Middle East. In 2009, Davutoğlu brokered a deal between Serbia and Bosnia by encouraging the Serbian Parliament to recognize and apologize for the Srebrenica massacres and this opened the way for Bosnia to name an ambassador to Serbia. Turkey and Brazil worked together to address the nuclear program of Iran.[33] During this period, Ankara consistently preferred negotiation as the first resort and volunteered to take on the mediating role to address regional issues.

Islamization of foreign policy (2010-2013)

The biggest transformation of Turkish foreign policy occurred during the Arab Spring. The external context of this shift is important to acknowledge. When Turkey did not receive unequivocal support for full EU membership, Davutoğlu argued that Turkey would wait no longer at the EU door and that Turkey should form its 'own axis' by developing closer ties with the Middle East, the Balkans, and the Caucasus. This strengthened the discourse surrounding Ottomanism and a shared Ottoman culture. Erdoğan and Davutoğlu openly supported the Tunisian and Egyptian revolutions and offered to help these countries. These rebellions also helped the AKP to shed the pretense of a Europhile identity and unfetter its Islamist identity, which had been long suppressed in official Turkish diplomatic circles. Davutoğlu presented the Turkish experience as an example of 'inspiration' for what nascent democracies in the region could accomplish. The dominant justification for Turkey's pro-revolutionary policy was that 'Ankara has to be on the right side of history' by supporting the Arab people against the corrupt governments. The AKP leaders presented Turkey as an ideal model in reconciling modernity and Islam, along with democracy. The AKP elite even insisted that the Arab Spring created new opportunities for Turkey to become an 'order-instituting country' to reconfigure the state-society relations in some countries.

The most fruitful period of Erdoğan's foreign policy occurred when the Arab Spring was unfolding and the Muslim Brotherhood networks were winning elections or joining the coalition governments throughout the region. The Arab Spring demonstrations were framed by Erdoğan as the manifestation of the will of the people against the secularist, Westernized, and puppet rulers of the Middle East who received aid from the West. The AKP leadership defended its policy of supporting Muslim Brotherhood organizations and the change in Arab world governments on the basis of supporting the will of the people and Turkey's return to a constructive role in the Middle East. As developed more in Hakki Taş's contribution to this Special Issue, this policy also played to the strategic interests of Turkey, as the AKP welcomed the end of Western hegemony in the region by siding with Islamic and pro-Turkey groups to remake the region's geopolitics.[34] Mohammed Morsi, Rashid Ghannouchi, Khaled Mashal, and many other prominent members of the Muslim Brotherhood would regularly attend AKP meetings as guests. Their presence, in turn, reminded AKP supporters that Erdoğan is the natural leader of the Muslim world and that the AKP works toward achieving the broad goal of Islamic solidarity. During this time Erdoğan also championed the rights of various downtrodden Muslim groups, such as Palestinians, Rohingya Muslims, Moro people in the Philippines, and Kashmiri Muslims (with the notable exception of Uighurs in China) in his project of cementing Islamic solidarity.

However, contrary to expectations, the Arab Spring did not lead to democratization but rather the formation of more authoritarian regimes in the region. The July 2013 Egyptian coup overthrew Morsi, and the civil war in Syria hammered the last nail in Turkey's hope of leading and shaping the Middle East. Instead, Turkey now had a failed states on its border and Kurdish secessionists occupying much of northern Syria.

Meanwhile, Turkey's pro-Muslim Brotherhood policy throughout the region led to forming a major axis against Turkey, fostered by Saudi Arabia and the United Arab Emirates (UAE). When the Gulf countries imposed an embargo on Qatar in 2017 to force the country to halt support for the Muslim Brotherhood and close the Turkish military base inside Qatar, Turkey responded by strengthening military and economic ties with Qatar and upgrading its military presence in Qatar. The clash between the Saudi-Emirati axis and Turkey/Qatar alliance continued to destabilize the region. In return, Saudi Arabia and the UAE targeted Turkey and used financial resources to weaken Erdoğan and his political standing in the Muslim world. Saudi Crown Prince Muhammed bin Salman described Turkey as part of a 'triangle of evil,' along with Iran and the Muslim Brotherhood.[35] The horrific killing of Saudi dissident journalist Jamal Khashoggi in the Saudi consulate in Istanbul not only shredded its ties with Turkey but also ruined the public image of Saudi Arabia. Turkey accused the Saudi Crown Prince of orchestrating Khashoggi's murder and shared critical evidence with international media to amplify the damage to the Crown Prince's image and credibility.

Turkey was now in a weakened position and faced a number of crises, particularly along its Syrian border, where a Kurdish insurgency and Islamic

State in Iraq and Syria (ISIS) were both active, and due to the Syrian refugee crisis. Ankara worried about the consolidation of the Syrian Kurdish forces and their close cooperation with the Kurdistan Workers' Party (PKK). The situation worsened when the US cooperated with the Kurdish Democratic Union Party (PYD) to defeat ISIS. This act of cooperation was part of Barack Obama's surrogate war doctrine, which in the Syrian context meant outsourcing warfare in whole or in part to the Kurdish militias to minimize the cost of war for US troops.

US alignment with the PYD in Syria became a nightmare for the Turkish military. Turkey was also concerned when the Kurdistan Regional Government (KRG) in Iraq organized an independence referendum in September 2017. Some US officials and NGOs openly called for the establishment of an independent Kurdish state along the Turkish border. This cooperation occurred at the time when the peace process between the Turkish government and the PKK collapsed and the AKP government used full force to suppress a Kurdish urban rebellion in 2015. The Kurdish issue was reclassified as an urgent security matter and Erdoğan closed the doors on seeking a democratic solution to the Kurdish problem. These security challenges forced Turkey to use military might to cope with the issues. After the 2015 national elections, the AKP could not form a new government on its own and allied itself with the far-right Nationalist Movement Party This Islamo-nationalist coalition, known as the People's Alliance, emboldened the shifts in foreign policy with claims that Turkey's domestic and external enemies were seeking to partition the country and weaken the state structure.

The quest for strategic autonomy and the militarization of foreign policy (2013-present)

The last stage of the AKP's foreign policy evolution is defined by several characteristics: it is motivated to serve for the security of Erdoğan's regime rather than national security; it is militarized and prioritizes the use of force; it is decoupled from the West and has 'moved' toward Russia; it is anti-American; and it seeks strategic autonomy.

US support for the PKK-affiliated Kurdish militia groups in Syria and refusal to sell a new air defense system to Turkey debilitated the already strained Turkish-US relations. As Turkey became isolated in the region, it had to rely more on military might to protect its vital interests. Nihat Ali Özcan, a professor at TOBB University, argues that.

> the militarization of the foreign policy was not an option but rather a necessity to cope with the problems around Turkey such as the conflict in Syria, Iraq and the Mediterranean area. Turkey is dealing with armed non-state actors in the region and has no option but to use force. When the use of force brings the expected result, you replicate the same strategy in other regions. Can you

trust the EU or the US to solve these problems? Absolutely not. So, Ankara has had to build and rely on the military force.[36]

The shift toward militarization, however, was more a response to domestic politics than the matter of security surrounding the regional conditions. A closer examination of the militarization of Turkish foreign policy indicates the prominent role of Erdoğan's insecurity and fear of being removed from power. This fear has resulted in authoritarianism inside the country and the militarization of foreign policy. Erdoğan's personal and domestic priorities have dominated foreign policy decisions and the use of force in Iraq, Syria, Libya, and the Karabakh region. As Erdoğan has enhanced his ties with the Nationalist Action Party of Devlet Bahceli, both political leaders have stressed the ontological security and survival objectives of the Turkish state, known as *beka sorunu* in Turkish. Erdoğan and Bahceli, along with their grassroot constituencies, which also include large segments of the population that identifies as secular nationalists, believe that hostile domestic forces and sinister international actors have collaborated to threaten Turkey's survival and its prosperity.

This alliance has produced more militancy in Turkish foreign policy. After establishing closer ties with its nationalist allies, the Erdoğan government carried out a series of cross-border operations against the PKK/PYD. These operations helped mobilize nationalists and conservative grassroot groups and the general public's willingness to 'rally around the flag.' The militarization of foreign policy correlates to the rise of fear-driven nationalism which sees domestic opposition forces such as the Kurds, Gülen followers, and the Europhiles as existential threats to the country's security. The majority of the public believes that the survival of Turkey is at risk due to internal and external attacks. As a result, there is a consensus among the large sector of the population on several foreign policy areas, such as responding militarily to the PKK insurgency, defending Turkey's rights in Eastern Mediterranean waters, protecting the rights of the Turkish Cypriot community, and supporting Azerbaijan's territorial claims in the Nagorno-Karabakh region. The public also does not see the EU as an effective and reliable actor to address problems in the region. Moreover, it remains very anti-American. Erdoğan's foreign policy has morphed into anti-Americanism, divorced from Turkey's long-term national interests, as he seeks to consolidate his regime and justify it on the basis of an Islamic-inspired nationalistic vision.

Strategic autonomy and the move toward Russia

One final element of Turkish policy that deserves some mention here, although it is covered in more detail in Paul Kubicek's contribution to this Special Issue[37], is Turkey's relationship with Russia. This reflects three interrelated trends: the lack of unity in the West regarding geopolitical priorities and strategies; the inevitable decline of the Western (US)-dominated international system; and the emerging bilateral and multilateral security arrangements in Europe as a replacement for the traditional collective security system. The framework of Turkey's Cold War foreign policy, where NATO was the reference point, is inadequate for Ankara to address fresh needs and challenges in security and international relations. Thus, Turkey's dependence on NATO and the US has lost its appeal, as Turkish officials and the public generally agreed that the time was ripe for Turkey to exercise its strategic autonomy. The message took hold, especially as Erdoğan and his supporters relied on instilling the sense of nostalgia for the old empire's historical heritage. This translated to a new message emphasizing self-sufficiency, independence, and national identity (e.g. neo-Ottoman) for articulating the twenty-first century principles of Turkey's foreign policy and without outside pressure and guidance.

However, Turkish officials and influential policy analysts also understood the realities of still needing to work with the great powers of the international community if Turkey was to preserve and enhance its interests. Thus issue-based policy alignments were necessary for the sake of flexibility if Ankara was to achieve the autonomy it desired in its foreign policy decision-making infrastructure. As a comparison, Rohan Mukherjee offers an interesting definition of strategic autonomy in the case of India:

> Strategic autonomy for most countries is akin to negative liberty, or freedom from external interference. Strategic autonomy for India is akin to positive liberty, or freedom to pursue certain goals and projects. In India's case, the primary long-term goal is to attain the status of a great power, whicentails recognition by other states of India's preeminent position in the international system. India resists strong alignment with a much stronger power such as the US because this puts India in a secondary or subordinate position.[38]

To reiterate, Turkey seeks freedom from external interferences and freedom to pursue its own goals. The governing AKP elites contend that maintaining close ties with the US constrain Turkey's freedom to act without the former benefits afforded by Western dependence. Although this made sense during the Cold War, today's Turkey has no major external security threats from the former Soviet bloc countries, although this could change if the war in Ukraine morphs into something much larger. Turkey's quest for strategic autonomy evolved with its policy of military intervention, which coincided with the American withdrawal and EU indifference regarding situations in the Caucasus, the Middle East and the Balkans.

In response, Turkey moved step by step to protect its interests by working with Russia. For Ankara, relations with Russia, a closer neighbor, are vital as they directly affect Turkey's national security. Moreover, Erdoğan treats

Russia as a balancing force against the US and the Western powers.[39] The AKP-dominated media, universities and think-tanks are spreading anti-Western ideas and sentiments. The AKP also closely works with the Turkish Eurasianists, known as *ulusalcılar*, to distance Turkey from US-dominated international institutions.[40] As the West continues to criticize Erdoğan's autocratic policies, Erdoğan, in return, reacts with anti-Western rhetoric by accusing the West of neo-imperialism, colonialism and racism. Meanwhile, the political elite in Europe and the US treats Turkey as a revisionist power, which seeks to challenge the Western dominated international environment and reap opportunities from the dynamic of 're-emerging empires' such as Russia and China.

However, Turkey's current policy toward Russia is characterized by caution, confusion, and contradiction.[41] Russia is Turkey's primary strategic rival in various areas. Ankara and Moscow do not agree on their respective support for different sides in Syria, Libya and the Karabakh region. Moreover, Turkey declared Russia's seizure of Crimea as an illegal annexation and has never recognized Crimea as part of Russia and has provided weaponry, including very effective drones, to Ukraine. But, Turkey also remains on Russia for energy, military technology, nuclear projects, and trade and tourism, and thus Erdoğan fears antagonizing Russia and thus is willing to work with them in certain areas. Ankara has become more sensitive to Russian redlines than those articulated by the US.

While Erdoğan's quest for strategic autonomy reduced Turkey's dependence on the West, it also inadvertently enhanced the country's dependence on Russia. Thus, by autonomy, Erdoğan means independence from the West and even resistance against the West with the support of non-Western countries, such as Russia, Venezuela, or Iran. As one pair of analysts noted, 'Turkey has moved a long way from being an essential pillar of NATO during the Cold War, a reliable member of the Council of Europe, and a promising EU candidate country to adopting the posture of a disruptive partner for the West.'[42] Although this assessment is correct about the radical shift, it falls short in examining the causes of this shift and especially the role of short-sighted EU policies. The EU has treated Turkey not as a partner but rather as a 'buffer state' to shield Europe from waves of refugees, and it sees Turkey as a source of industrial production because labor is cheap and the environmental rules are less rigid. Unquestionably, in 2022, Turkish foreign policy has become heavily militarized, nationalistic and defiant. Although some are quick to blame the governing Islamist elite for this shift in Turkish foreign policy, they ignore the damage inflicted as a result of the EU's policies toward Turkey, especially in the Cyprus issue along with the positions of former German chancellor Angela Merkel and former French president Nicolas Sarkozy, which opposed Turkey's application for full EU membership.

Shifts in international politics are having a profound effect on Turkish foreign policy. The abrupt withdrawal of American forces from Afghanistan and Iraq convinced Erdoğan and his innermost circle that the US role in the region was trending toward long-term decline. By realizing the ongoing need for close economic ties with the EU and a security partnership with the US, albeit it on a revised scale and more limited in scope, Erdoğan redefined relations with the West from a utilitarian perspective to a solely transactional one. Erdoğan does not want to subordinate Turkey's national interests to the demands or preferences of Western or US-led institutions. Meanwhile, Ankara is more prone to use the military to realize its foreign policy goals in the eastern Mediterranean, Syria, Iraq, Libya, and in the Caucasus.

Conclusion

To conclude, Erdoğan's foreign policy is based on a new sense of the Turkish identity as neo-Ottoman and Islamic. His foreign policy decisions are also personally dictated, where Erdoğan makes the decisions and has minimized the advisory and guiding role of the foreign ministry hierarchy, essentially reducing them to administrative assistants filing and disseminating the dossiers representing Erdoğan's decisions. Moreover, as discussed previously, Turkish foreign policy seeks strategic autonomy from the US and Europe. Policy decisions are frequently predicated on assuming the West as colonial, racist, and anti-Muslim, none of which serve Turkey's needs. Finally, the Turkish government is willing to take risks associated with militarizing its foreign policy conduct.

However, it is also fair to say that The AKP elite's romanticized understanding of past and present have not had the desired effect, but instead have ended up as self-defeating in the process of trying to realize Turkey's aspirations to become a great power reflective of the Ottoman Empire's golden era. These policies have ignored the presence of deep resentment and negative collective memories about the Ottoman past that are evident in many countries within the region.

Notes

1. For different versions of neo-Ottomanism, see Yavuz, *Nostalgia for the Empire*, 70-71; Erdogan's Islamized neo-Ottomanism, 162-178.
2. Lobell, et al. *Neoclassical Realism*.
3. For one of the best books on Turkish foreign policy, see Kösebalaban, *Turkish Foreign Policy*.
4. Yavuz, *Erdoğan*. 77-112.
5. Başkan. "Islamism."
6. Başkan, "Islamism," 272.
7. Davutoğlu, "Turkey's foreign policy."

8. Yavuz and Khan, "Turkish Foreign Policy," 70-71, and Robins, "Turkey's 'Double Gravity'".
9. Huntington, "The Clash of Civilizations?"
10. For one of the best books for examining the domestic evolution of Turkish political and social landscape with an emphasis on the impact of Ottoman influence, see Findley, *Turkey, Islam, and Modernity*.
11. Öztürk,. *Religion, Identity and Power*.
12. Onar, "Echoes."
13. Arısan, "From `client'."
14. Yavuz, *Erdoğan*, 282-313.
15. Aydın, "Determinants," 154-56.
16. Millman, "Turkish Foreign."
17. Hasanli, *Stalin and the Turkish Crisis*.
18. Laciner, "Turgut Özal."
19. Yavuz, *Islamic Political Identity*, 81-102.
20. Khan, "The Two Hundred Year Crisis."
21. Karaosmanoğlu, "The evolution."
22. Tziarras, "Turkish Foreign Policy."
23. Saraçoğlu and Demirkol, "Nationalism," 314. For the ideological underpinnings of neo-Ottomanism, see Uzer, "Conservative Narrative."
24. Kalin, "Debating Turkey," 91-92.
25. Davutoğlu, "Dışişleri Bakanı." See also Bashirov and Yilmaz, "The rise of transactionalism."
26. Quoted from Saraçoğlu and Demirkol, "Nationalism," 314-315, and Davutoğlu, *Stratejik Derinlik*, 143.
27. Lesser, "The Evolution," 261.
28. Holt, *The Balkan Reconquista*.
29. Yavuz, *Islamic Political Identity*.
30. Kaliber, "Securing the ground."
31. Nasr, "The Rise of 'Muslim Democracy'."
32. Uzer, "The downfall."
33. For more on Turkish-Brazilian cooperation on the Iranian nuclear deal, see Ozkan, "Turkey-Brazil Involvement." Also see "Text of the Iran-Brazil-Turkey Deal," Julian Borger's Global Security Blog, *Guardian*, May 17, 2010.
34. Taş, "Erdoğan and the Muslim Brotherhood."
35. "Saudi Prince Says Turkey Part of `Triangle of Evil': Egyptian Media." *Reuters*, 7 March 2018.
36. Interview with Nihat Ali Özcan, 12 June 2022.
37. Kubicek, "Structural dynamics."
38. Mukherjee, "Chaos as opportunity," 429.
39. Đidić and Kösebalaban, "Turkey's Rapprochement."
40. Erşen, "The Return of Eurasianism."
41. Kubicek, "Structural dynamics."
42. Pierini and Siccardi, "Why the EU."

Acknowledgements

The author would like to thank Behlül Özkan, Birol Başkan, Umut Uzer, Zenonas Tziarras, Mehmet Arısan, Paul Kubicek, Fumiko Sawae, and anonymous reviewers for helpful comments on the initial draft of this paper.

Disclosure statement

No potential conflict of interest was reported by the author(s).

Bibliography

Arısan, Mehmet. "From 'Clients' to 'Magnates': The (not so) Curious Case of Islamic Authoritarianism in Turkey." *Southeast European and Black Sea Studies* 19, no. 1 (2019): 11–30.

Aydın, Mustafa. "Determinants of Turkish Foreign Policy: Historical Framework and Traditional Inputs." *Middle Eastern Studies* 35, no. 4 (1999): 152–186.

Bashirov, Galib, and Ihsan Yilmaz. "The Rise of Transactionalism in International Relations: Evidence from Turkey's Relations with the European Union." *Australian Journal of International Affairs* 74, no. 2 (2020): 165–184.

Başkan, Birol. "Islamism and Turkey's Foreign Policy During the Arab Spring." *Turkish Studies* 19, no. 2 (2018): 264–288.

Davutoğlu, Ahmet. "Dışişleri Bakanı Sayın Ahmet Davutoğlu'nun Dış Ekonomik İlişkiler Kurulu Tarafından Düzenlenen Toplantıda Yaptıkları Konuşma." 2013, available at http://www.mfa.gov.tr/disisleri-bakani-sayin-ahmet-Davutoğlu_nun-dis-ekonomik-iliskiler-kurulu-tarafindan-duzenlenen-toplantida-yaptiklari-konusma_−9.tr.mfa.

Davutoğlu, Ahmet. *Stratejik Derinlik: Tukiye'nin Uluslararası Konumu*. Istanbul: Küre Yayınları, 2001.

Davutoğlu, Ahmet. "Turkey's Foreign Policy Vision: An Assessment of 2007." *Insight Turkey* 10, no. 1 (2008): 77–96.

Đidić, Ajdin, and Hasan Kösebalaban. "Turkey's Rapprochement with Russia: Assertive Bandwagoning." *The International Spectator* 54, no. 3 (2019): 123–138.

Erşen, Emre. "The Return of Eurasianism in Turkey: Relations with Russia and Beyond." In *Turkey's Pivot to Eurasia: Geopolitics and Foreign Policy in a Changing World Order*, edited by Emre Erşen, and Seçkin Köstem, 31–47. London: Routledge, 2019.

Findley, Carter V. *Turkey, Islam, and Modernity: A History, 1789-2007*. New Haven: Yale University Press, 2010.

Hasanli, Jamil. *Stalin and the Turkish Crisis of the Cold War, 1945–1953*. Washington, DC: Lexington Books, 2011.

Holt, William. *The Balkan Reconquista and Turkey's Forgotten Refugee Crisis*. Salt Lake City: University of Utah Press, 2019.

Huntington, Samuel. "The Clash of Civilizations?" *Foreign Affairs* 72, no. 3 (1993): 22–49.

Kaliber, Alper. "Securing the Ground Through Securitized 'Foreign' Policy: The Cyprus Case." *Security Dialogue* 36, no. 3 (2005): 319–337.

Kalin, Ibrahim. "Debating Turkey in the Middle East: The Dawn of a New Geopolitical Imaginations." *Insight Turkey* 11, no. 1 (2009): 91–92.

Karaosmanoğlu, Ali. "The Evolution of the National Security Culture and the Military in Turkey." *Journal of International Affairs* 54, no. 1 (2000): 199–216.

Khan, Mujeeb R. "The Two Hundred Year Crisis 1821-2021: The Fragmentation of the Ottoman State, Ongoing Western Imperialism, and the Tragedy of the Modern Muslim World." In *The Arab Spring: Past, Present, and Future*, edited by Sener Aktürk. Istanbul: TRT World Research Center, 2022.

Kösebalaban, Hasan. *Turkish Foreign Policy: Islam, Nationalism, and Globalization*. New York: Palgrave, 2011.

Kubicek, Paul. "Structural Dynamics, Pragmatism, and Shared Grievances: Explaining Russian-Turkish Relations." *Turkish Studies* 23, no. 5 (2022). doi:10.1080/14683849.2022.2060637.

Laciner, Sedat. "Turgut Özal Period in Turkish Foreign Policy: Ozalism." *USAK Yearbook* 2 (2009): 153–205.

Lesser, Ian O. "The Evolution of Turkish National Security Strategy." In *Turkey's Engagement with Modernity: Conflict and Change in the Twentieth Century*, edited by Celia Kerslake, Kerem Öktem, and Philip Robins, 258–276. Basingstoke: Palgrave, 2010.

Lobell, Steven E., Norrin M. Ripsman, and Jeffrey W. Taliaferro. eds. In *Neoclassical Realism, the State, and Foreign Policy*. Cambridge: Cambridge University Press, 2009.

Millman, Brock. "Turkish Foreign and Strategic Policy 1934-42." *Middle Eastern Studies* 31, no. 3 (1995): 483–508.

Mukherjee, Rohan. "Chaos as Opportunity: The United States and World Order in India's Grand Strategy." *Contemporary Politics* 26, no. 4 (2020): 420–438.

Nasr, Vali. "The Rise of &Quot;Muslim Democracy&Quot;." *Journal of Democracy* 16 (2005): 13–27.

Onar, Nora Fisher. "Echoes of a Universalism Lost: Rival Representations of the Ottomans in Today's Turkey." *Middle Eastern Studies* 45, no. 2 (2009): 229–241.

Özkan, Mehmet. "Turkey-Brazil Involvement in the Iranian Nuclear Issue: What is the Big Deal?" *Strategic Analysis* 32, no. 1 (2011): 26–30.

Özkan, Behlül. "Turkey, Davutoglu, and the Idea of Pan-Islamism." *Survival* 56, no. 4 (2014): 119–140.

Öztürk, Ahmet Erdi. *Religion, Identity and Power: Turkey and the Balkans in the Twenty-First Century*. Edinburgh: Edinburgh University Press, 2021.

Pierini, Marc, and Franceso Siccardi. Why the EU and the United States Should Rethink Their Turkey Policies in 2021." *Carnegie Europe*, January 21, 2021, available at https://carnegieeurope.eu/2021/01/21/why-eu-and-united-states-should-rethink-their-turkey-policies-in-2021-pub-83662.

Robins. "Turkey's 'Double Gravity' Predicament: The Foreign Policy of a Newly Activist Power." *International Affairs* 89, no. 2 (2013): 381–397.

Saraçoğlu, Cenk, and Özhan Demirkol. "Nationalism and Foreign Policy Discourse in Turkey Under the AKP Rule: Geography, History and National Identity." *British Journal of Middle Eastern Studies* 42, no. 3 (2015): 301–319.

Taş, Hakkı. "Erdoğan and the Muslim Brotherhood: An Outside-In Approach to Turkish Foreign Policy in the Middle East." *Turkish Studies* 23, no. 5 (2022). doi:10.1080/14683849.2022.2085096.

Tziarras, Z. *Turkish Foreign Policy towards the Middle East under the AKP (2002-2013): A Neoclassical Realist Account*, Department of Politics and International Studies, University of Warwick, Unpublished Dissertation. 2015.

Uzer, Umut. "Conservative Narrative: Contemporary neo-Ottomanist Approaches in Turkish Politics." *Middle East Critique* 29, no. 3 (2020): 275–290.

Uzer, Umut. "The Downfall of Turkish–Israeli Relations: A Cold Peace Between Former Strategic Allies." *Israel Affairs* 26, no. 5 (2020): 687–697.

Yavuz, M. Hakan. "Turkish Identity and Foreign Policy in Flux: The Rise of Neo-Ottomanism." *Critique: Critical Middle Eastern Studies* 7 (1998): 19–41.

Yavuz, M. Hakan. *Islamic Political Identity in Turkey*. New York: Oxford University Press, 2003.

Yavuz, M. Hakan. *Nostalgia for the Empire: The Politics of Neo-Ottomanism*. New York: Oxford University Press, 2020.

Yavuz, M. Hakan. *Erdoğan: The Making of an Autocrat*. Edinburgh: Edinburgh University Press, 2021.

Yavuz, M. Hakan, and Mujeeb R. Khan. "Turkish Foreign Policy Toward the Arab-Israeli Conflict: Duality and the Development (1950 - 1991)." *Arab Studies Quarterly* 14, no. 4 (1992): 69–94.

Populism, victimhood and Turkish foreign policy under AKP rule

Mehmet Arısan

ABSTRACT
This article explores how notions of conservative populism animate Turkish foreign policy. It explicates the construction of the 'us' and 'them' in conservative populism and how it became the dominant or hegemonic discourse of the AKP regime. While demonstrating various aspects of the peculiar conservative populism, the paper will try to point out the specific governmental ethos that conservative populism generates in the case of the AKP. By emphasizing how conservative populism is intermingled with Turkish-Islamist ideology, the paper explores the background of the AKP's pro-active and assertive foreign policy as well as the devastating effects of the de-institutionalization of the bureaucratic state structure and decision-making mechanisms.

Introduction

A common understanding of populism is that rests on a majoritarian understanding of government and anti-elitist modes of discourse, as a populist government purports to serve the 'common people'. However, most studies of populism suggest that each populist regime differs according to its particular and peculiar circumstances that initially led to that particular regime in a given country. Thus it may be difficult to determine and define a 'populist foreign policy' because it is not possible to describe the common features of it as a universal phenomenon.[1]

However, one can detect the populist features of a particular country's foreign policy by focusing on the peculiar historical, sociological, economic and cultural circumstances that prepared the ground for a populist government and/or leader coming to power. One distinction between different forms of populism is whether they are driven by demand or supply. By demand, we refer to upheavals generated by populist demands coming from below. By supply, we refer to governments and/or leaders utilizing populist rhetoric to mobilize people around a dichotomous and divisive discourse, which defines the 'native and authentic' people against a fictive evil-other, usually in the form of establishment elites or minority groups, who are often accused of serving their own narrow or even 'foreign' interests.[2] Furthermore, there is a reciprocal relation between supply and demand. Mudde and Kaltwasser, prominent theorists of populism, emphasize that 'for populists to continue winning the hearts and minds of supporters, they, as the supplier of populism, must meet the needs of the latter on the demand side.'[3] In addition to focusing on how the 'we' and 'others' are constructed by the ruling Justice and Development Party (*Adalet ve Kalkınma Partisi*, AKP) and government affiliated media, this study will also point out the historically continuous populist discourse in Turkey that has prepared the ground for contemporary authoritarian and a populist political regime, which in turn has produced some serious repercussions in Turkish foreign policy.[4]

In terms of the methodological approach, this article utilizes comparative analysis in order to define the varieties of populist governments as well as to determine the unique form of populism in Turkey. As described below, populism is a thin-centered ideology, which always needs an ideological supplement to attach itself. In the Turkish context, this is defined as Turkish-Islamism. In this regard, this article depends on an analysis of an ideology,[5] thereby aiming to elucidate how a particular group in Turkish society began to define itself or its own identity vis-à-vis 'evil others', and how this identity became the identity of the state, especially through AKP rule. Consequently, it demonstrates populism's impact on foreign policy and how this particular identity has become a basis to claim a particular *lebensraum* that exceeds the nation's current borders.

In short, this article expects to contribute mainly to a constructivist understanding of Turkish foreign policy, generally by focusing upon how the 'we' of the populist AKP and President Recep T. Erdoğan have been constructed. For this purpose, it elucidates the historical and socio-political circumstances related to the construction of the binary logic of 'we' and 'others' in the Turkish context and thus, analyzes the reflections and repercussions of this binary logic upon Turkish foreign policy, particularly within the last decade.

One of this article's basic arguments is that Erdoğan and AKP were not the only creators of the populist discourse including a specific 'we' and evil 'others'. The populist discourse that the AKP depends upon has firm historical and social roots going back to before the Cold War and can be traced even further to the Republican Revolution in the earlier part of the twentieth century. This conservative populist discourse contains a blend of Turkish nationalism and Islamism as well as a certain amount of vague and awkward Ottomanism. This discourse began to manifest itself in the 1950s, gradually expanded after the 12 September 1980 military coup and finally became the official discourse or mentality the regime in the first decades of the twenty-first century.

This discourse, like all populist discourse, draws a boundary, sometimes physically, but mostly symbolically, separating the people into separate' people 'into 'us' and 'them.'[6] This boundary drawing is a performative act in a double sense: it declares who is one of 'us' and who is not, and it evokes fear and a sense of threat from those declared 'others'.[7] Erdoğan's unique example, which separates him from the historically continuous line of populist conservatism, is that he expands the boundaries of the 'we' beyond Turkey and tries to form a peculiar *umma*, an Islamic community.[8] Another factor is the vague, awkward discourse of Ottomanism, discussed more in Hakan Yavuz's contribution to this Special Issue,[9] which tries to establish a link between Muslims living in the Middle East and the Balkans with the Ottoman heritage. Certainly, it is quite disputable whether or not these attempts of boundary construction have been successful, but we also see that in the second half of the 2010s the AKP's boundaries of 'we' shrunk back to Turkey itself, which has resulted in the visibility of a more nationalistic tone in foreign affairs.[10]

This article has three primary objectives. First, it reviews the basic literature on 'populist foreign policy' and how contemporary Turkish foreign policy can be situated within this framework. In this section it also highlights studies on how Turkey's conservative populist discourse was formed, what are the features of its 'we'/'others' dichotomy, and how it produces and reproduces this binary logic. While demonstrating various aspects of this peculiar conservative populism, it focuses on the specific governmental ethos that conservative populism generates in the case of the AKP. Second, it will demonstrate a specific logic of conservative populism which completely penetrates Turkish foreign policy. By emphasizing and analyzing how conservative populism is intermingled with the enduring Turkish-Islamist ideology, the article tries to point out both the background of the AKP's recently assertive foreign policy as well as the devastating effects of the de-institutionalization of the bureaucratic state structure and decision-making mechanisms, which are the outcomes of the AKP's particular governmental logic. Finally, the article will reflect on the discourse of victimhood, an important component of Turkish populism, and the dangers this poses for Turkish foreign policy.

A populist foreign policy?

As noted above, it is not possible to define specific features of a 'populist foreign policy' valid for all eras and countries. As Verbeek and Zaslove suggest:

> Populist parties do not pursue identical foreign policies despite their shared distinction between the corrupt elite and the pure people: the variation in their foreign policy preferences can be understood via the specific ideology populism as a thin-centered ideology attaches itself to; and populism as a domestic phenomenon, which varies from case to case and may well have a strong impact on the foreign policies of states, thus affecting the relations between states.[11]

Thus, the 'pure people versus the corrupt elite' formulation manifests itself differently in each case by means of utilizing a specific ideology to construct such a simplistic binary. This is the basic reason why populism is called a 'thin-centered ideology,' which always needs an ideological supplement to empower and manifest itself in a particular context. Focusing on European, Latin American, and North American countries, Verbeek and Zaslove claim that populism and nationalism can generally be seen as complementary, but both are still thin-centered ideologies, which require yet another discursive and/or ideological supplement to function in a particular socio-political setting. However, for nationalism, there is no need for a binary of elite versus the 'pure people'. There can even be an elitist nationalism, but this cannot be said for populism. Even if the leader of a populist movement or party comes from an elite background, that individual has to deploy a 'people'-oriented anti-elite discourse.

As demonstrated below, nationalism does not always accompany populism because sometimes populism is supplemented with some civilizational discourses such as Islam, which alters the functioning base of populism from a national level and expands it to a larger geographical area. However, even the deployment of such a civilizational discourse is closely related to some domestic and national dynamics, which are linked to peculiar historical and socio-political factors as well as an international context. It should also be noted, it is primarily the domestic historical and socio-political contexts that determine the ideology attached to the populist discourse. The attached ideology becomes important in determining the foreign policy of the populist party in question. As Verbeek and Zaslove note:

> We do not expect populist parties to take identical foreign policy positions. Rather we expect them to differ in their assessment of the impact that the international environment will have on their own understanding of who the pure people are.[12]

In order to generalize various populist foreign policy approaches, Verbeek and Zaslove have determined four basic categories.[13] The first is the radical right, which basically depends on a nationalist approach and mostly in an isolationist sense. They offer examples of the French National Front, the Austrian Freedom Party, the Danish People's Party, and Jobbik in Hungary. The second depends on the market-oriented liberalism's projection of the 'pure, authentic people', who are portrayed as honest and hardworking citizens endangered by the elite run state. Berlusconi's *Forza Italia!*, the Belgian List Dedecker, the Dutch List Pim Fortuyn, and Peruvian president Alberto Fujimori in the 1990s are examples in this category. This form of populism can be paralleled to that which emerged after the 12 September 1980 military coup in Turkey, which provided the necessary sociopolitical climate to make the transformation into a market economy with a new constitution.[14]

After Turgut Özal's Motherland Party (*Anavatan Partisi*, ANAP) came to power in 1983, a populist dichotomy was deployed in the political discourse of the incumbent party. This populist binary depended upon a particular reading of Turkish political modernization in the form of the modernist Kemalist elites versus the pure and authentic people of Anatolia. A highly visible blend of Turkish nationalism and Islamism was in play here. Turkish-Islamism can be said to be the basic ideology attached to such a populist understanding, which manifested itself as authentic Muslims and Turks of Anatolia versus alienated and overly Westernized Kemalists who founded the modern republic. In such a market-oriented populist discourse, the claim is that the elite is generally accepted as the clumsy and corrupt state bureaucracy that prevented the pure people from reaping the fruits of a true market economy. In the Turkish case, Kemalism is generally equated with that clumsy and corrupt state bureaucracy, which notably in the AKP's populist discourse involves the military bureaucracy as well.

However, Özal and ANAP never adopted an anti-Western stance. Özal was always ready to cooperate with the Western world. However, he also referred to the Japanese model by emphasizing that economic and technological advancement could be modelled on the West, and that Turkey should always be vigilant to keep its pure Turkish-Islamist spirit and culture as inherited from the Ottoman Empire. While promoting such a populist discourse, Özal carried out a radical privatization project, which aimed to integrate Turkey into the rising trend of global neoliberalism. Although there is considerable evidence of a continuous pattern in AKP's populist discourse, there are also significant differences between the AKP's populism and ANAP's version. While the AKP adopted neoliberal policies and maintained a pragmatic relationship with the West (at least in its early years in office), it also adopted a more civilizational populist identity, that is Islam, in order to make regional claims and to construct a powerful domain of influence in the Middle East, North Africa and the Balkans. Both invoked neo-Ottomanism.[15] However, while Özal utilized 'being a part of Ottoman heritage' in Turkey's relations with the Balkans, notably during the Bosnian crisis in the 1990s, the AKP has been more persistent in its use of Ottoman nostalgia as well as invoking the Sunni Muslim *umma*. In this sense the AKP's populism, contrary to many theories of populism, has never been anti-cosmopolitan, as long as this sentiment of cosmopolitanism was limited within a Sunni Islamic identity.

Verbeek and Zaslove's third mode of populism is regionalist populism which is limited to the people of a particular territory who claim to belong to a particular territory historically. They mention the Italian Northern League and the Belgian Flemish Interest as examples of this mode of populism, which also might be considered a type of 'separatist populism'. The final mode is 'left-wing' populism, which perceives the people as a social phenomenon rather than as a nationalist one and, most importantly, demarcates the capitalist class and 'imperialists' as the evil-other. Examples of this last type include the late Hugo Chavez in Venezuela, Evo Morales in Bolivia, and Rafael Correa in Ecuador, along with certain populist left parties such as Podemos in Spain and the Dutch Socialist Party.

Post-1980 Turkish populism has little or nothing to do with leftist populism because it has always been a predominantly conservative one. However, the two share a few common points. Latin American left-wing populism, for example, has a high degree of anti-American sentiment, which can be found in the AKP's foreign policy in the 2010s, in particular efforts to establish alliances with various actors in the Middle East and develop in a general sense a more independent role in global politics. This is especially evident in AKP's relations with various branches of the Muslim Brotherhood (MB), which reached its zenith in the aftermath of the Arab Spring. This topic is covered in more detail in Hakki Taş's contribution to this Special Issue.[16] In terms of leftist populism's critique of capitalism, the AKP does not oppose neoliberalism as an economic form and ideology (quite the contrary), but it does oppose what it views as the global hegemony of the leading capitalist countries of the West that often, in its view, acts against Turkey's interests.[17]

The most important point in detecting the form or model of a particular populism is to understand who the 'elite' is or who is or will be the 'threat' to the 'pure people'. This issue is also crucial in detecting the international reflections of populism in a particular country and how it might affect the foreign policy of that country. For the populist radical right in Europe, this means the European elites in Brussels. Meanwhile, for the regionalist populists, the elite is slightly blurred, as it can be elites in the center or the European Union. For the populist left parties, the 'evil' elites can be local politicians but they can also be transnational financial elites or leaders of other countries who push for globalization. For the populist (neo)liberals, the elite 'other' is a member of the state bureaucracy which obstructs the people's entrepreneurial freedom.[18]

In the Turkish case, the post-1980 political and economic climate allowed (neo)liberal populists to cast the state bureaucracy as an intransigent, corrupt elite which was associated with Kemalism. Actually, such an antipathy against the state bureaucracy long existed in Turkish politics, especially within the center-right parties which been dominant since 1950. Metin Heper has stated that the main tension in most periods of the Turkish Republic's history has been between the state elites and political (party) elites.[19] However, political elites have never seen themselves as 'elites'. They have always pretended and presented themselves as the true embodiment of the pure and authentic 'Muslim' people of Anatolia, a point especially true of center-right politicians. This has climaxed with the rise of the AKP. The key point here is that Islam has always been the invariable ingredient of Turkish populism, whereas Kemalism (which features Westernization and *laicité*) is characterized as an obstacle for the pure Anatolian Muslim people to discover and express their 'true' identity.[20]

The Turkish conservative populist discourse and foreign policy

In many scholarly papers and studies on the rise of AKP, there is a common point: the AKP came to power with great hope on behalf of a large portion of society that extended far beyond the Islamist groups. This was based on AKP's promise of constructing a truly democratic regime, integrating with the European Union (EU), and encouraging the conservative masses to support a democratic understanding and a more global outlook by reconciling their Islamist political identity with democratic norms and principles. Notably, the AKP managed to appeal to some leftists, who had been repressed after the 1980s coup and had grown disillusioned with Kemalism.[21] Islamists could also claim to be victims of the Kemalist establishment, insofar as they had been repressed after the Welfare Party-led government was ousted under pressure from the military in 1997 and expressions of Islamic faith and identity, such as wearing a headscarf, had been banned in universities and other institutions.[22] There was a large underground Islamist organization, sustained through the religious societies (*tarikats*), whose members included many officials in ANAP, but these too had been repressed by the state bureaucracy, particularly the military, which positioned itself as the guardian of the secular (*laic*) republic.[23] Liberals and center-right voters were also searching for an alternative, especially after the fragmentation and weakening of the center-right parties in the second half of the 1990s.[24] Thus, AKP came to the rescue for all of these political groups and succeeded in uniting them against Kemalism, which had been seen as a perennial obstacle to both true democratization and a true integration with the world economic system. The moment when AKP came to power can thus be defined as the ultimate populist point in terms of the mobilizing and unifying power of the populist discourse by 'othering' the Kemalist state bureaucracy.

However, in many of these scholarly studies, the first term of AKP rule has not been defined as populist. According to these studies, the AKP is accepted as the true process of democratization and integration with the EU and the West. Indeed, in the early 2000s, AKP

> followed a liberal internationalist path, seeking EU membership and adopting reforms aiming to democratize Turkey's political system in conjunction with the EU's 'harmonization packages'. The party also remained committed to the NATO alliance, the defining feature of Turkey's relationship with the West since World War II.[25]

One should emphasize, however, that being in favor of democratization and having a concern for international connection do not mean a particular government is not populist. As explained in detail above, one cannot talk about a single form of populism. Populists may take various positions according to the particular ideology or ideologies to which they would attach themselves. Even though it deployed a predominantly liberal discourse in this period and even adopted some features associated with the left, one cannot claim that the populist stance of AKP during its first term was attached extensively to a liberal cosmopolitan worldview. Many of the current studies on the AKP also emphasize that the AKP had a predominantly Islamist ideological orientation that determined its genuine mode of a populist stance, but which it also concealed in order to make an alliance with the liberals and a certain part of the left as well as to make the AKP appealing to center-right voters.[26] These other groups provided very good initial leverage and partners for an openly Islamic-oriented party which always presented itself as the representative of the 'long-lasting victims' of the Kemalist republic.

However, in its subsequent terms of rule, the AKP consolidated its power in the state bureaucracy and dominated the military by orchestrating a series of allegations against various Kemalist military officers about coup plotting. AKP thus consolidated its power by eliminating Kemalist elements in military and judiciary and started to pursue a more markedly conservative and majoritarian (even plebiscitarian) line. Former Prime Minister and now President Erdoğan, began to view the ballot box as the only legitimate instrument of democratic accountability and subsequently described anti-government demonstrations (e.g. the Gezi protests in 2013) as an attempt by the minority to impose its will on the majority by unlawful means.[27] After these developments, AKP revealed its genuine mode of populism with a strong attachment to an Islamic identity of *umma* and a great sense of vengeance against the secular republican institutions. This manifested itself in a form of anti-institutionalism rather than as an urge for re-institutionalization. According to Hakkı Taş:

> Populists often exhibit strong disdain for intermediary institutions and treat the procedural and institutional requirements of modern liberal democracy only as impediments to their conception of general will. This people-centrism

in the form of anti-institutionalism has two main consequences for foreign policy decision-making along with the centralization of power in the hands of the populist leader. The prioritization of the hyper-empowered populist leader, rather than the long-established patterns, defines the foreign policy agenda.[28]

Although Taş explained AKP's disdain for institutionalism by connecting it to populism, it should not be solely referred to populism as if populism has only one agenda or orientation. As demonstrated above in some cases, a populist government may exist on quite good terms with inherited institutions and institutional regulations. What bears emphasis in the Turkish case is that populism is tightly connected to Islam and Islamic identity, which in turn is strongly associated with victimhood and victimization and thus produces a critical or even cynical stance toward the country's long-standing institutions. According to Zafer Yılmaz, 'victimhood' is the most determining feature of a continuing discourse of Turkish-Islamist ideology, which is the basic ingredient of Turkish conservative populism that existed long before the AKP era. However, as he also suggests, AKP can be said to be the most successful entity in utilizing this continuous conservative populism in modern Turkey. He states that Erdoğan effectively articulated this assertion in his public speeches.[29] He adds that Turkish-Islamist identity is in a sense a 'permanent wound' related to being deprived of their true Islamic identity and being alienated from their own essential culture and tradition by the Kemalist republic. In a sense this discursive stance portrays the republic as a colonial power, which has colonized the pure and authentic Muslim people of Anatolia.[30] This logic of victimization also perceives the countries that were once a part of the Ottoman Empire as 'colonized' countries, which were colonized and fragmented by the Western policies and interventions after the conclusion of the Sykes-Picot Agreement. Thus, only a regional power with a strong sense of the past imperial and Islamic unity, namely Turkey, can now bring order and development to the region.[31]

One of the most important political outcomes of this discourse of victimization is, as Yılmaz suggests, a vengeful political subject. He states that:

'Turkish-Islamist identity is also deeply invested in its own impotence, even while it seeks to compensate its historical suffering by sublimating political power and the vengeful moralization of its fight against the 'West,' 'Kemalist elites' or the 'cosmopolitan Left,' who are seen as depriving the Turkish-Islamist subject of its object of desire and the 'golden era.'[32]

The golden era that Yılmaz mentions varies according to the different circumstances in which the Turkish-Islamist ideology is put forward as the fundamental ingredient of populist policies. In some instances, it could be the imperial grandeur of the Ottoman Empire in the fifteenth and the sixteenth century. In another instance, the golden era could be introduced as the period of the four Caliphs, as many Muslims accept it. However, generally there is a parallel usage of these two instances that is relevant to the vagueness of the conservative populism and the Turkish-Islamist ideology that it employs.[33] In any case, when vengefulness meets with an idea of the 'golden age,' it would naturally contribute to a legitimate base for the growing militarism and expansionist moves of the AKP, which became much more visible in the post-2016 era.[34]

Yılmaz emphasizes that the conservative populist discourse reproduces a series of binary oppositions and constructs its simplistic dualist logic upon these binaries, such as the East versus West, Kemalist power versus the Islamist opposition, the authoritarian (Kemalist) state versus the democratic-populist Islamist opposition, center versus periphery, immoral and materialist secular elites versus big-hearted spiritual lower classes, and 'black Turks' versus 'white Turks'.[35] The consequence of this binary logic is the continuous production of resentment, irresponsibility and a continuous form of paranoid conspiracy thinking, which has serious implications for Turkish foreign policy:

> Resentment is one of the most efficacious emotions in that context, since it calls out surpassed emotions of wrath, which awakens reactive forces as a result of an earlier wound, pain, and a feeling of impotence. Such kind of resentment 'retains real or imagined holdings of its subject as object of desire' concurrently. It immanently imagines itself as powerful as the West, as culturally acceptable as secularist elites, and as self-confident as powerful nation states. However, its captured imagination always discloses the wounded character of its identity and its sense of impotency, followed by the fetishization of its wound. Thereafter, every step toward power and success creates more fragility and intensifies its impotency instead of underlining its subjecthood.[36]

This clearly reflects the AKP's constant drive to be on the forefront and to have the upper hand in dealing with the issues related to the region. This is manifested in intensified militarization. In the last 10 years, Turkey has deployed troops and established bases in Iraq, Syria, Qatar, Somalia, Libya and Cyprus. Moreover, it has been involved in other conflicts (e.g. Nagorno-Karabakh) with its newly developed military technology, especially drones. In addition, some aggressive moves in the Eastern Mediterranean also brought Turkey to the brink of war with Greece and caused great distress amongst the countries who have interests in the region. It becomes quite clear that, starting with the former Prime Minister Ahmet Davutoğlu's time in power (2014-2016), Turkey 'assumed an active and determinant position in every issue in the region.'[37] However, as noted below, this foreign policy activism occurs far from realistic and rational considerations.

Rather than calculated acts, these moves depend on motivations mostly based on reactive ideological considerations.

In this context, irresponsibility appears to be another important consequence of the binary logic that runs parallel with the victimization discourse. Yılmaz successfully sketched out the discursive construction of the Turkish conservative populist discourse, which he claims can be traced back to Necip Fazıl Kısakürek's writings in which one can see a continuous discourse of 'suffering' in defining the agony of the 'true Muslims of Anatolia' under the rule of the alienated, Westernist Kemalist elite. Kısakürek is also admired by President Erdoğan and he has referred to him and his works numerous times in political speeches.[38] The victimization discourse always goes hand-in-hand with a discourse of suffering, which involves self-pity, impotence and, most importantly, 'irresponsibility'. Yılmaz explains the relationship between suffering and irresponsibility by employing reference to Nietzsche:

> ... every sufferer instinctively seeks a cause for his suffering, more exactly an agent, still more specifically, a *guilty* agent who is susceptible to suffering, in short, some living thing upon which he can, on some pretext or other, vent his affects, actually or in effigy... This causes the actual psychological cause of *resentment,* vengefulness, and the like: a desire to *deaden pain by means of affects*... (emphasis in the original)[39]

This quotation powerfully explains and summarizes the victimhood position in the Turkish populist conservative discourse, which is most successfully embodied in the AKP. From the particular angle of conservative populism, the AKP embodies the masses victimized by the Western-oriented Kemalist republicanism. In this sense, the subject of 'victimhood' (the AKP) is a passive one and cannot be held responsible for any wrongdoings because it is the 'victim'. If the victim commits anything wrong, it is because they are being forced to by the ones who made them victims and who stole their true identity. Referring to the writings of Garrath Williams, Yılmaz explains the irresponsibility of the victimhood logic: 'That our hands have been dirtied becomes further evidence of the wrongs that are being done to us ('look what they have made us into')'.[40]

Such discursive logic can be dangerous when one considers foreign policy. If a group of people are postulated as the true descendants of the 'glorious Ottoman imperial legacy', who were suppressed by the alienated and Westernized elites of the Republic, then every claim or reclaim about the imperial legacy becomes legitimate, especially if this discursive assumption is embraced by the ruling party. In a sense, they can still play the victim while turning the institutional structure of the state upside down or making expansionist moves into neighboring countries. When this populist victimization discourse comes into play then it becomes irrelevant if such moves have some rational basis or not. There is no need to 'rationalize' the moves because they can be rationalized from a quite irrational source when both the rulers and the people see themselves as ultimately passive victims of history. Referring to the work of Fethi Açıkel, Yılmaz further explains this notion of 'irresponsibility' in a relevant way:

> The Turkish-Islamist victim emerges constantly as a passive subject of the history of wrongdoings and attributes every mishap to the external world. Hence, concerning negative results of his/her actions, he/she evades agency and in taking any responsibility in its narcissist ego-centrism. Relatedly, with its strong incentive to self-dramatize its own situation and destiny, the Turkish-Islamist subject always mentions the tragic dimension of his/her existence and adheres mythical accounts of its history and activity to sustain his/her group identity.[41]

Such logic, embedded in a longstanding ideology which depends on a hostile relationship with the foundations of the Turkish Republic, contributes to a reactionary and irrational longing for power. However, this cannot be related to a shift of axis in Turkish foreign policy in the last ten years of AKP rule. As Başer rightly points out, there is a gradual change towards an ambitious attitude rather than a clear shift of axis.[42] The reason is that there is neither any clear rationale nor any institutional base of a determined alternative foreign policy, except an uncalculated and unrealistic desire to dominate the region (or an unrealistic will to power). It can be sometimes anti-Western and sometimes pro-Western, depending on its immediate needs that are shaped within a political identity of 'the victim'. While this was an identity of Turkish conservatives in general, it has become the state identity of Turkey in the last ten years of AKP rule.

Moreover, the 'irresponsible' victim, who rejects any responsibility of his/her actions as being the 'passive subject of history', can never act in a proactive way. According to this logic of victimization, there is always a 'mastermind' that allocates the roles in the international stage, an eternal, secret agent of a nearly absolute power, who is always able to shape and dominate world politics.[43] In this sense, not only is every problem that bothers the state (like the Gezi protests or the Kurdish issue) perceived as a conspiracy of that all-powerful 'mastermind', but also any of the state's expansionist moves could not be defined as arising from its own will.[44] Rather, it would be defined as something which the all-powerful 'mastermind' 'forced' Turkey to do. Turkey thus only acts defensively. In this sense, both the Syrian incursions and the direct and indirect military acts in Iraq, Libya and Africa are just 'moves against the imperialist mastermind' to protect the victimized brothers and a reclamation of an imperial glory that was supposedly taken away by the evil, all-powerful mastermind. Consequently, it is quite possible to claim that this discourse of the evil, all-powerful mastermind functions as an efficient cover for the pathological desire for power, which relies on the inferiority complex of victim identity.

Another significant manifestation of the sense of irresponsibility can be observed in the gradual de-institutionalization of the state structure, including the Ministry of Foreign Affairs. In explaining the issue of de-institutionalization, Taş refers to the gradual personalism and personalization of the Turkish mode of government and the state mechanism that became visible after the Gezi protests in 2013 and reached its peak after the transition to the presidential regime, which likely was the outcome of the paranoiac political atmosphere that the coup attempt in 2016 generated.[45]

However, it cannot be solely attributed to a personal will to power of a particular leader or a couple of particular events. As mentioned before, the antipathy against the civil and military bureaucracy has been the basic characteristic of conservative populist discourse from Menderes in the 1950s through Erdoğan today. In the late 1960s, and throughout the 1970s and 1980s, the leaders of the conservative center-right parties such as Süleyman Demirel and Özal always complained about the limitations and pressures of the state bureaucracy by emphasizing that they were the elected ones and they were the representatives of the people and it was not the appointed bureaucrats' job to direct them in one way or another.[46] However, it was only Erdoğan who was able to penetrate the whole bureaucratic mechanism, including the military, and was able to eliminate bureaucrats in significant posts who opposed him or were known to interfere with his policies. Although it may seem a personal and/or personalist move, it has a strong discursive legitimation basis in Turkish conservative populism, which has been effective in Turkish politics for many decades. Engaging with the state bureaucracy and abiding by the state's principles, legal procedures and institutional mechanisms have always been seen as a nuisance by the conservative center-right politicians.

As Taş also suggests, the established diplomatic procedures and protocols have also become the victim of the logic inherent in Turkish conservative populism and activated in de-institutionalizing the state structure. Referring to many other populist cases, Taş points to the gradual sidelining of established diplomatic and bureaucratic institutions, shifting the core of decision-making from the Ministry of Foreign Affairs to the office of chief executive, which have resulted in eliminating the accumulated knowledge and experience of senior bureaucrats.[47]

In place of conclusion: the impact of victimhood and conspiracy thinking on Turkish foreign policy

As mentioned earlier, three basic features can be located in the Turkish conservative populist discourse, which can be defined as a legitimating pretext for the foreign policies that the AKP has carried out in the last decade. These are 'resentment', 'irresponsibility' and 'conspiracy thinking', all of which may sometimes lead to paranoiac approaches. The functioning of the first two in the Turkish domestic and foreign policy contexts was briefly defined above. In place of concluding remarks, I would like to explain the impact of conspiracy thinking in the Turkish context, in so doing refer to the work of Evren Balta, who categorizes AKP's foreign policy into three periods.[48]

The first period is associated with the first term of AKP's rule in which it continued its unofficial alliance with liberals and some leftist circles that it formed during its initial election campaign. The second period started with AKP's second term of rule and extended to 2014. Balta characterizes this period as 'civilizational expansionism,' as marked by Davutoğlu's tenure as Foreign Minister. This 'civilizational expansionism' can also be defined by the internationalization of the victimization discourse, which has manifested itself by postulating an *umma* victimized both by the West and by the Westernized elite. In this period, AKP presented itself as the 'decolonizer' of Muslims in the Middle East, Caucasus and the Balkans. However, this victimized *umma* was generally limited to Sunni Muslims.[49] This is the point where the AKP utilized Sunni Islam as one of the most efficient tools of foreign policy, including using the Presidency of Religious Affairs (*Diyanet İşleri Başkanlığı*) as an alternative Ministry of Foreign Affairs, as it engaged in many foreign policy issues and worked with Islamic organizations in other countries, including Europe and North America. This issue is explored much more extensively in this Special Issue by Öztürk and Baser.[50] In this second period, one can observe both resentment and the issue of being 'the passive and irresponsible victim-agents of history'.

In the third period, however, populist discourse becomes embedded in conspiracy thinking, which was exacerbated by the military coup attempt in 2016. Balta also emphasizes the role of the 2013 coup against the Muslim Brotherhood in Egypt, the regional Islamist movement supported extensively by the AKP. In a sense, the coup in Egypt and the overlapping Gezi protests in Turkey can be said to be the starting points of the process that led the AKP to conspiracy thinking, which climaxed with the 2016 coup attempt. At the same time, Western support for Erdoğan and the AKP diminished during the 2010s, due to the country's aggressive and expansionist foreign policy moves. Being fully aware of this situation, the AKP, which had already loaded ideological baggage with anti-Western sentiments, distanced itself even further from the West. Even though it did not drop its civilizational claims, such as being the leader of victimized Muslims of the world, the AKP came closer to ultra-nationalist circles.[51] As Kara rightly points out, the alliance of AKP with the ultra-nationalist Nationalist Action Party 'is based on the creation of external problems and military engagement abroad like the 'forever war' where conflicts constantly remain in the political background.'⁵² Even though more recently AKP has begun to adjust its course by de-escalating conflicts in the Eastern Mediterranean and trying to (re)establish good relations with Israel, Saudi Arabia, and other Middle East countries, this is largely related to its rising anxieties of losing the upcoming elections due to the deteriorating economy, which has seriously decreased domestic support.

Finally, it should be emphasized that populism is not something merely related to the AKP or Erdoğan's leadership. It has long-lasting ideological company, Turkish-Islamism, which can be traced to the 1950s, a period that also witnessed the emergence of Islamic-oriented activism. The AKP, perhaps more so than any other party in Turkish history, has openly embraced this ideology, with serious repercussions both in domestic and foreign policy.

Notes

1. For the varying features of "populist foreign policy" in different cases and the peculiar features of the Turkish case see Taş, "The formulation."
2. For the varying significance of the supply and demand side of populism see Sawae, "Populism."
3. Mudde and Kaltwasser, *Populism*.
4. Zafer Yılmaz's sophisticated study demonstrates how the AKP's popularity Turkish-Islamists' populist ideology depends on a repeating discourse of victimization and self-pity. However, he firmly argues that those feelings and self-perception of the people are the result of a continuous process of "deliberate construction" by the assistance of Turkish-Islamist intellectuals and later by the help of mass-media which can be traced back to the 1950s. See Yılmaz, "The AKP and the Spirit," as well as Kaliber and Kaliber "From De-Europeanisation."
5. It may be necessary to indicate that the notion "ideology" is used interchangeably with the notion of "discourse," because at some point, the term "discourse" becomes more suitable to define some socio-political formations. However, this article does not rely on "discourse analysis" in the sense of a "rhetorical analysis" but it instead tries to demonstrate the parameters, mindset and logic of an ideologically created socio-political identity or 'subjectivity', its internalizations and externalizations which, in turn, corresponds to what is meant by "discourse" See Purvis and Hunt, "Discourse, ideology. . ."; Howarth and Stavrakakis, "Introducing Discourse Theory"; Howarth, *Discourse*, 1-15; and Laclau, "Identity and Hegemony."
6. Yuval-Davis, *The Politics of Belonging*, 10.
7. Sawae, "Populism," 264.
8. The substitution of the national "people" with a transnational "*umma*" as a civilizational identity was also appropriated by the former Prime Minister Ahmet Davutoğlu. See Başkan and Taşpinar, *The Nation*.
9. Yavuz, "The Motives."
10. See Balta, "The AKP's Foreign Policy"; Öztürk, "Turkey's Post-2016"; and Ege, "Foreign Policy"

11. Verbeek and Zaslove, "Populism," 611.
12. Verbeek and Zaslove "Populism," 619
13. Verbeek and Zaslove "Populism," Most other studies make no such categorization, often acknowledging the peculiarity of each case in producing a populist foreign policy. For an extended discussion and examples, see Chrissogelos, "Populism in Foreign Policy."
14. Arısan, "From Clients."
15. For the different articulations of "Neo-Ottomanism" in the Özal and Erdoğan eras, see Yavuz, *Nostalgia for the Empire*, 116–125 and 162–178
16. Taş, "Erdoğan and the Muslim Botherhood." See also Gürpınar, "Turkey and the Muslim Brotherhood," and
17. Demir, Morieson, and Yılmaz, "The Islamist Populism"; Kaliber and Kaliber "From De-Europeanisation"; and Ege, "Foreign Policy," 13.
18. Verbeek and Zaslove "Populism," 627.
19. Heper, *State Tradition in Turkey*.
20. Ege, "Foreign Policy." For a critical account of this specific utilization of Kemalism by conservatives, see Aytürk, "Post-post Kemalizm" and Aytürk, "Post-Kemalizm Nedir."
21. The September 12, 1980 military coup and the following military regime eliminated the leftist articulations of Kemalism and instead employed a rigidly state centered and national security oriented Kemalism, which caused a radical rupture between the Turkish socialist left and Kemalism. See Durgun, "Left-Wing Politics in Turkey" and Yılmaz, "Sol-Kemalizmin Tasfiyesi"
22. See, Özdalga, *The Veiling Issue*,; Secor, "Islamism"; and Saktanber and Çorbacıoğlu, "Veiling and Headscarf."
23. Heper and Güney, "The Military and Democracy," and Narlı "Concordance and Discordance."
24. Özbudun, "The Institutional Decline," and Taşkın, "AKP's Move."
25. Balta, "The AKP's Foreign Policy," 14.
26. See Balta, ibid., Özpek and Yaşar, "Populism and Foreign Policy", Sawae, "Populism", Kaliber and Kaliber "From De-Europeanisation"; and Taş, "The formulation," 4.
27. Özbudun, "AKP at the Crossroads," and Kubicek, "Majoritarian democracy."
28. Destradi and Plageman, "Populism and International Relations," 14–17 quoted in Taş, "The Formulation," 6y.
29. Yılmaz, "The AKP and the Spirit," 483
30. Çapan and Zarakol, "Post-colonial Colonialism."
31. Yavuz, *Nostalgia for the Empire*, 198. Also see Erdoğan, "Yeni Türkiye Vizyonu."
32. Yılmaz, "The AKP and the Spirit," 484-85.
33. Although Özal introduced a version of (neo-)Ottomanism and Islamism when ANAP was in power, it was employed more systematically as the ideological and/or philosophical basis of the Turkish foreign policy in the 2010s by Ahmet Davutoğlu, who emphasized Turkey's civilizational identity. See Davutoğlu, *Stratejik Derinlik*.
34. Mikhail, "Why Recep Tayyip Erdoğan's."
35. Of course, this particular dichotomy does not rely on actual racial differences in Turkey because there are none. This completely depends on an allegorical reference that is based on class difference appropriated and employed by the AKP and Erdoğan. The arrogant, elitist, and anti-Islamist "White Turk" is

also a particularly popular theme among Turkish-Islamist media intellectuals. Erdoğan has proudly declared that he is a "Black Turk" and that Muslims are Turkey's "Blacks". As argued by Demiralp, Erdoğan was "Black" not just because he was a practicing Muslim, but also because he was from provincial Anatolia. See Demiralp, "White Turks, Black Turks?" 511, See also Bora, "Muhafazakar ve İslamcı Söylemde Beyaz Türk Hıncı" and, specifically for the binary discourse of Turkish conservatism, see Bora and Erdoğan "Biz, Anadolu'nun Bağrı Yanık Çocukları … " For Erdoğan's speech, see "I am Proud To Be A Black Turk," *Daily Sabah*, June 25, 2015.
36. Brown, *States of Injury*, 60.
37. Öztürk, "Turkey's Post-2016," 4-5.
38. Yılmaz, "The AKP and the Spirit," 487, and Singer, "Erdoğan's Muse." Also see Anatolian Agency (AA) News, "Cumhurbaşkanı Erdoğan: Necip Fazıl bu millete ruh kökünden aldığı kuvvet ve cesaretle var olabileceğini gösterdi," May 13, 2022, available at https://www.aa.com.tr/tr/gundem/cumhur baskani-erdogan-necip-fazil-bu-millete-ruh-kokunden-aldigi-kuvvet-ve-cesar etle-var-olabilecegini-gosterdi/2587391
39. Yılmaz, "The AKP and the Spirit," 500.
40. Williams, "Dangerous Victims," 88, quoted in Yılmaz, "The AKP and the Spirit," 500.
41. Açıkel, "'Kutsal mazlumluğun psikopatolojisi," 190, quoted in Yılmaz, "The AKP and the Spirit," 500.
42. Başer, "Shift of Axis."
43. Kara, "Linking," 11
44. See "İbrahim Kalın: FETÖ'cüleri Türkiye Cumhuriyeti'ne İade Etsinler." *Milliyet*, October 26, 2017.
45. Taş, "The formulation."
46. Heper claims that from the transition to multi-party politics in 1946 up to recent times, Turkish political history is basically composed of the tensions between state-bureaucrats (state elites) and politicians (political elites). See Heper, *State Tradition in Turkey*.
47. Taş, "The formulation," 6-8.
48. Balta, "The AKP's Foreign Policy."
49. Erdoğan, "Yeni Türkiye Vizyonu."
50. Öztürk and Baser, "The Transnational Politics."
51. Öztürk, "Turkey's Post-2016," 4.
52. Kara, "Linking," 14.

Disclosure statement

No potential conflict of interest was reported by the author(s).

References

Açıkel, Fethi. "Kutsal mazlumluğun' psikopatolojisi." *Toplum ve Bilim*, no. 70, Güz (1996): 153–198.

Arısan, Mehmet. "From Clients to Magnates, The (Not So) Curious Case of Islamic Authoritarianism in Turkey." *Southeast European and Black Sea Studies* 19, no. 1 (2019): 11–30.

Aytürk, İlker. "Post-post Kemalizm: Yeni Bir Paradigmayı Beklerken." *Birikim* 319 (2015): 34–48.

Aytürk, İlker. "Post-Kemalizm Nedir? Post-Kemalist Kimdir? Bir Tanım Denemesi." *Varlık*, no. 1337 (February 2019): 4–7.

Balta, Evren. "The AKP's Foreign Policy as Populist Governance." *Middle East Report* 288 (2018)(Fall 2018): 14–18.

Başer, Ekrem T. "Shift-of-axis in Turkish Foreign Policy: Turkish National Role Conceptions Before and During AKP Rule." *Turkish Studies* 16, no. 3 (2015): 291–309.

Başkan, Birol, and Ömer Taşpınar. *The Nation or the Ummah: Islamism and Turkish Foreign Policy*. Albany, NY: SUNY Press, 2021.

Bora, Tanıl. "Muhafazakâr ve İslamcı söylemde Beyaz Türk hıncı: Beyaz Türk'e kahretmek." *Birikim* 350 (2014): 6–45.

Bora, Tanıl, and Necmi Erdoğan. "Biz Anadolu'nun Bağrı Yanık Çocukları... Muhafazakar Populizm." In *Modern Türkiye'de Siyasi Düşünce, Cilt 5: Muhafazakarlık*, edited by Tanıl Bora, and Murat Gültekingil, 632–644. İstanbul: İletişim Yayınları, 2003.

Brown, Wendy. *States of Injury, Power and Freedom in Late Modernity*. Princeton: Princeton University Press, 1995.

Çapan, Zeynep Gülşah, and Ayşe Zarakol. "Postcolonial Colonialism? The Case of Turkey." In *Against International Relations Norms: Postcolonial Perspectives*, edited by Charlotte Epstein, 193–210. London: Routledge, 2017.

Chrissogelos, Angelos. "Populism in Foreign Policy." In *Oxford Research Encyclopedia of Politics*, edited by William R. Thompson. Oxford: Oxford University Press, 2017. https://oxfordre.com/politics/view/10.1093/acrefore/9780190228637.001.0001/acrefore-9780190228637-e-467

Çorbacıoğlu, Gül, and Ayşe Saktanber. "Veiling and Headscarf-Skepticism in Turkey." *Social Politics: International Studies in Gender, State & Society* 15, no. 4 (2008)(Winter 2008): 514–538.

Davutoğlu, Ahmet. *Stratejik Derinlik: Türkiye'nin Uluslararası Konumu*. İstanbul: Küre Yayınları, 2014.

Demir, Mustafa, Nicholas Morieson, and İhsan Yılmaz. "The Islamist Populism, Anti-Westernism and Civilizationism of Turkey's Directorate of Religious Affairs." *European Center for Populism Studies* (May 19, 2021). Accessed on June 30, 2022 at https://www.populismstudies.org/the-islamist-populism-anti-westernism-and-civilizationism-of-turkeys-directorate-of-religious-affairs/

Demiralp, Seda. "White Turks, Black Turks? Faultlines Beyond Islamism versus Secularism." *Third World Quarterly* 33, no. 3 (2012): 511–524.

Destradi, Sandra, and Johannes Plageman. "Populism and International Relations: (Un)predictability, Personalisation, and the Reinforcement of

Existing Trends in World Politics." *Review of International Studies* 45, no. 5 (2019): 711–730.

Durgun, Şenol. "Left-Wing Politics in Turkey: Its Development and Problems." *Arab Studies Quarterly* 37, no. 1 (2015)(Winter 2015): 9–32.

Ege, Aslı. "Foreign policy as a means of AKP's Struggle with Kemalism in relation to domestic variables." *Turkish Studies* 23, no. 5 (2022). Available at https://doi.org/10.1080/14683849.2022.2066527

Erdoğan, Recep Tayyip. *Yeni Türkiye Vizyonu: Mazlumların Sığınağı.* Ankara: Cumhurbaşkanlığı Yayınları, 2019.

Güney, Aylin, and Metin Heper. "The Military and Democracy in the Third Turkish Republic." *Armed Forces & Society* 22, no. 4 (1996): 619–642.

Gürpınar, Bulut. "Turkey and the Muslim Brotherhood: Crossing Roads in Syria." *Eurasian Journal of Social Sciences* 3, no. 4 (2015): 22–36.

Heper, Metin. *State Tradition in Turkey.* North Humberside: Eothen Press, 1985.

Howarth, David. *Discourse.* Philadelphia: Open University Press, 2000.

Howarth, David, and Yannis Stavrakakis. "Introducing Discourse Theory and Political Analysis." In *Discourse Theory and Political Analysis: Identities, Hegemonies and Social Change*, edited by David Howarth, Aletta J. Norval, and Yannis Stavrakakis, 1–23. Manchester: Manchester University Press, 2000.

Kaliber, Alper, and Esra Kaliber. "From De-Europeanisation to Anti-Western Populism: Turkish Foreign Policy in Flux." *The International Spectator* 54, no. 4 (2019): 1–16.

Kara, Mehtap. "Linking Turkey's domestic politics and foreign policy: The Justice and Development Party's political strategies and their divergent foreign policy effects." *Turkish Studies* (2022). Published Online May 8 2022, Available at https://doi.org/10.1080/14683849.2022.2060082

Kubicek, Paul. "Majoritarian democracy in Turkey: causes and consequences." In *Democratic Consolidation in Turkey: Micro and Macro Challenges*, edited by Cengiz Erisen, and Paul Kubicek, 123–143. London: Routledge, 2016.

Laclau, Ernesto. "Identity and Hegemony: The Role of Universality in the Constitution of Political Logics." In *Contingency, Hegemony, Universality: Contemporary Dialogues on the Left*, edited by Judith Butler, Ernesto Laclau, and Slavoj Zizek, 44–89. London: Verso, 2000.

Mikhail, Alan. "Why Recep Tayyip Erdoğan's Love Affair With the Ottoman Empire Should Worry the World." *Time* (September 3, 2020). Accessed on June 30, 2022 at https://time.com/5885650/erdogans-ottoman-worry-world/

Mudde, Cas, and R. Kaltwasser. Cristobal. *Populism.* Oxford: Oxford University Press, 2017.

Narlı, Nilüfer. "Concordance and Discordance in Turkish Civil-Military Relations, 1980-2002." *Turkish Studies* 12, no. 2 (2011): 215–225.

Özbudun, Ergun. "The Institutional Decline of Parties in Turkey." In *Political Parties and Democracy*, edited by Larry Diamond, and Richard Gunther, 238–265. Baltimore: Johns Hopkins University Press, 2001.

Özbudun, Ergun. "AKP at the Crossroads: Erdoğan's Majoritarian Drift." *South European Society and Politics* 19, no. 2 (2014): 155–167.

Özdalga, Elizabeth. *The Veiling Issue, Official Secularism and Popular Islam in Modern Turkey.* London: Routledge, 1998.

Özpek, Burak Bilgehan, and Nebahat Tanrıverdi Yaşar. "Populism and Foreign Policy in Turkey Under the AKP Rule." *Turkish Studies* 19, no. 2 (2018): 198–216.

Öztürk, Erdi. "Turkey's Post-2016 Foreign Policy Drivers: Militarization, Islam, Civilization and Power." *Hellenic Foundation for European and Foreign Policy (ELIAMEP) Policy Paper, No. 58* (2021): 3–10.

Öztürk, Ahmet Erdi, and Bahar Baser. "The Transnational Politics of Religion: Turkey's Diyanet, Islamic Communities, and Beyond." *Turkish Studies* 23, no. 5 (2022). Forthcoming, Available at https://doi.org/10.1080/14683849.2022.2068414.

Purvis, Trevor, and Alan Hunt. "Discourse, Ideology, Discourse, Ideology, Discourse, Ideology ... " *The British Journal of Sociology* 44, no. 3 (1993): 473–499.

Sawae, Fumiko. "Populism and the Politics of Belonging in Erdoğan's Turkey." *Middle East Critique* 29, no. 3 (2020): 259–273.

Secor, Anna. "Islamism, Democracy and the Political Production of the Headscarf Issue in Turkey." In *Geographies of Muslim Women: Gender, Religion and Space*, edited by Ghazi-Walid Falah, and Caroline Rose Nagel, 203–225. London: Guilford Press, 2005.

Singer, Sean R. "Erdoğan's Muse: The School of Necip Fazıl Kısakürek." *World Affairs* 176, no. 4 (November/December 2013): 81–88.

Taş, Hakkı. "The formulation and implementation of populist foreign policy: Turkey in the Eastern Mediterranean." *Mediterranean Politics* (2020). Published On-Line, October 2020, https://doi.org/10.1080/13629395.2020.1833160.

Taş, Hakkı. "Erdoğan and the Muslim Brotherhood: An outside-in approach to Turkish foreign policy in the Middle East." *Turkish Studies* 23, no. 5 (2022). Published Online on 13 June 2022, Available at https://doi.org/10.1080/14683849.2022.2085096

Taşkın, Yüksel. "AKP's Move to 'Conquer' the Center-Right: Its Prospects and Possible Impacts on the Democratization Process." *Turkish Studies* 9, no. 1 (2008): 53–72.

Verbeek, Bertjan, and Zaslove Andrej. "Populism and Foreign Policy." In *The Oxford Handbook of Populism*, edited by Cristobal R. Kaltwasser, Paul Taggart, Paulina Ochoa Espejo, and Pierre Ostiguy, 611–631. Oxford: Oxford University Press, 2017.

Verbeek, Bertjan, and Andrej Zaslove. "The counter forces of European integration: nationalism, populism and EU foreign policy." In *The Sage Handbook of European Foreign Policy*, edited by Knud Erik Jørgensen, Asne Kalland Aarstad, Edith Drieskens, Katie Laatikainen, and Ben Tonra, 530–544. London: Sage Publications, 2015.

Williams, Garrath. "Dangerous Victims: On Some Dangers of Vicarious Claims of Victimhood." *Distinktion: Journal of Social Theory* 9, no. 2 (2008): 77–95.

Yavuz, M. Hakan. *Nostalgia for the Empire, The Politics of Neo-Ottomanism*. New York: Oxford University Press, 2020.

Yavuz, M. Hakan. "The Motives Behind Erdoğan's Foreign Policy: Neo-Ottomanism and Strategic Autonomy." *Turkish Studies* 23, no. 5 (2022). Forthcoming. Available at https://doi.org/10.1080/14683849.2022.2100700.

Yılmaz, Zafer. "The AKP and the Spirit of the 'New' Turkey: Imagined Victim, Reactionary Mood, and Resentful Sovereign." *Turkish Studies* 18, no. 3 (2017): 482–513.

Yılmaz, Onur Alp. "Sol-Kemalizmin Tasfiyesi: 12 Eylül'ün Atatürkçülüğü ve Kökenleri." *Atatürk Yolu Dergisi* 70 (2022): 473–485.

Yuval-Davis, Nira. *The Politics of Belonging, Intersectional Contestations*. London: Sage, 2011.

The transnational politics of religion: Turkey's Diyanet, Islamic communities and beyond

Ahmet Erdi Öztürk and Bahar Baser

ABSTRACT
The article builds on current academic debates pertaining to the use of religion in global politics. By examining how and why religion is used as a tool for foreign policy aims as well as for perpetuating a state's identity and institutional capacity at home and abroad; the article presents a theory-informed discussion on Turkey's transnational politics of religion from a comparative perspective. The country's use of religion as a political tool outside of its borders has been studied in Western Europe, Africa, Asia and the Balkans thanks to extensive fieldwork and interviews conducted between 2016 and 2020. The article investigates how and why Turkey has implemented similar policies with different aims in different geographic territories and the underlying material and normative motivations for this pursuit. The main argument presented in the article is that Turkey, under the rule of the AKP (Justice and Development Party), employs religion for three fundamental reasons: to bolster its regional and global influence, to access regions or groups that are difficult to reach through traditional foreign policy tools and to alter domestic political balances or amass power.

Introduction

In recent years, the intricate and multifaceted role that religion plays in domestic politics and foreign policy has become one of the most studied subjects in the fields of politics and international relations.[1] Researchers have investigated the various roles that Abrahamic religions such as Islam, Christianity and Judaism play in global politics[2] and discussed how and why some particular countries explicitly and implicitly utilize religion in both domestic and foreign policy.³ Numerous academic studies and policy papers make a series of assertions regarding the use of religion in global politics that can be categorized along three objectives which generally fit into the instrumentalization of religion both in domestic and foreign policy areas: (**a**) to bolster regional and global influence (**b**) to access regions and groups that are difficult to reach through conventional foreign policy tools and (**c**) to alter domestic political balances or amass power. These three objectives are debated in relation to the personal characteristics of the leaders and/or political groups which use religion in foreign policy as well as the state's identity and its institutional capacity. Beyond that, the causal factors driving the use of religion in foreign policy is still an important subject which should be scrutinized through the lens of multiple theories.

In accord with this Special Issue's goal of presenting a theory-informed perspective on Turkish foreign policy, this article uses the three objectives listed above as a starting point for discussion and further analyzes what countries seek to achieve by using religion as a foreign policy tool. It uses the contemporary Republic of Turkey's *sui generis* secular (*laik*) state structure[4] and its intricate instrumentalization of Sunni Islam in the new millennium both at the level of the ruling party—namely the Justice and Development Part (*Adalet ve Kalkınma Partisi* – AKP)—and throughout society as a case study into how state and non-state actors use religion in international relations[5] for different reasons. Furthermore, semi-non-state religious organizations that maintain an indirect relationship with the state have also been using religion in global politics for various aims and these are also affecting Turkey's image outside its borders, as some policy makers have underlined that 'after the beginning of 2010s we have been observing Turkey's abuse of Islam beyond its territories'.[6] In this context, Turkey's use of religion as a political tool outside of its borders has been studied in Western Europe, Africa[7], Asia[8] and the Balkans.[9] Using this background, this article presents a comparative analysis by discussing these regions and beyond. It also investigates how and why Turkey has implemented similar policies with different aims in different geographic territories and the underlying material and normative motivations for this pursuit.

This study relies methodologically on two foundations. The first is ethnographic findings acquired from field studies conducted between 2016 and 2020 in the Balkans, Western Europe and the United States. These findings rely on 52 semi-structured interviews with elites in Turkey, Bulgaria, North Macedonia, Serbia, Albania, Sweden, France, Germany, England and the US.[10] Most of the interviewees preferred to stay anonymous due to the political sensitivity of the issues discussed. Additionally, even though the general aim of the interviews was to understand the impact and transformation of Turkey's religious-oriented foreign policy and the host countries' reactions, all of the interviews have unique characteristics due to the different structures of each country. These interviews generally were conducted with the representatives of the Presidency of Religious Affairs (hereinafter *Diyanet*) in host countries, prominent figures of Turkey's various Islamic groups such as the Gulen Movement and Suleymanci communities, and Turkish diplomats and employees of foreign ministries in the host countries. Conducting these interviews offered an opportunity to examine how and in what manner Turkey utilizes religion and how elites and ordinary citizens in these countries react. The second methodological foundation is based on the secondary resources covering the activities of Turkey's religious apparatuses in Africa, Asia and the Caucasus. The article also examines official publications of the *Diyanet* and statements made by Turkish President Recep Tayyip Erdoğan on some political issues.

The article is structured as follows: the first section investigates how various structures and actors have utilized religion in the changing world order. The second section explicates how Turkey has used Sunni Islam in different ways throughout history. This section particularly focuses on Turkey's use of religion in domestic and foreign policy as well as the period of AKP rule during which religion has been used to a greater extent. The subsequent sections will discuss how Turkey and various Turkey originated actors have utilized religion in the Balkans, Western Europe, the Anglo-Saxon world, Africa, and Eurasia. The final section addresses conclusions that may be made by comparing Turkey's actions in various regions.

The use of religion in international relations and those who use it: state, non-state and intermediary actors

Some have noted that the world has witnessed in the past century the near disappearance of religion from political spaces with the growth of secularism and its profound influence on global politics.[11] However, this situation has ended with renewed influence of religion in world politics. This influence continues in a multifaceted and layered manner. The evolving situation has precipitated a number of debates since the early 2000s[12], and the extent to which various actors utilize religion in global politics is studied in greater depth with novel questions in this article.

The first issue is one of sequencing, namely the use of religion by states first in domestic politics then in foreign policy. According to Fox, the use of religion in foreign policy – especially by states – relates to those states' domestic political environments.[13] Often, countries' deliberate use of religion in foreign policy can be traced back to domestic political developments.[14] Some leaders, such as Turkey's Erdogan, have frequently tried to use religion for domestic political gain.[15] However, one should not present religion solely as an instrument to be (ab)used by leaders. Religion is one of the most important determinants of a state's identity and its institutions,[16] and thus on a most basic level studies exploring connections between and use of religion in foreign policy would fall under the constructivist paradigm. How states conceptualize and use religion as a foreign policy tool, however, depends on their political systems, state structures and the identities and objectives of their political actors.[17] The use of religion as a foreign policy tool typically has mixed results, as constructivist Kubálková argues, and it is thus essential to study the ontological differences between states that use religion in foreign policy.[18] In light of this, it is useful to return to the research question to ask how and why a given state uses the same tools with different aims in different geographic territories and what would be the underlying material and normative motivations for this pursuit.

Secondly, it is important to note that non-state actors also use religion as a foreign policy tool. Although a state's instrumental se of religion in the international arena may appear to conform to realist theory, the utilization of religion by non-state actors on the global stage can be better explained with a constructivist interpretation that gives primacy to identity, norms and culture. Therefore, the use of religion in foreign policy for mostly non-state actors is not directly related with power relations.[19] Such a reading reveals how these actors differentiate their own norms over time with changing conditions around the world and how they alter their foreign policy decision making accordingly. While the activities of some actors serve the purpose of searching for peace and rapprochement[20], some actors use religion as an instrument to disseminate violent narratives.[21] This is beyond the limits of realism and neo-realism which study world politics through mostly, but not fully with a state-centered positivist lens.

When considering the comprehensive nature of Islam, compared to the other Abrahamic religions, and the authoritarian structures of many states with Muslim-majority populations,[22] it is important to mention the existence of a third actor instrumentalising religion in foreign policy. Definitely, this issue is not related to the nature of Islam, but to states and their objectives. These actors may appear to be non-state actors and may claim to be so, but when contemplating the relationships they form with the state in the name of partnership with ruling authorities, it would be more accurate to describe them as semi-civic organizations. Although these organizations generally operate in an interests-based manner within authoritarian state structures, they appear in quite different forms in different geographical spaces. These organizations, which are not autonomous, endeavor to establish global influence pursuant to their own identities and religious views and strive to gain visibility. The relationships, consistencies and conflicts between states, non-state actors and semi-civic structures that use religion in the international arena affect their influence and visibility across the world and how countries that allow them to operate within their borders perceive them.

Important questions here are how states, non-state actors and semi-civic structures use religion in international politics, and why. It is apparent in this context that religion is a source of power, suggesting it can be analyzed from a realist perspective, but also a given that it includes norms, values and identity, factors given more weight under constructivist approaches. Clearly, religion is not a classical form of (hard) power. This compels us consider the connection between religion and soft power, an issue that arose with the first articulation of the concept of soft power by Joseph Nye in very early 1990s.[23] Jeffrey Haynes was one of the first to seriously include religion within the scope of soft power. Haynes argues that both religion and religious actors are determinants of foreign policy influence and that this influence must be defined as religious soft power.[24] However, this influence may also appear in both positive and negative contexts in various indirect manners when considering the ambivalent nature of religion. Although the past decade has seen a significant increase in discussions over how religion and religious institutions and actors can be used as elements of soft power in global politics[25], the number of studies approaching the topic through collective readings of domestic and foreign policy is rather small and sceptical. Mandaville and Hamid, who further expanded on this trajectory,[26] identified three ways in which states exercise religious soft power transnationally. First is the institutional and normative capacity of states and their civilizational affinity, second is the socio-political circumstances of states and the aims of those seeking to wield religious soft power, and third is the double-edged sword structure of religious soft power. Finally, Bettiza suggests that some states act as important religious institutions and that their use of religion with and as a symbolic, cultural and network-based element in foreign policy compels us to broaden the scope of what is typically meant by soft power.[27]

It is certainly possible to synthesize all these definitions, especially when studying Turkey's use of religion as a foreign policy tool. However, the advantage of the constructivist approach is that it enables us to study the instrumentalization of religion in global politics both vertically and horizontally by scrutinizing it within a matrix of power, norms, values, and identity. Furthermore, it also enables us to interpret different actors' use of religion in various forms. Therefore, constructivism would a more suitable lens through which Turkey's transnational politics of religion under the AKP rule, which has different dimensions and actors, can be studied.

Scrutinising Turkey's history along the axis of religion

'Islam will not act according to us; we will act according to Islam'

Recep Tayyip Erdogan 2019[28]

Although Turkey's founding elite claimed to have established an entirely new republic amid the ruins of the Ottoman Empire, the Republic of Turkey, in certain respects, rests upon continuities with its predecessor. A complete departure from history was not realistic. One of the most important points at which a sort of paradoxical logic emerged was when the ostensible secular Turkey began to utilize and instrumentalize religion. Although the Republic of Turkey asserts that it withdrew religion from the core of the state and enshrined *laiklik* as one of the building blocks of the state's structure, it borrowed a method of governance directly from the Byzantines and the Ottomans. This method entails the state's use and administration of religion through certain institutions or agencies. The *Diyanet*, founded in 1924, assumed this responsibility during the Republican era, as did a council during the Byzantine era and the office of the Shaykh al-Islam during the Ottoman era.[29]

The *Diyanet* is tasked with governing Sunni Islam for the benefit of society on behalf of the state and within the limitations the state has imposed. The principle of *laiklik* and the foundational philosophy of Turkey, which sought to seize control of religion through the *Diyanet*, legally banned autonomous religious organizations/communities, though it did not eliminate them entirely.[30] Discreetly operating religious communities have become important political actors. Religion remained inextricable from politics and continued to be even after the collapse of the Ottoman state. This continuity is apparent in the cadres of the *Diyanet*, particularly after the 1960s. As Professor Mehmet Görmez, who served as the director of the *Diyanet* between 2010-2017, noted a 2016 interview:

> In the late 1960s and in the 1970s, the *Diyanet*, perhaps unintentionally, entered into a relationship with other religious structures without being fully aware of it. Individuals close to religious organizations began to be employed to meet the personnel needs in Anatolia and various parts of the country. This was necessary and unavoidable.

This situation was the outcome of the interests-based unification of religion and state, as we noted above, while the 1960s and 1970s witnessed Turkey's exportation of various religious structures. The exportation of religion was a consequence of Turkish nationals and other Muslims choosing to migrate to various parts of the world, particularly Continental Europe.[31] The swelling numbers of migrants necessitated the establishment of organizations that would provide religious services for them in their new home countries. Due to the significant population of Turkish citizens in places such as Germany, Austria, France and Sweden and because Turkish citizens adopted a more moderate interpretation of Islam relative to other Muslim-majority countries, Western states chose Turkey to fill this role. The

Diyanet as well as other religious organizations thus began to operate internationally in the late 1970s and its role grew in the 1980s. Following the end of the Cold War in the early 1990s, some Turkish religious organizations became more active in the Balkans, Central Asia and Africa.[32] One of the most prominent of these organizations was the Gülen Movement, which embedded itself in Turkish politics in the 2000s. The Gülen Movement, which adopted a para-political character, became a key determinant of how Turkey utilized religion in foreign policy.[33]

In 2001, a political cadre of former defenders of Islamic ideology founded the AKP under the leadership of Erdoğan and, after winning elections in 2002, assumed sole control of the government. Particularly after 2006-2007, the AKP was certainly not alone in its use of religion and religious organizations. The Gülen Movement became one of the AKP's most important foreign policy partners through a coalition based on mutual interests and collaboration. Within this relationship, the Gülen Movement guided the AKP internationally and provided it with human resources and the AKP provided legal and normative legitimacy in return. However, especially after 2013, the deterioration of the Turkish economy, Erdoğan's adoption of an exclusive discourse that threatened certain sects of Turkish society, his oppressive use of religion and nationalism in domestic politics, and the interests-based battle he started with various groups, particularly the Gülen Movement, altered both Turkey's image and Erdoğan's policymaking. Following the 2016 coup attempt, Ankara's relations with the West became cooler than ever before due to the Islamization and nationalization occurring in Turkey.[34] Although Turkey is still governed by a secular constitutional system, Ankara uses religion in every societal domain in a rigid and intense manner, never before seen in its history.[35] Its heavy use of religion has far-reaching consequences throughout the world as well as in its domestic politics.

The balkans: neo-Ottomanism and imaginary reality

> 'Turkey establishes its Balkans policy from Ankara, but there are different realities of the region which Turkey could not manage to understand properly.'

These are the words of a prominent former member of the North Macedonian Parliament explaining the intricacies of Turkish-Balkan relations in 2019. While a sizable portion of the Balkans was ruled by the Ottomans for over three hundred years and consequently has some religious, cultural, and linguistic connections with modern Turkey, the Balkans is politically, economically, culturally and historically distinct from Turkey. Nevertheless, Turkey recognized the Balkans as part of its sphere of influence and made policy accordingly during the early Republican era and especially during the 2000s after the end of the Cold War and the wars in the former Yugoslavia.[36] This situation is a key reason why Turkey's Balkan policy is flawed, but it is progressively more differentiated during the AKP era for many different reasons. The main ones are the differences between Turkey and the Balkans' norms, values and identity perceptions. A key reason for this differentiation was Turkey's use of religion in every facet of its relationship with the Balkans and often to a much greater extent than necessary.

> 'We invited Turkey and its religious institutions to our country so that no sort of radical movement would disturb our country.'

This quote is from an interview we conducted in 2017 with Mihail Ivanov, an advisor to former Bulgarian President Zhelyu Zhelev, who invited the Turkish *Diyanet* to Bulgaria in the 1990s. The *Diyanet* also became active in Albania and North Macedonia in the 1990s. Turkey subsequently provided financial assistance and other support to the offices of muftis in these countries, and the *Diyanet* trained and assisted their imams when necessary. Similarly, other Turkish religious organizations, such as the Suleymanci community, began to establish influence through schools, student dormitories and other institutions after the birth of the Gülen Movement. These activities continued in the Balkans after 2002 due to the good relationship Turkish religious organizations maintained with the AKP, Turkey's economic growth, and the AKP's affinity for the West. Speaking in a 2018 interview on this matter, a former Albanian State Minister observed:

> '[When] the AKP rose to power, it seemed to prove that Islam and democracy were functioning collectively, and we viewed this situation positively. For us at the time, this demonstrated development and progress. But Turkey under the AKP later began to distance itself from democracy and implemented a slew of foreign policies based on religion, and this evoked questions perhaps not within society but among state elites.'

The AKP pursued serious investments and initiatives in the Balkans through the *Diyanet* and other institutions such as the Turkish Cooperation and Coordination Agency (*Türk İşbirliği ve Koordinasyon İdaresi Başkanlığı*, TIKA). For example, the *Diyanet* constructed the largest mosque in the Balkans in the Albanian capital of Tirana and built many others throughout the region. The *Diyanet* also began to support the offices of muftis in these countries through official agreements. It provided scholarship opportunities for youth in the region to study in Turkey, and both the public and elites in the region greeted these developments positively as they bolstered Turkey's visibility in the Balkans. However, the foreign policy initiatives Turkey implemented after 2013 based on domestic political changes occurring during these years provoked various reactions in the Balkans. These reactions were provoked by Turkey's widespread use of religion and religious apparatuses as foreign policy instruments.

One of the most significant issues was the international nature of the battle between the Gülen Movement and the AKP, especially after the 15 July 2016 coup. The Turkish government accused Fethullah Gülen of being the mastermind behind the coup attempt and demanded that countries such as Serbia, Bosnia and Herzegovina, North Macedonia, Albania and Kosovo outlaw Gülen Movement activities. While some countries, such as North Macedonia, complied with Turkey's demands, others, such as Albania, did not. Turkey made considerable investments in some Balkan countries in an effort to break the influence of the Gülen Movement, but these investments began to directly and indirectly influence religious spaces due to their religious character. An official from the North Macedonia Ministry of Foreign Affairs whom we interviewed in 2019 said;

> 'Especially after the failed coup attempt in Turkey, Erdoğan's Turkey sought to pacify oppositional Islamist actors in the region through the *Diyanet* and similar institutions and to situate its own Islamist agenda in the spirit of the Balkan people by building mosques and appointing loyal imams.'

This statement contains two differing explanations for Turkey's evolving use of Islam in foreign policy. It also exposes the manner in which Turkey uses religion internationally. Senior Turkish bureaucrats have also expounded upon this situation. In a 2020 statement, *Diyanet* Director Ali Erbaş emphasized that Turkey has incredibly strong relations with Balkan countries and that this cooperation will continue through religious education, services and religious publications. Erbaş, stressing the importance of the Balkans to Turkey, said, 'Our historical ties will continue as they have in the past.' This situation was predominantly met with satisfaction among the Muslims of the Balkans but evoked some questions within the region's non-Muslim communities. Turkey's use of religion in a more multifaceted manner in its Balkans policy after 2010 positively and negatively impacted the states and different religious groups in the region. This demonstrates that Turkey under the AKP is an extremely effective yet contentious actor in the Balkans. Turkey has acted on its nostalgic neo-Ottoman desires by dreaming up an imaginary reality in the Balkans by instrumentalizing its religious power in the region. Likewise, a constructivist interpretation would argue that Turkey's religious oriented foreign policy in the Balkans has different vertical and horizontal dimensions that use norms, belief, ideas, and institutions.

Western Europe: from helping to controlling the diaspora

> 'Turkey's use of religion has increasingly overreached its legal limits and involved diaspora politics in various ways. It is thus difficult to understand

which activities are related with religious service and which with diaspora control.'

These are the words of a French Ministry of Foreign Affairs official whom we interviewed in 2018 highlighting this situation. Turkey's religious-oriented relations have a storied history and are important to understanding the current situation. The motivations of Turkish religious institutions in Western Europe are different from their motivations in other parts of the world. This history is interwoven in the history of Turks' migration to Europe over the past century. Starting in the 1960s, a need to provide religious services to Turkish nationals migrating to Europe for economic reasons and individuals coming to Europe from other countries emerged. Similar to other regions, European states invited Turkey and organizations affiliated with the *Diyanet* into their countries or allowed them to establish the legal institutions necessary to operate in their borders because they believed the Turkish organizations could be more compatible with their social and political atmosphere. Therefore, starting the mid-1970s, Turkish religious organizations began to provide services to Turkish nationals and other Muslims in numerous countries including Germany, France, Austria, Sweden, and the Netherlands.[37]

These official religious institutions and other organizations became more active during the 1980s and 1990s and especially after the AKP rose to power in the 2000s. There are three underlying reasons for this: (a) Turkey's economic growth and ability to move resources internationally particularly between 2002 and 2011; (b) the growing areas of influence for the Turkish state as it used its religious organizations to operate internationally; (c) Turkey's use of religion in foreign policy for various reasons especially after 2011 and unification of its diaspora with other Muslims to exert influence in Western Europe.

For instance, as of 2020, Turkish institutions run more than nine hundred mosques in Germany. The Turkish-Islamic Union for Religious Affairs (*Diyanet İşleri Türk-İslam Birliği*, DITIB), a *Diyanet* institution, has sent more than one thousand imams—whose wages are paid by Turkey—from Turkey to Germany. Additionally, the *Diyanet* has representative offices, mosques and organizations operating on its behalf in countries including France, the Netherlands, Belgium, Sweden and Austria. Other religious organizations such as the Gülen Movement, Sulaimanis and Naqshibandis also have a number of associations, dormitories and institutions in these countries. However, all these organizations have left complex and oftentimes negative impressions on European political elites due to Turkey's changing domestic political balances and their consequences in the international arena. An official from the French Ministry of Foreign Affairs whom we interviewed in 2018 highlighted this situation:

'Turkey's religious institutions have operated in our country and other countries for years. We are – or were – very happy that they are present in our country. But as a result of some changes in recent years, we are seeing that these institutions sometimes engage in activities beyond the domain of their operations such that it piques our suspicions of these institutions. This compels us to seek out alternatives.'

Such sentiments also exist outside of France. The spill-over of the conflict between the Gülen Movement and the AKP went beyond Turkish borders[38] and led to different types of activities being enacted in Europe after 2014 by the *Diyanet* as well as institutions with which it has direct and indirect relationships. For instance, an investigation that began in Germany in 2015 and later spread to Austria and France showed that local institutions affiliated with the Turkish *Diyanet* and other Turkish religious structures operated in coordination with Turkish intelligence against both the Gülen Movement and other oppositional organizations. In other words, the Turkish state used mosques and Muslim institutions as tools to exert influence over the diaspora. These institutions also used propaganda to advertize Erdoğan's domestic and European policy. Erdoğan's Turkey grew more authoritarian, utilized religion excessively as a tool of legitimation and began to collect intelligence and propagate an evolving state identity in the diaspora in line with its authoritarian tendencies.[39] However, these operations were met with different reactions in Western Europe than in the Balkans, the fundamental reason for which was the divergent formation of power relations between the countries. For example, French President Emmanuel Macon considered banning or, at the very least, limiting the operations of the *Diyanet* and spoke about rumors that had emerged before 2021 regarding the institution's interference with France's upcoming elections:

'In Continental Europe today, there are community organizations, local groups and political groups, among which is the *Diyanet*, which [has been] mobilized by Turkey's official organs of propaganda ... They sometimes interfere with our elections and other times finance [European] organizations. We have seen this again in recent days.'

The institutional response from senior positions in the French government was not the only reaction in Europe. Many countries, including Germany, Austria and Sweden, reacted like this or in similar ways. This demonstrates that Turkey's religious institutions have become powerful in Western Europe during the AKP era while at the same time changing their focus from merely providing services to govern or control the diaspora.[40] This evokes a number of questions about autonomy and certainly falls outside of the space for the historical use of religion and religious institutions. This is also related the ambivalent use of religion and limited capacity of religious soft power as it was argued previously.

The Anglo-Saxon world: the struggle to close the gap in a race entered late

Comparatively speaking, Turkey's religious institutions and structures began to organize relatively in the Anglo-Saxon world, which includes the United States (US) and the United Kingdom (UK). There are four main reasons for this: (a) Turkey does not have the historical relationship with the US and UK that it does with the Balkans or Continental Western Europe; (b) the Turkish diaspora in the Anglo-Saxon world is smaller than its Continental West European counterpart, and Turkey thus lacks the direct channel for the provision of services in the US and UK that it has in other parts of Europe; (c) the share of Turkish nationals within the Muslim populations in these countries is relatively small compared to those from other regions, and there is no role that Turkey could fill in religious spaces in these countries because the other Muslim communities in these countries are already well organized; and (d) the religion-state and community relations in Anglo-Saxon countries are subject to less government control relative to those in the Balkans and Continental Western Europe, so Turkey's ability to establish relations with the states is thus considerably weaker. Isobel Ingham-Barrow, head of policy at Muslim Engagement and Development, spoke about this situation in a 2020 interview:

> 'I can say, particularly for the UK, that most of the Muslims here come from Asia, and Turkish Muslims have not been in the most visible position, at least until recently. However, the fact that Turkey has become discussed in the context of religion around the world in recent years brought the subject of Turkey to the agenda. But it is still not a very widespread topic.'

Turkey's organizational efforts in the UK with religious institutions, at least officially, began much later compared to its efforts in other parts of Europe. The Diyanet Foundation of England began providing services in 2001 through organic ties to the Turkish Embassy in London's Religious Services Consultancy, and it is now one of many Turkish organizations engaging in religious and cultural activities with Turks in the UK. There are more than seven mosques affiliated with the Turkish Diyanet Foundation of England, with the Luton Turkish Islamic Centre Mosque and the Bristol Turkish Islamic Centre Mosque being two key examples. The foundation also installs cadres of religious officials to the mosques or masjids that the various Turkish organizations build. Additionally, the Gülen Movement and Naqshibandis have various religious institutions, mosques and organizations throughout England. The advent of these groups' organizational efforts dates back to the 1980s before they were affiliated with the *Diyanet*. Despite all these initiatives, there is currently no evidence confirming assertions that Turkish organizations attempt to control the diaspora, interfere with domestic politics, or export Turkish political trends using religious institutions. It can be confirmed, however, that Turkey's religious institutions have become more visible and active both domestically and internationally.

Similar to the UK, the *Diyanet*'s operations began late in the US relative to those in Europe. The Diyanet Centre of America was founded in 1993 as an institution functioning in coordination with the Turkish *Diyanet*. Prior to this, however, Turkish Muslims had already taken advantage of religious freedom in the US and founded Turkish mosques and religious associations. However, these mosques have strong cultural and nationalist undertones and have thus isolated Turks from other American Muslims. The buildings have mainly been named after Ottoman Sultans, similar to mosques in Turkey. A Turkish flag flies above each mosque, and the interior decor in each pays homage to Turkish culture, making them less appealing to non-Turks. The fact that the Turkish-American community and other Muslim groups do not share religious spaces is also caused by a linguistic gap between Turkish Muslims and non-Turkish Muslims. Religious officials serving at these mosques generally do not know much English and therefore their communications are limited with Turkish originated diaspora members. Therefore, Turkey's religious oriented influence is limited when compared to the other parts of the world. It is important to note that the *Diyanet* and other Turkish religious institutions engage in far fewer initiatives in the UK and US, and this is due to the social and political configurations in these countries as well as the character of their Turkish diaspora. This also demonstrates the limited power of religion alone.

Africa: the religious dimension of neo-colonialism and neo-ottomanism

Turkey's efforts to hasten political, military, cultural and economic relations with African countries began with the 'African Expansion Action Plan' prepared in 1998, but this plan remained merely an idea until the AKP rose to power in 2002 and announced 2005 as the 'Year of Africa'. That same year, Turkey attained observer status at the African Union. The cumbersome progression of relations with the West and European Union in the late 2000s and early 2010s and the wave of rebellions known as the 'Arab Spring' after 2010 motivated Turkey to strengthen its relationships with African states. Accordingly, in the early 2010s Turkey turned to Africa in search of new trade partners and to reinforce its diplomatic influence on the continent. One of the most important contributions to Turkey's strength in Africa was the Gülen Movement, which had operated there for years through educational institutions and other organizations. As a result of these initiatives, the number of Turkish diplomatic missions in Africa rose from 12 in 2002–42 in 2020. Both public and private companies in Turkey including Turkish

Airways, TIKA, the Humanitarian Relief Foundation, the Maarif Foundation, the Yunus Emre Institute, the Red Crescent and the Anadolu Agency maintained relations with Africa. There are a few underlying motivations for Turkey's growing presence in Africa.

The first is the neo-Ottomanism that first entered Turkish political spaces with Turgut Özal in the 1980s but became dominant in the late 2000s as a consequence of Ahmet Davutoğlu's influence in the AKP and Turkish politics. Davutoğlu and Erdoğan's neo-Ottomanism, which would later emerge as a leader-oriented ideology, not only called for Turkey to influence former Ottoman territories but also encouraged Ankara to use religious and cultural partnerships to influence regions with significant Muslim populations around the world.[41] This influence indicates a relationship predicated on neo-colonialism and hegemony, as it gave the appearance of a tutelary system over these geographic regions. Turkey began to aspire to a degree of dominance over North Africa in particular but also over the entire continent.

The second reason for Turkey's growing presence in Africa was the struggle for global dominance Turkey entered with some Western states after 2014. Turkey competed with countries such as France, which has historically dominated North African countries, that were former Ottoman territories. This process can be seen as a combination of neo-colonialism and neo-Ottomanism, and was, in a sense, a geopolitical battle in which religious institutions were used as weapons. While Turkey's growing presence in Africa may not appear to be explicitly religious, former *Diyanet* Director Mehmet Görmez clearly underscored its religious character in a 2016 interview:

> 'We have a legacy from the Ottoman Empire in that region and a responsibility to our religious brothers. We cannot leave them struggling or abandoned.'

The *Diyanet* and other Turkish transnational state apparatuses opened wells and provided health services and food aid, especially on religious holidays, in countries including Somalia, Nigeria and Angola.[42] The Turkish Diyanet Foundation also provides urgent humanitarian assistance to regions experiencing crises such as civil wars and natural disasters. Additionally, the *Diyanet* prints and distributes the Quran in nine languages in 24 African countries and provides imam support to African mosques.

While all these activities were not directly organized by the Gülen Movement, which was very active in Africa between 2007 and 2013, they were indirectly supported by it. However, just as in the Balkans and in Western Europe, the close relationship between the Turkish state and the Gülen Movement devolved into a conflict that spread beyond Turkey's borders and into Africa after 2013. Although there is not currently evidence that the *Diyanet* or other Turkish religious structures directly clashed in Africa as they did in the Balkans or Western Europe, Turkey expanded relations with African countries to hinder the Gülen Movement's operations, and increased its own religious, cultural and economic activities in Africa, legitimizing these actions with a neo-Ottomanist discourse. Turkey also features alongside China, India, Russia, Brazil, the US, the EU, and the Gulf states, which have all recently increased their presence in Africa. It is important to note, however, that Turkey is trying to establish its presence and power in Africa through religious and cultural partnerships, though African political elites largely do not view these efforts positively, as in the Balkans. This also demonstrates that religion can serve cover different socio-political purposes and therefore it has the double-edged sword structure.

Eurasia: the fusion of islamism and turkism

During the Cold War, Turkey did not – or was unable to – meaningfully influence the Soviet Turkic republics and the broader Eurasian region due to the bipolar world order and the secular ideas defining Soviet identity. However, the AKP began to penetrate these regions using religion in the early 2000s and attempted to assume a tutelary role. After the collapse of Soviet Union in 1991, the *Diyanet* implemented numerous initiatives directed at the region to meet the growing demands of Muslim communities living in Caucasus and Central Asia. Furthermore, has started to play a role of protecting and preserving Islam in the region. One of the highly ranking *Diyanet* official commented on this situation in a 2016 interview:

> 'Our services, especially during the Soviet era, pertain to the urgent needs emerging in the fields of religious education and services that have been ignored and denied for almost a century under the inhumane and tyrannical policies of hostile and atheist regimes. As the Muslim nations and communities in the Eurasian region gained independence and autonomy, our regional activities prioritised, as an urgent matter, the reconstruction and betterment of the culturally interwoven religious identities and senses of belonging, with a consideration of the needs of the era.'

In this regard, the Islamic Council of Eurasia (*Avrasya İslam Şurası*), an organization sponsored by the *Diyanet*, provides nearly all the services which were mentioned in the above quotation. The Islamic Council of Eurasia is a collaborative initiative launched in 1995 primarily to facilitate cooperation in the areas of religious services and education between indigenous religious institutions in Muslim countries and the institutions of Muslim society in Eurasia. The fundamental objective of this collaborative initiative, which is thought to serve as a forum for counsel to address contemporary religious issues, is to facilitate cooperation between Muslim religious institutions and organizations to provide religious services and education needed by Muslim communities in a uniform and coordinated manner.

The fact that the Islamic Council of Eurasia operates under the auspices of the *Diyanet* in the Turkic republics bolsters the religious and ethnic tutelary system Turkey maintains in the region. Although this tutelage may be symbolic, the Islamic Council of Eurasia normatively engages in religious spaces on contemporary religious issues such as the determination of new approaches and methods in the provision of religious services and education. This is the very classical and successful examples of Turkey's religious soft power in the region.

However, they also connect to Turkey's wider ambitions. For example, Erdoğan attended the 2018 opening ceremony of the Bishkek's Imam al-Sarakhsi Mosque that the *Diyanet* and the Turkish Diyanet Foundation had constructed in the capital of Kyrgyzstan. This mosque is the largest in Central Asia. Erdoğan, speaking at the ceremony, stated, 'Our mosque and its complex will, God willing, be conducive for the rejuvenation, of the religion, language, history, culture and conversation that previously existed between Anatolia and Central Asia. This project has appeared after six years of considerable efforts and will remain at the heart of Central Asia for centuries as a gift from the Turks to the Kyrgyz people.'[43] We can understand from this statement that Turkey uses its religious institutions in these countries as both symbols and instruments of visibility, similar to what it has been doing in the Balkans and in Africa. That is to say, Turkey's religious oriented activities in the region have multidimensional aims.

Conclusion

This study examined how Turkey has historical utilized religion in its foreign policy while also discussing contemporary international activities and the interconnectedness of Turkish institutions (state, religious organizations, and non-state actors) in their operations in various regions. It predicated its arguments on interviews and on an analysis of these institutions' operations and made comparison across regions. Although 2002, when the AKP came to power, was not the starting point for Turkey's use of religion in foreign policy, its utilization certainly grew after this year and accelerated throughout the 2010s. Turkey's operations in this space are too complex and interwoven to be singularly labelled as neo-colonial, hegemonic or from a simple realist perspective. In recent years, Turkey has employed religion in foreign policy for three fundamental reasons: (**1**) to bolster its regional and global influence (a Realist interpretation), (**2**) to access regions or groups that are difficult to reach through traditional foreign policy tools (a more Constructivist interpretation that speaks to the role of identity and culture) and (**3**) to alter domestic political balances.

Turkey's shift of its domestic political trends and agenda to the international arena and its use of material force while doing so prevents us from arguing that it has used religion only as soft power in foreign policy. Nevertheless, Turkey's use of religion in foreign policy indicates a certain change that has unfolded in its state identity, as constructivists would argue. It is important to note, however, that regardless of the degree to which Turkey appears to utilize religion and religious organizations, the degree in which these activities generate influence relies on three factors. The first one is the relationships and power dynamics that foreign countries maintain with Turkey. The second one is the characteristics of the Turkish diaspora and other Muslim diasporas in those countries. And lastly, the normative and practical connections with Turkey that are held Muslims of other countries and the power and influence of Turkish religious organizations in that region. In this context, the use of religion in foreign policy, especially for Turkey, cannot be studied on a single level or through a single lens because of its horizontally and vertically multidimensional structure.

Notes

1. Warner and Walker, 'Thinking about the role'; Sandal and Fox, *Religion in international relations theory*; and Haynes, *Religion in Global Politics*.
2. Mandaville, *Islam and Politics*; Cesari, *What is Political Islam*; and Marshall, 'Roman Catholic Approaches'
3. Bettiza, *Finding Faith in Foreign Policy*; Henne, 'Government interference in religious institutions'; James and Ozdamar, '"Religion as a factor in ethnic conflict'
4. Ozturk, 'Turkey's Diyanet under AKP rule'.
5. Haynes, *Religion and International Relations*, 5, and Sandal and James, 'Religion and international relations theory,' 9.
6. Interview with high-ranking French Interior Ministry staffer in May 2018.
7. Ozkan, 'Turkey's Religious and Socio-Political Depth'.
8. Korkut, 'The Diyanet'.
9. Ozturk and Gozaydin, 'A Frame'
10. A majority of the interviews were conducted by the first author. Both authors contributed to the theoretical framework and conceptual analysis of the data gathered as a result of multi-sited ethnographic fieldwork.
11. Philpott, 'The rise and fall'.
12. Micklethwait and Wooldridge, *God is Back*.
13. Fox, 'Religion as an overlooked element,' 53.
14. Fox and Sandler *Bringing Religion*, 168.
15. Yavuz, and Öztürk. 'Turkish secularism and Islam under the reign of Erdoğan'.
16. Brown and James, 'The religious characteristics of states,' 1345.
17. Henne, 'The two swords'.
18. Kubálková, 'Towards an international political theology'.
19. Sandal and Fox, *Religion in International Relations Theory*, 176.
20. Sandal, 'Religious actors'.
21. Gurses, 'Is Islam a cure?'.
22. Kuru, *Islam, Authoritarianism, and Underdevelopment*.
23. Nye, 'Soft power.'

24. Haynes, *Religious Transnational Actors*.
25. Ciftci and Tezcur, 'Soft power'.
26. Mandaville and Hamid, 'Islam as statecraft'.
27. Bettiza, 'States, Religions and Power'.
28. Cumhurbaskani Erdogan; 'Biz Islam'a Gore Hareket Edecegiz Islam Bize Gore Degil https://www.youtube.com/watch?v=v80YpZ-I1cI
29. Ozturk and Sozeri, 'Diyanet as a Turkish Foreign Policy Tool'.
30. Öztürk, 'Transformation of the Turkish Diynaet'.
31. Citak, 'National conceptions'.
32. Öztürk, 'Religion, Identity and Power'.
33. Watmought and Ozturk, 'The future'.
34. Candar, *Turkey's Neo-Ottomanist Moment*.
35. Yilmaz and Albayrak, *Populist and Pro-Violence*.
36. Bechev, 'Turkey in the Balkans'.
37. Citak, 'The institutionalization'.
38. Tas, 'A history'.
39. Yabanci, 'Home State Oriented Diaspora Organizations,' and Baser and Ozturk, 'Positive and negative'.
40. Baser and Feron, 'Host state reactions'.
41. Yavuz, *Nostalgia for the Empire*.
42. Ozkan, 'Turkey's Religious'.
43. 'Erdogan Kirgizistan'da Cami Acilisi Yapti,' *Haberler.com*, September 2, 2018, accessed April 12 2022 at, https://www.haberler.com/guncel/erdogan-kirgizistan-da-cami-acilisi-yapti-11196649-haberi/

Acknowledgement

This project has received funding from the European Union's Horizon 2020 research and innovation programe under the Marie Skłodowska-Curie grant agreement No 891305.

Disclosure statement

No potential conflict of interest was reported by the author(s).

References

Baser, Bahar, and Élise Féron. "Host State Reactions to Home State Diaspora Engagement Policies: Rethinking State Sovereignty and Limits of Diaspora Governance." *Global Networks* 22, no. 2 (2022): 226–241.

Baser, Bahar, and Ahmet Erdi Ozturk. "Positive and Negative Diaspora Governance in Context: From Public Diplomacy to Transnational Authoritarianism." *Middle East Critique* 29, no. 3 (2020): 319–334.

Bechev, Dimitar. "Turkey in the Balkans: Taking a Broader View." *Insight Turkey* 14, no. 1 (2012): 131–146.

Bettiza, Gregorio. *Finding Faith in Foreign Policy: Religion and American Diplomacy in a Postsecular World*. Oxford: Oxford University Press, 2019.

Bettiza, Gregorio. "States,: Religions and Power: Highlighting the Role of Sacred Capital in World Politics." Working Paper, Berkley Center for Religion, Peace, and World Affairs, Washington DC, 2020.

Brown, Davis, and Patrick James. "The Religious Characteristics of States: Classic Themes and new Evidence for International Relations and Comparative Politics." *Journal of Conflict Resolution* 62, no. 6 (2018): 1340–1376.

Çandar, Cengiz. *Turkey's Neo-Ottomanist Moment*. London: Transnational Press, 2021.

Cesari, Jocelyne. *What is Political Islam?* Boulder, CO: Lynne Rienner Publishers, 2018.

Ciftci, Sabri, and Güneş Murat Tezcür. "Soft Power,: Religion, and Anti-Americanism in the Middle East." *Foreign Policy Analysis* 12, no. 3 (2016): 374–394.

Çitak, Zana. "The Institutionalization of Islam in Europe and the Diyanet: The Case of Austria." *Ortadoğu Etütleri* 5, no. 1 (2013): 167–182.

Citak, Zana. "National Conceptions,: Transnational Solidarities: Turkey, Islam and Europe." *Global Networks* 18, no. 3 (2018): 377–398.

Fox, Jonathan. "Religion as an Overlooked Element of International Relations." *International Studies Review* 3, no. 3 (2001): 53–73.

Fox, Jonathan, and Shmuel Sandler. *Bringing Religion Into International Relations*. New York: Palgrave Macmillan, 2004.

Gurses, Mehmet. "Is Islam a Cure for Ethnic Conflict? Evidence from Turkey." *Politics and Religion* 8, no. 1 (2015): 135–154.

Haynes, Jeffrey. *Religion in Global Politics*. London: Routledge, 2014.

Haynes, Jeffrey. *Religious Transnational Actors and Soft Power*. London: Routledge, 2016.

Haynes, Jeffrey. "Religion and International Relations: What do we Know and how do we Know it?" *Religions* 12, no. 5 (2021): 328.
Henne, Peter S. "The two Swords: Religion–State Connections and Interstate Disputes." *Journal of Peace Research* 49, no. 6 (2012): 753–768.
Henne, Peter S.: "Government Interference in Religious Institutions and Terrorism." *Religion, State & Society* 47, no. 1 (2019): 67-86.
James, Carolyn C., and Özgür Özdamar. "Religion as a Factor in Ethnic Conflict: Kashmir and Indian Foreign Policy." *Terrorism and Political Violence* 17, no. 3 (2005): 447–467.
Korkut, Şenol. "The Diyanet of Turkey and its Activities in Eurasia After the Cold War." *Acta Slavica Iaponica* 28 (2010): 117–139.
Kubálková, Vendulka. "Towards an International Political Theology." *Millennium* 29, no. 3 (2000): 675–704.
Kuru, Ahmet T. *Islam, Authoritarianism, and Underdevelopment: A Global and Historical Comparison.* Cambridge: Cambridge University Press, 2019.
Mandaville, Peter. *Islam and Politics.* London: Routledge, 2020.
Mandaville, Peter, and Shadi Hamid. Islam as statecraft: How governments use religion in foreign policy." Brookings Institution, November 2018, accessed on March 31, 2022 at https://www.brookings.edu/research/islam-as-statecraft-how-governments-use-religion-in-foreign-policy/, 2018.
Marshall, David. "Roman Catholic Approaches to the Qur'an Since Vatican II." *Islam and Christian–Muslim Relations* 25, no. 1 (2014): 89–100.
Micklethwait, John, and Adrian Wooldridge. *God is Back: How the Global Revival of Faith is Changing the World.* New York: Penguin, 2009.
Nye, Joseph S. "Soft Power." *Foreign Policy* 80 (1990): 153–171.
Ozkan, Mehmet. "Turkey's Religious and Socio-Political Depth in Africa." *Emerging Powers in Africa, LSE IDEAS Special Report* 16 (2013): 45–50.
Öztürk, Ahmet Erdi. "Turkey's Diyanet Under AKP Rule: From Protector to Imposer of State Ideology?" *Southeast European and Black Sea Studies* 16, no. 4 (2016): 619–635.
Öztürk, Ahmet Erdi. "Transformation of the Turkish Diyanet Both at Home and Abroad: Three Stages." *European Journal of Turkish Studies. Social Sciences on Contemporary Turkey* 27 (2018).
Öztürk, Ahmet Erdi. *Religion, Identity and Power: Turkey and the Balkans in the Twenty-First Century.* Edinburgh University Press, 2021.
Öztürk, Ahmet Erdi, and İştar Gözaydın. "A Frame for Turkey's Foreign Policy via the Diyanet in the Balkans." *Journal of Muslims in Europe* 7, no. 3 (2018): 331–350.
Öztürk, Ahmet Erdi, and Semiha Sözeri. "Diyanet as a Turkish Foreign Policy Tool: Evidence from the Netherlands and Bulgaria." *Politics and Religion* 11, no. 3 (2018): 624–648.
Philpott, Daniel. "The Rise and Fall of Secularism in International Relations." In *Handbook on Religion and International Relations*, edited by Jeffrey Haynes, 24–37. Cheltenham UK: Edward Elgar Publishing, 2021.
Sandal, Nukhet A., and Patrick James. "Religion and International Relations Theory: Towards a Mutual Understanding." *European Journal of International Relations* 17, no. 1 (2011): 3–25.
Sandal, Nukhet Ahu. "Religious Actors as Epistemic Communities in Conflict Transformation: The Cases of South Africa and Northern Ireland." *Review of International Studies* 37, no. 3 (2011): 929–949.

Sandal, Nukhet, and Jonathan Fox. *Religion in International Relations Theory: Interactions and Possibilities*. London: Routledge, 2013.
Taş, Hakkı. "A History of Turkey's AKP-Gülen Conflict." *Mediterranean Politics* 23, no. 3 (2018): 395–402.
Warner, Carolyn M., and Stephen G. Walker. "Thinking About the Role of Religion in Foreign Policy: A Framework for Analysis." *Foreign Policy Analysis* 7, no. 1 (2011): 113–135.
Watmough, Simon P., and Ahmet Erdi Öztürk. "The Future of the Gülen Movement in Transnational Political Exile: Introduction to the Special Issue." *Politics, Religion & Ideology* 19, no. 1 (2018): 1–10.
Yabanci, Bilge. "Home State Oriented Diaspora Organizations and The Making Of Partisan Citizens Abroad: Motivations,: Discursive Frames, And Actions Towards Co-Opting The Turkish Diaspora In Europe." *Diaspora* 21, no. 2 (2021): 139–165.
Yavuz, M. Hakan. "Understanding Turkish Secularism in the 21th Century: A Contextual Roadmap." *Southeast European and Black Sea Studies* 19, no. 1 (2019): 55–78.
Yavuz, M. Hakan. *Nostalgia for the Empire: The Politics of Neo-Ottomanism*. Oxford: Oxford University Press, 2020.
Yavuz, M. Hakan, and Ahmet Erdi Öztürk. "Turkish Secularism and Islam Under the Reign of Erdoğan." *Southeast European and Black Sea Studies* 19, no. 1 (2019): 1–9.
Yilmaz, Ihsan, and Ismail Albayrak. *Populist and Pro-Violence State Religion: The Diyanet's Construction of Erdoğanist Islam in Turkey*. Singapore: Palgrave Macmillan, 2022.

OPEN ACCESS

Erdoğan and the Muslim Brotherhood: an outside-in approach to Turkish foreign policy in the Middle East

Hakkı Taş

ABSTRACT
Amidst multiple foreign policy flip-flops of the Turkish government, the Middle East is where observers agree most about the explanatory priority of ideational factors over realpolitik calculations. The assertive foreign policy activism to extend the country's role in the region has largely been linked to the Islamist leanings of the ruling Justice and Development Party (AKP). This study revisits Turkey's Middle East policy with a particular focus on the AKP's relations with the Muslim Brotherhood (Ikhwan al Muslimin), which marked Turkish foreign policy formulation and implementation in multiple theatres from Yemen to Egypt to Libya. Using a neoclassical realist approach, it argues that the AKP's ideological ties to the Ikhwan are significant for the availability of new resources but Turkish foreign policy behavior in the Middle East, including relations with the Ikhwan, reflects a grand strategy to respond to systemic and sub-systemic stimuli.

Introduction

In 2011, scholar Tariq Ramadan, grandson of the founder of the Muslim Brotherhood (*al Ikhwan al Muslimin*, hereafter Ikhwan), suggested that "Democratic Turkey is the template for Egypt's Muslim Brotherhood."[1] In the heyday of the Arab Uprisings, Turkey's ex-Islamists-turned-conservative-democrats were believed to inspire Islamists in the Middle East, in particular the various affiliates of Ikhwan, which were the "Arab Spring's largest immediate beneficiaries."[2] However, while the conventional idea of a Muslim-democratic "Turkish Model," as embodied in the ruling Justice and Development Party (*Adalet ve Kalkınma Partisi*, AKP), soon lost its relevance, some began to argue that the AKP and its leader, Recep Tayyip Erdoğan, were pursuing an Islamist foreign policy based on Ikhwan links

This is an Open Access article distributed under the terms of the Creative Commons Attribution License (http://creativecommons.org/licenses/by/4.0/), which permits unrestricted use, distribution, and reproduction in any medium, provided the original work is properly cited.

and ideology. Put differently, the template identified by Ramadan had, arguably, been reversed. This article casts a more critical view on such claims.

Invoking the glories of the Ottoman period, the AKP has engaged in a (neo)imperial project, a phenomenon well-described in Hakan Yavuz's contribution to this special volume.[3] Throughout its two-decades of rule, it has been invested in the Middle East more than in any other region. When compared to the Republic's history, this unmatched level of Middle Eastern involvement—along with the country's drift away from its Western orientation in the 2010s—has been subject to ideational readings and related to the AKP's Islamist identity as an "independent driver" of its foreign policy.[4] For many observers, the AKP's approach to Ikhwan and the Middle East is devoid of instrumental rationality. Some argue that Erdoğan, despite his pragmatism, has been "a captive of his ideological convictions."[5] Others even question the mental condition of Turkey's "Islamist" strongman and project him as the nearest approximation of a mad king pursuing over-ambitious foreign policy activism in the region.[6]

Countering the overwhelming domestic and ideational readings in the academic literature,[7] this article suggests that a fine-tuned, outside-in approach anchored in several systemic factors is better-suited to explain the underlying dynamics beneath Turkey's Middle East policy. It employs neoclassical realism, which offers a holistic understanding of whether foreign policy behavior is exogenously determined by the material conditions of the international system or endogenously by collective ideas and other domestic factors.[8] A growing body of literature draws on this approach to examine Turkish foreign policy in general,[9] and Middle East policy in particular.[10] This article seeks to contribute to the literature by delving into the heart of the debate and, in a most likely case design, calls into question the validity of a more ideational reading of Turkish foreign policy in the area where it is likely to be most persuasive. It focuses on the AKP's Middle East policy vis-à-vis its relationship with the Ikhwan, which, allegedly, forms the basis of its "Islamist" foreign policy reflexes.

Despite the centrality of the topic, references to various Ikhwan branches in the academic field are thin and scattered. This paper intends to develop a holistic outlook on the AKP-Ikhwan relations. It is not exhaustive, but suggestive of the rich scope of the developments in the post-Arab Uprisings era. The central argument is that, while the AKP's ideological ties to Ikhwan made resources available in the competitive logic of proxy warfare, Turkey's grand strategy and Ikhwan's role in it largely follow systemic incentives and constraints envisioned in structural perspectives. It begins with a brief critique of the ideational readings that grant Islamist/Ikhwan ideology a central explanatory role in Turkey's Middle East policy. As an alternative explanation, it analyzes systemic and sub-systemic imperatives and their implications for Turkish foreign policy towards the region. In the following sections, it discusses Ikhwan's role in Turkey's vision for a new regional order and assesses how the unit-level variables affected the decisions of the foreign policy executive in this regard.

Ikhwan ideology and foreign policy

The recurrent emphasis on the AKP's Islamist orientation in Middle East policy establishes a sharp contrast between the old Kemalist politics of avoidance and Turkey's current assertiveness in the region. Since 2009, the "shift of axis" debate has highlighted the AKP's increasing involvement in the Middle East as a foreign policy manifestation of its Islamist identity and, consequently, Turkey's retreat from Kemalist secularism and Westernization.[11] At the regional level, too, Turkey is part of a supposedly ideational struggle for the soul of Islam, depending on one's affinity for Ikhwan. This rivalry is framed ideologically as "'moderate versus Islamist' for Riyadh and Abu Dhabi, and 'competitive democracy versus authoritarian monarchy' for Ankara."[12] Whether religion is seen either as a primordial entity or social construct, ideational readings treat it as a self-standing referent that informs foreign policy perceptions and choices. From a broader perspective, ideas and beliefs matter a) as a meaning-making heuristic and cognitive short-cut, guiding policymakers' actions; b) as an institutional framework, building the *Zeitgeist* or shared systems of thought in any setting; or c) as strategic tools used to craft political discourse and mobilization.[13] Neoclassical realism recognizes the significance of ideas and beliefs such as religion as a transmission belt between systemic stimuli and foreign policy outputs. However, they are "analytically subordinate to the systemic factors, the limits and opportunities of which states cannot escape in the long run."[14]

Against the purported parochialism of area studies, Turkey-focused readings need to be put under comparative lenses for validity. Islamism, as an independent variable in foreign policy, is not enough to explain similar foreign policy behaviors of other regional players. For instance, the United Arab Emirates (UAE), dubbed "Little Sparta," has been equally aggressive in filling the perceived void left by the United States' (US) indifference and imposing its vision on the region.[15] From building a rimland of militias in Yemen to arm transfers for the rebels and Emirati fighters in Libya, this power projection hardly relates to any religiously-inspired agenda. Similarly, the prime motivation of Qatar's Wahhabi leaders in siding with Turkey in several regional conflicts was power maximization, not religion.[16] While it is true that as a small state with grand ambitions and few constraints, Qatar's support for actors in the Islamist spectrum makes it an essential part of the key conversations shaping the region, this support is largely considered instrumental, if not opportunistic, since Doha has sought influence through access to various political actors (Islamist and non-Islamist) abroad. In a similar vein, ideational readings attribute too much substance and coherence to the AKP's political identity and ideology. Erdoğan's dance with diverse political ideologies, from conservative democracy to Islamism to Turkish nationalism, invites a more nuanced reading.[17]

In terms of agent orientation, several observers point to the AKP's ideological kinship with Ikhwan, even referring to the party as its Turkish branch.[18] The AKP's antecedent, the National Outlook (*Millî Görüş*) Movement and its affiliated political parties under Necmettin Erbakan had a larger overlap with Ikhwan's world view, with the connections even gaining a personal level when Erbakan's niece married Ibrahim el-Zayat, the head of Ikhwan's organization in Germany. Erbakan's Welfare Party hosted several top Ikhwan figures at its party congress in 1993, including Mustafa Mashhur and Mahdi Akif. The AKP maintained such ties, as evidenced by Hamas leader Khaled Meshal's 2006 visit to Ankara or the AKP's hosting of Mohamed Morsi, the head of the Ikhwan's Freedom and Justice Party, at its 2012 party congress.[19] Following the 2013 post-coup suppression of Ikhwan in Egypt, Erdoğan showed his solidarity for the victims with the then popularized four-finger Rabaa salute. These existing ties later made available to the AKP some of the resources of the Ikhwan.

However, one should not overlook the bumpy trajectory of the AKP-Ikhwan relationship. In retrospect, the Ikhwan's leaders initially did not welcome the foundation of AKP as a split-away from the National Outlook. This formation was reminiscent of Ikhwan's own experience when some of its defectors founded the Wasat Party in 1996 and divided the movement. Moreover, in its early years, the AKP was constantly reassuring outside observers of its commitment to secularism and maintaining good relations with Israel. Obviously, such developments ran counter to Ikhwan's founding ideology, and its leaders did not accept the AKP as Islamist, but secular.[20] Finally, having learned its lesson from the fate of the National Outlook parties, which were shut down by the Constitutional Court for being a hub for anti-secular activities, AKP leaders worked hard to persuade the state elite of the absence of a hidden Islamist agenda, and acted cautiously to avoid overtly close relations with other Islamist actors at home and abroad.

The Arab Uprisings, however, marked a new phase in bilateral relations. Unlike former portrayals of the AKP as a splinter movement embracing Western secularism, Ikhwan began, at least strategically, using the popular "Turkish Model" discourse for its own political legitimation against the widespread charges of terrorism. By framing the AKP as a successful fusion of Islam and democracy, Ikhwan could now position itself as a rightful actor in the pursuit of a similar, viable, pro-Western project in Egypt. This was not an unrequited love, as Turkey, being an aspiring middle power, also wanted to get the best out of the turmoil in the region. While the

2013 coup moved Ikhwan much closer to Turkey, the rapprochement was replaced gradually by an embedded relationship, in which Ikhwan's prospects became increasingly tied to the AKP. After years of unceasing domestic and transnational repression, the Ikhwan weakened considerably in both organizational and financial terms, becoming a diaspora movement in exile with internal schisms. Although the divide over the leadership continues between Ibrahim Mounir's camp in London and Mahmoud Hussein's camp in Istanbul, Istanbul has become the new hub, hosting Ikhwan's several foundations, organizations, and TV channels.[21] In April 2016, Ikhwan leaders from all over the world gathered in Istanbul for an event titled "Thank you, Turkey," declaring their gratitude and allegiance to the Turkish leader as the only hope for the Islamic Ummah.[22]

While support for Ikhwan abroad did not start with Erdoğan and had precedence in Kemalist Turkey,[23] Erdoğan intensified Turkey's relations with Ikhwan not at the peak of its pan-Islamist vision but when he leaned more towards a nationalist foreign policy discourse. In an iconic twist, following the failure in 2015 of the Kurdish resolution process, the reference point of the Rabaa salute changed from support for Ikhwan to the AKP's new nationalist dictum of "one homeland; one state; one flag; one nation." Nevertheless, the recent militarized foreign policy behavior, to which Ikhwan is attached, is not merely an AKP phenomenon, but rests on a consensus within the state bureaucracy on several fronts. Turkey's incursion to Libya, for instance, was not mainly motivated by an Islamist urge to support the Ikhwan affiliates in a civil war but related to its power calculations to counterbalance other countries in the Eastern Mediterranean dispute through the well-supported Eurasianist "Blue Homeland" project.[24]

The question of the AKP's Ikhwan-based foreign policy expectably puts Turkey at the center and yet largely poses the diverse Ikhwan branches as passive recipients of Turkey's foreign policy decisions. When Morsi himself came to power in 2012, his regional leadership aspirations were harshly limited by material capabilities, and Egyptian foreign policy did not change much except for a few symbolic moves, like his visit to Tehran the same year. Besides forging strong relations with revolution supporters, Morsi adopted a non-confrontational approach towards Egypt's traditional allies, signaling no drastic foreign policy change at both the regional and global levels.[25] Moreover, Turkey's relations with diverse Ikhwan branches have taken different trajectories depending on the balances of power. Unlike the Egyptian Ikhwan, which was bound to Turkey's favors, the Yemeni front has a more transactional relationship with Turkey, shifting according to the involvement of other actors, such as Saudi Arabia and Iran. Especially since its 2015 launch of Operation Decisive Storm, Saudi Arabia has backed the Ikhwan-affiliated al-Islah Party in Yemen despite leading, at a broader regional level, the anti-Ikhwan campaign. Likewise, al-Islah seeks to keep its relations with Saudi Arabia safe in recognition of the latter's political, military, and economic clout in Yemen.[26] Ennahda in Tunisia remains at a cautious distance from Erdoğan, who, in contrast with his harsh reaction to the 2013 military intervention in Egypt, sufficed with a single statement calling the 2021 dismissal of the Tunisian government a "coup."[27] Overall, such diversity cannot be attributed to the primacy of a single ideological constant. Taking into account these phenomena, this paper adopts neoclassical realism to explain how Turkey's Middle East policy has been shaped by the global and regional dynamics.

Systemic and sub-systemic factors

When the collapse of the Soviet Union transformed the Cold War's bipolar international system into a unipolar one, the new structure led some scholars to claim US hegemonic exceptionalism in the absence of any balancing against the preponderant material capabilities of the US in the international distribution of power.[28] For pessimists, however, the unipolar system was just a temporary phase until a new multipolar system would emerge due to the inevitable pattern of hegemonic failure.[29] In fact, American decline has been a recurring narrative in academic debates since the 1950s. Yet, in its last wave, scholars citing the Great Recession (2007-2009) observe the power of the US shrinking in the face of rising challengers[30], a transformation producing a shift towards a nascent multipolar order. Even Francis Fukuyama, who once claimed the end of history, argued in 2021 for the end of the American era, with its peak period lasting less than twenty years from the 1989 fall of the Berlin Wall to the Great Recession.[31] Of course, the US still maintains a preeminence in multiple metrics of material capabilities. However, the Great Recession and the subsequent Eurozone Crisis not only underlined the shift of wealth and power from the (Transatlantic) West to the (Indo-Pacific) East but also raised doubts about the economic and financial robustness of US primacy. This marked the emergence of a de-centered "post-western world,"[32] in which the US ceased its commitment to defend the liberal international order and non-western authoritarian powers such as China and Russia emerged as alternative models of development.

The fading unipolar moment and the US's retrenchment played out most evidently in its withdrawal of overseas military deployments. Since the 1991 Gulf War, the US has had a strong direct military presence in the Middle East, with more than 200,000 troops stationed in the region (mostly in Iraq) in the early 2000s and cemented its position as the chief guarantor of the regional security order.[33] However, with the economic crisis constraining the interventionist impulse and growing fatigue with inconclusive military interventions, successive US administrations under Barack Obama, Donald

Trump, and Joe Biden have sought to devote fewer resources to and diminish the US troop presence in active conflict zones such as Syria, Iraq, and Afghanistan. The US cut down its military presence in part by a retreat to offshore balancing, e.g. reluctantly leading from behind during the Syrian war, or, even, as in the case of Afghanistan, a direct withdrawal of US troops.[34] The feasibility of this "right-sizing" policy is open to debate. However, the Middle East has been increasingly de-prioritized and replaced by a pivot toward Asia-Pacific to counter China's rise. As shown by the lack of retaliation against Iran, which was widely blamed for the attacks on Saudi oil facilities at Abqaiq and Khurais in 2019, the US did not want to be entrapped by the regional conflicts any longer. This also relates to energy issues—a prime motive behind US Middle East policy. Whereas the US's annual energy imports incrementally increased since the 1950s, reaching a record high in 2005, the numbers have decreased since then, making the country a net total energy exporter in 2019 for the first time since 1952 and signaling much less dependence on the Gulf energy supplies.[35]

At the sub-systemic level, the post-Arab Uprisings geopolitical turmoil, combined with multiple cases of state failures and conflict, has multiplied the impact of the US's perceived disengagement. In the absence of a regional hegemon, Washington's retreat from where it had previously overextended itself has created a perception of a power vacuum, stimulating two foreign policy behaviors in the Middle East: power maximization and balancing.

Strategic autonomy as power maximization

The perceived void left by the US withdrawal encouraged multiple regional actors to take a maximalist approach in pursuit of greater "strategic autonomy."[36] Unlike "restrictive strategic environments" that entail greater systemic impediments to a state's use of material power to achieve its interests, "permissive strategic environments," as in the case of Middle Eastern politics under a waning unipolar system, provide states with a broader range of strategies to respond to potential threats and opportunities.[37] Besides international players like Russia, opportunistically keen to fill the power vacuum, several ambitious aspirants in the region, such as Turkey, Iran, and the UAE, adopted power-maximizing behaviors under less systemic imperatives in an effort to move up the regional and global hierarchy.

If grand strategy is broadly defined as the organizing principle informing a state's relations with the outside world, the Turkish case represents a recent slide from integrationist revisionism to autonomous expansionism, both aiming to revise the existing regional order (see Table 1).[38] Previously, the rigid bipolar international system of the Cold War era pushed Turkey to align itself with the Western bloc in order to counterbalance potential

Table 1. The systemic and sub-systemic dynamics shaping Turkey's Middle East Policy

		Period		
		1945–1989	1989–2009	2009-now
System Level	Stimuli	World War II	The Demise of the Soviet Union	The Great Recession
	Global Order	Bipolar	Unipolar	Post-Unipolar
Subsystem Level	Stimuli	1952 Egyptian Revolution	1991 Gulf War	US Retreat, Arab Uprisings
	Regional Order	The Arab Cold War	US Hegemony	Power Vacuum
Unit Level	Turkey's Foreign Policy	Status Quo	Integrationist Revisionism	Autonomous Expansionism

Soviet aggression. Throughout this period, Turkish foreign policy was anchored in its traditional Western orientation and geopolitical position as the southern bastion of NATO. The advent of a unipolar system at the end of the Cold War altered Turkey's grand strategy from calculated pacifism to regional activism, adding new regional components to its foreign policy and redefining its position with multiple identities and historical assets.[39] After the US invasion of Iraq in 2003, Turkey found systemic incentive for more active involvement in the Middle East as well, and projected itself as a functioning Muslim democracy with a pro-Western orientation that could serve as an anchor for a new Middle East with Western-friendly democratic governments—known as the US's Greater Middle East Initiative. This revisionist policy meant improving cultural and economic ties to other countries and enhancing mediator and facilitator roles in regional conflicts. In fact, the AKP government opposed the motion allowing US troops to use Turkey's military bases and facilities in Iraq's 2003 invasion. Moreover, it also established contacts with Hamas, which was listed as a terror organization by the US and European Union (EU) but won the 2006 legislative election in the Palestinian territories. In general, however, the AKP thrived on a multidimensional and proactive foreign policy, mostly overlapping the national interests with those of the US and the EU.

In the permissive environment of the post-unipolar global system, Turkey, like other rising powers as potential gravity centers of the global economy and political order, has increasingly aimed to carve out more space and autonomy in the pursuit of raising its global and regional profile.[40] At the sub-systemic level, Turkey reoriented its foreign policy to respond to the dramatic political transformations in its immediate neighborhood. It pursued a maximalist, regional-hegemony-seeking behavior with the calculation that the authoritarian regimes in the region would sooner or later crumble through the Arab Uprisings, paving the way for the rise of Ikhwan offshoots across the region. With the same discursive claim of reinvigorating Pax Ottomana, the integrationist approach of the early years of AKP rule has been replaced by a more autonomous, interventionist policy with a more hawkish tone after the siege of Kobani in 2015 and, more pronouncedly, the 2016 abortive coup.[41] Turkey has pursued assertive, bellicose, and largely unilateral involvements such as oil and gas drilling in the Eastern Mediterranean basin or preemptive cross-border military operations in Northern Iraq and Syria.[42] It competed with other powers such as the UAE and Saudi Arabia for regional leverage, particularly through its involvement in the Libyan conflict, but also extended its direct presence from the Eastern Mediterranean basin to the Horn of Africa.

Balancing as security maximization

Another consequence born of perceived US apathy has been the new pattern of alliances. While the hegemon was extricating itself from the conflict-ridden region, the growing security challenges led to a latent-anarchic, self-help system in which security and survival were at stake. The Middle East, already marked by long-standing internal clashes, has heated up with the constant proliferation of threats under the increasing permeability of borders and power rivalries. In a volatile region, states have used different foreign policy tools, such as balancing, strategic hedging, and bandwagoning, as part of a strategy that includes both conflict and cooperation.[43] As power is more diffused and fragmented among a wider range of competing state and non-state actors, the security concerns primarily lead to new pacts and alliances.

Although neither Russia nor China can match the US presence in the Middle East, regional powers have tended to cooperate with non-Western powers in the post-unipolar world. The systemic incentives and constraints have led to a series of back and forth plays in Turkish foreign policy,[44] with the power-maximizing behavior accompanied by a balancing strategy. As Turkey and the US gradually lost their shared strategic outlook in multiple regional conflicts, Ankara played a delicate balancing game between major powers to increase its room to maneuver and pursue its own interests. The AKP sought to forge greater military and economic cooperation with Russia and China by declaring its intention to join the Shanghai Cooperation Organization or, more recently, via the 2019 Asia Anew Initiative.[45] Yet, Turkey's politics of aggregate balance via rapprochement with Russia went only so far, as they have divergent interests in the Middle East, and Russia imposed geographic limits on Turkey's zone of influence, especially in Syria, via its 2016–2017 Operation Euphrates Shield and the 2020 Idlib offensive.[46]

The more consistent pattern has been the emergence of new alliances. Israel aside, three competing axes have been confronting each other from Morocco to Afghanistan. The divide between the Iranian-led Axis of

Resistance and the Saudi-led Sunni Arab bloc has a long history; however, the more recent rift within the Sunni bloc dates back to the Arab Uprisings. Alarmed by the contagious revolutionary fervor and the rise of Ikhwan affiliates throughout the region, Saudi Arabia, the UAE, Bahrain and Egypt —known as the Arab Quartet—designated Ikhwan as a terrorist organization and worked together to contain the "democratic threat" and re-establish the *status quo ante*. In contrast, Turkey and Qatar, which did not feel threatened by the Ikhwan's rise, have harbored and supported the movement on multiple fronts in order to establish a new regional order with Ikhwan-led governments in power. Despite their divergent visions, both alliances could maintain cordial relations through the mid-2010s and cooperate in cases such as Syria or Yemen. However, following the 2017 Gulf Cooperation Council (GCC) Crisis, in which Saudi Arabia, the UAE, Egypt, and Bahrain severed diplomatic ties with Qatar due to its support for Ikhwan, Turkey backed Qatar, deploying troops and supplies to the country. The murder of Saudi dissident journalist Jamal Khashoggi in 2018 at the Saudi consulate in Istanbul (allegedly by the security aides to Crown Prince Mohammed bin Salman) deteriorated bilateral relations further. A Cold-War-like rivalry between the alliances with several proxy confrontations on multiple fronts, such as Syria and Libya, has reached a stalemate, putting the regional security order under a lot of strain and consuming the political and economic resources of all involved parties.

The countries of the Middle East, consumed by this intra-regional zero-sum competition, found an incentive to keep tensions low in the face of rising security challenges and the US's waning role as a security guarantor to its allies. The 2020 Abraham Accords to normalize relations between Israel and several Arab states and the 2021 re-entry negotiations to revive the Joint Comprehensive Plan for Action, marking a softer stance on Iran, also triggered diplomatic de-escalation in the region.[47] Having realized the limitations of its expansionist foreign policy, most notably in Syria as the most calamitous example, the AKP government, too, has worked since 2020 to recalibrate its foreign policy and made more pronounced overtures for rapprochement with countries in the region. While initially condemning the Abraham Accords, Turkey gradually expressed an understanding, eventually leading to Israel's President Isaac Herzog's official visit to Turkey in 2022 – the highest-level visit in 14 years. Reflecting the new wind of rapprochement, the GCC Crisis was resolved at its 2021 summit in al-Ula, ending the dispute with Qatar, and this was followed by some fence-mending between the Arab Quartet and Turkey, such as Erdoğan's visits to Abu Dhabi and Riyadh.[48] Likewise, in April 2022, a Turkish court ruled to stop the trial of 26 Saudis accused in the Khashoggi killing and to transfer the case to Saudi Arabia. Overall, uncertainty exists as to whether political leaders of the region are simply seizing the moment or whether this de-escalation heralds a new era despite the continuation of hot conflicts.

Ikhwan's role in Turkey's power projection

The AKP's calculation was that the Arab Spring would be the Ikhwan Spring in practice, and AKP's stance as the advocate of the Arab street against the crumbling authoritarian regimes was in line with its broader agenda of democratic transition in the region. Initially, Western powers also supported the revolutions.[49] The global dynamics that once favored the rise of the AKP would now promote the AKP model of political governance throughout the region. The new Middle East with Turkey-allied Sunni governments would then usher in a new era in the AKP's own projection. The sudden surge in Arab streets required swift action. To export its model and transfer its know-how, the AKP government financially subsidized the Ikhwan-affiliated political parties and organized workshops in 2011 and 2013 to train the Arab Islamists in political campaigning and party formation.[50] It convinced the Egyptian Ikhwan to run a candidate for president in 2012, although the movement had previously pledged not to do so.[51] Turkey gave the movement "geographical depth" via its material capabilities, and Qatar offered "rhetorical breadth" via its media and intellectual organizations.[52]

In this cost–benefit analysis, Turkey, unlike the Gulf monarchies, had little to fear regarding the security of its regime due to its support for Ikhwan. Both Qatar and Turkey felt immune to an Ikhwan-led uprising. Quite the contrary, such a proxy power minimizes Ankara's strategic costs, such as the legal consequences of its foreign operations and potential human and material losses. Working with local actors instead of crude interventions could also be used to legitimize Turkish involvement in the broader region. For Turkey and Qatar, Ikhwan provided a wieldy political identity with which local populations could identify.

In the aftermath of the Arab Uprisings, aspirants such as Iran and Saudi Arabia employed their already-existing transnational networks and proxies for their divergent templates for regional order, e.g. the Shia organizations like Hezbollah and Salafi Islamist groups, respectively. This power competition operated in a setting where transnational non-state actors such as the Kurdish armed forces and Salafi jihadis were challenging nation-state borders. In security terms, the post-2011 alliances are marked by the rise of armed non-state actors as proxies for regional powers.[53] With similar regional-hegemony-seeking behavior yet lacking the political infrastructure to do so, Turkey aimed to alter the regional distribution of relative material capabilities by first targeting the low hanging fruits and activated its links to Ikhwan offshoots across the Middle East and North Africa. Though not hierarchically interconnected, the movement possessed strong grassroots organizations across the region. As seen in Figure 1, Ikhwan-affiliated political parties operated in several countries, including Algeria, Jordan, Kuwait, Libya, Morocco, Sudan, Tunisia, and Yemen.

Enabled by these linkages, Erdoğan embarked upon a wholesale region-building process with a new imagination for the Middle East. For instance, he suddenly brought up the Köroğlu Turks in Libya, whom the Turkish public had never heard of before but came into the picture during Ankara's cooperation with the Ikhwan-affiliated Government of National Accord (GNA), stating: "In Libya, there are Köroğlu Turks remaining from the Ottomans [...] and they are being subjected to ethnic cleansing. Haftar is bent on destroying them, too. As is the case across North Africa, in Libya, too, one of our main duties is to protect the grandchildren of our ancestors."[54] In 2017, the Sudanese island of Suakin popped up in the Turkish news as a former Ottoman port, one that Erdoğan hoped to use as a military base to impose Turkish prerogatives in the Horn of Africa. As such, the AKP's reimagination of the region, or Pax Ottomana, rests on the present network and strength of Ikhwan offshoots rather than a deeper shared history. This network has enabled Ankara to project its influence in areas where doing so used to be unthinkable until recently. Besides such political leverage, the Ikhwan identity also offered a religious legitimation to Turkish interventionism. Notably, Turkish support for Hamas outbid Arab leaders in the Palestinian cause, which resonated most among the Arab populations.

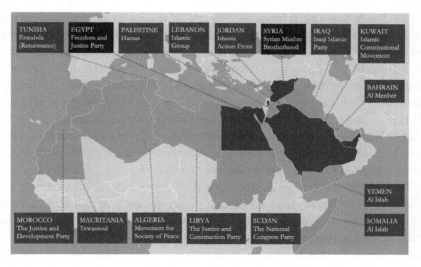

Figure 1. Ikhwan-affiliated political parties. Source: Author's illustration.
Note: Countries in a dark red shade have designated the Ikhwan as a terrorist organization.

Initially things were lining up and the fortunes seemed to rise for Ikhwan in Egypt, Tunisia, Libya, and Somalia. AKP aggressively supported the reconstruction of these countries to export the "Turkish model." Mohamed Morsi's victory in Egypt's 2012 presidential elections and Ennahda leading Tunisia's transitional government after 2011 marked the zenith of this project. Turkey also supported the Ikhwan-affiliated JCP in Libya and pushed Syrian President Bashar al-Assad to legalize the Syrian Ikhwan and hold free elections.[55] While diplomatic channels failed and the rising star of Ikhwan faded, most notably with the 2013 military intervention that ousted Morsi, Ankara did not hesitate in flexing its muscles to confront major setbacks on multiple fronts and adopted a proxy warfare strategy by making use of Ikhwan networks. In Syria, for instance, Turkey backed Faylaq al-Sham, an Ikhwan-affiliated armed group, which, together with Ahrar al Sham, joined the Turkish army's 2016 Operation Euphrates Shield. In order to restructure and unify nationalist Islamist armed groups in Idlib, Turkey also supported the National Front for Liberation in 2018, which was led by Ikhwan-affiliated groups, political Salafists, and nationalists.[56] In Libya, Turkey assumed the command of militias in Tripoli that were aligned with the GNA and empowered them with Syrian mercenaries. Reinforcing this proxy architecture, Istanbul has increasingly become a transnational center of Ikhwan activities, such as hosting the intra-party elections of Yemeni al Islah and the formation of the Syrian National Council which included the exiled Ikhwan members.

Because Turkish foreign policy is so tied to Ikhwan offshoots, the AKP elite saw the coups overthrowing Ikhwan in Egypt (2013) and Sudan (2019) as a direct attempt to reduce Turkish influence.[57] Deep ties make it more difficult to use Ikhwan as a bargaining chip to normalize relations with the new governments. Nevertheless, when responding to the sub-systemic stimuli, the Turkish government did not hesitate to make concessions and diminish its support for these groups. Turkey's Ikhwan links within its overstretched foreign policy have increasingly become a liability. To mend the fences with the Arab Quartet and show its good will in that regard, the Turkish authorities, for instance, asked the Ikhwan's Istanbul-based TV channels in 2021 to tone down their criticisms of Egypt's military-dominated government. Due to the continuing pressure, several critical Arab reporters left Istanbul and Ikhwan's most popular satellite channel, Mekameleen, shut down its Turkey offices in March 2022.[58] Especially in the case of the relations with Egypt, the extradition of prominent Ikhwan figures is an open question and Turkey denies allegations against them. However, the current rapprochement has concerned many Ikhwan exiles and pushed them to consider moving to another country such as Malaysia.

One of the reasons that facilitated the Quartet's initiative to normalize relations and Turkey's to soften its pro-Ikhwan stance is the movement's much weakened position. The Ikhwan-affiliated governments fell one by one, from Egypt to Sudan to Tunisia, and the movement overall faced catastrophic setbacks with the authoritarian backlash to the Arab Uprisings. It has also been wracked by internal frictions, reflected in the two camps that have emerged in London and Istanbul. The Ikhwan ran out of steam in general and its potential power as a threat to the regime security of the Gulf countries has waned immensely. For the very same reason, Ikhwan seems to have lost the value Erdoğan once saw in it. Ankara has showed its willingness to curb some activities and voices of Ikhwan. While the considerable use of Ikhwan links as a proxy power in foreign policy and as a discursive asset in domestic politics still makes it difficult to cut off links entirely, Turkey's recent track record and the current regional rapprochement, widely expected to take place only in the post-Erdoğan era, indicate that relations with Ikhwan did not primarily evolve out of Islamist convictions.

Unit-Level variables
Systemic incentives and constraints explain longer trends, but divergence in foreign policy responses to the same systemic stimuli often hinge on the domestic processes "as transmission belts that channel, mediate and (re)direct policy outputs in response to external forces (primarily changes in relative power)."[59] Especially, in permissive settings, such unit-level factors may have a greater influence on the process of foreign policy making and implementation. This holds true for Turkey's relations with the Middle East and Ikhwan in the last decade as well.

In neoclassical realist theory, strategic assessment of the geopolitical structure of the international and regional systems can be heavily affected by the personality, core values, beliefs, and ideas of the foreign policy executive. As Kitchen argues in his analysis of the unit-level impact of ideas as an intervening variable, uncertainty about threats and opportunities, derived from imperfect intelligence, may also create a void to be filled by ideas and beliefs.[60] When interpreting the Arab Uprisings as a historic moment for its foreign policy ambitions, AKP leaders overestimated not only Turkey's material capabilities in comparison to those of other regional forces, but also the Ikhwan's fortunes. In addition to Erdoğan being prone to risk-taking, the potential transformative power attributed to Ikhwan in the aftermath of the Arab Uprisings steered Turkey's foreign policy in a particular direction under the aforementioned permissive systemic conditions. Regarding the cognitive filters processing systemic signals and threat perceptions, Erdoğan also internalized regional developments and saw Ikhwan and himself as having an overlapping fate under the threat of Western powers and the Saudi-UAE alliance. The ousting of Morsi coincided with the massive, anti-government 2013 Gezi Protests, which Erdoğan claimed were driven by dark, outside forces in an attempt to bring him down. "Those, who dream that I will end up like Adnan Menderes (Turkish Prime Minister ousted from power in 1960 and later executed) and Morsi, hear me! This journey will not be left unfinished. There are millions of Anatolian people who will shoulder the new Turkey ideal," Erdoğan stated.[61] This perceived vulnerability pushed him harder to build the strength needed to defuse internal and external threats as much as systemic conditions would permit doing so. Another element of grand strategy formulation is the selection of means to address systemic stimuli. This brings questions of "what means are available, which will work most effectively, and whether their use can be justified."[62] Here, ideological affinity ensured the availability of resources as the AKP used its old links with Ikhwan branches. This move was also "justified" by the AKP's Islamist foreign policy discourse, which not only provided the shared ground to work together in multiple regional conflicts but also raised the party's profile at home as the protector of the *ummah*.

One should also note that not all the unit-level variables are ideational. Turkey's institutional structure has functioned as a moderating variable in the AKP's Middle East policy. While states consist of diverse, competing actors, the centralization and personalization of political power in contemporary Turkey eliminated the traditional veto players and the systems of checks and balances, further fast-tracking foreign policy making and implementation. The process reached its zenith with the 2018 transition to the presidential system.[63] Another moderating variable conditioning the state's ability to respond adequately to external pressures and opportunities, is state-society relations. While the AKP elite is able to harness the country's power potential in general, social and elite cohesion to support foreign policy objectives defines the level of responsiveness. In this regard, the ruling alliance between the AKP and the ultranationalist Nationalist Action Party, as well as the presence of several Eurasianist groups in the state bureaucracy, affected the scope of Turkish interventionism in the region in line with a populist expansionist rhetoric. Finally, transborder military operations can stimulate a "rally around the flag" effect, increasing public support for government policies at least in the short run,[64] and act as a diversionary effect in times of successive economic crises, which have only been exacerbated by the Russian invasion of Ukraine. Considering the sagging approval ratings for his presidency and the Turkish economy wracked with high inflation, Erdoğan sought success abroad. Besides systemic stimuli, domestic challenges and the desperate need for Gulf capital further motivated him to repair the fractured relations with Saudi Arabia and the UAE.

Conclusion

The AKP's Middle East policy, widely considered as foreign policy adventurism, represents more than a passing twist, but a deeper change in Turkey's foreign policy orientation. Despite its domestic use for the authoritarian practices, the AKP's pursuit of strategic autonomy reflects a grand strategy to respond to the shifts in the balance of power in the post-unipolar world. The AKP's ideological ties to the Ikhwan made available new resources and opportunities and helped legitimize its foreign policy activism, particularly among its conservative base. However, the AKP approached Ikhwan as part of its power-maximizing strategy because it offered the greatest benefit (as the most organized group in the region) at the lowest cost (posing no threat to its own regime security). When regional conditions changed, the AKP was willing to downplay its Ikhwan card as well. The domestic ideational, institutional, and social factors mediating systemic and sub-systemic stimuli have affected the scope and pace of AKP's relations with the Ikhwan within its broader Middle East policy.

Amidst theoretical quarrels about the overriding importance of material or ideational factors, a neoclassical realist approach suggests a holistic perspective in which systemic imperatives explain a state's strategic orientation and unit-level variables account for the variance in concrete foreign policy choices. As a remedy to the disconnect between the International Relations of the Middle East and Foreign Policy Analysis, it provides a systemized, generalizable, outside-in approach that is also attuned to factors of domestic politics. Yet, neoclassical realism still maintains a state-centric approach to foreign policy analysis. A more complete approach requires the incorporation of non-state actors in order to grasp proxy power politics and transnational governance in the Middle East. While this study on the AKP's entanglement with the Ikhwan's offshoots as a force multiplier can provide an entry point, future studies need to take into account the interests, incentives, and constraints various non-state actors face.

Notes

1. Ramadan, "Democratic Turkey."
2. Berman, "Islamist Mobilization."
3. Yavuz, "The Motives."
4. Başkan and Taşpınar, *The Nation or the Ummah*, 9.
5. Cagaptay, *Erdogan's Empire*, 133.
6. *Duvar English*, "CHP leader."
7. For a recent overview of Turkish foreign policy, see Aydın, "Grand Strategizing"; Dalacoura, "Turkish foreign policy"; Şahin, "Theorizing the Change"; and Siri et al., "Turkey as a regional security actor."
8. Ripsman et al, *Neoclassical Realist Theory*, and Schweller, "Unanswered Threats."
9. Aydın, "Grand Strategizing"; Kutlay and Öniş, "Turkish foreign policy"; Ovalı and Özdikmenli, "Ideologies and the Western Question"; and Şahin, "Theorizing the Change".

10. Han, "Paradise Lost"; Kardaş, "Revisionism and Resecuritization"; Yeşilyurt, "Explaining Miscalculation and Maladaptation"; and Yilmaz, "A Government Devoid."
11. Hintz, *Identity Politics*.
12. Aydıntaşbaş and Bianco, "Useful Enemies."
13. Swinkels, "How Ideas Matter."
14. Kitchen, "Systemic pressures," 118.
15. Mashino, "The Bipolar Conflict."
16. Yüksel and Tekineş, "Turkey's love-in."
17. Taş, "The Formulation and Implementation."
18. *T24*, "Çandar."
19. Gurpinar, "Turkey and the Muslim Brotherhood," 24–28.
20. Ayyash, "The Turkish Future."
21. Yavuz, "Erdoğan's Soft Power Arm."
22. Taş, "AKP and the Muslim Brotherhood."
23. Özkan, "Relations between Turkey and Syria."
24. Taş, "The Formulation and Implementation."
25. Fouad, *Missing Influence*, 35.
26. Al-Sofari, "An Exceptional Case."
27. Yaşar and Aksoy, "Making Sense."
28. Wohlforth, "The Stability."
29. Layne, "This Time," 204.
30. Nye, "The rise."
31. Fukuyama, "Francis Fukuyama."
32. Stuenkel, *Post-western World*.
33. Barnes-Dacey and Lovatt, *Principled Pragmatism*, 4.
34. Hinnebusch, "The Arab Uprisings," 16.
35. Barnes-Dacey and Lovat, *Principled Pragmatism*, 6.
36. Kutlay and Öniş, "Turkish foreign policy."
37. Ripsman et al, *Neoclassical Realist Theory*, 52–56.
38. Ibid., 84.
39. For a historical account of Turkey's grand strategies, see Aydın, "Grand Strategizing."
40. Kanat, "Theorizing the Transformation," 71.
41. Yeşilyurt, "Explaining Miscalculation," 79–80.
42. The latter required tacit US approval.
43. El-Dessouki and Mansour, "Small states."
44. Dalacoura, "Turkish foreign policy."
45. Taş, "The Formulation and Implementation," 17.
46. Şahin, "Theorizing the Change," and Kubicek, "Structural dynamics."
47. Jabbour, *After a Divorce*, 12.
48. Mashino, "The Bipolar Conflict," 4.
49. Kardaş, "Revisionism and Resecuritization," 494.
50. Jabbour, *After a Divorce*, 9.
51. Çevik, "Erdogan's Endgame."
52. Cinkara, "Interpreting Turkey."
53. Darwich, "Foreign Policy Analysis."
54. International Crisis Group, "The View," 3.
55. Yeşilyurt, "Explaining Miscalculation," 72.
56. Yüksel, "Turkey's approach," 142.

57. Aydıntaşbaş and Bianco, "Useful Enemies."
58. Taş, "AKP and the Muslim Brotherhood."
59. Schweller, "Unanswered Threats," 164.
60. Kitchen, "Systemic pressures," 134.
61. Erdoğan, "President."
62. Kitchen, "Systemic pressures," 135.
63. Taş, "The Formulation and Implementation."
64. Siri et al, "Turkey as a regional security actor," 14.

Disclosure statement

No potential conflict of interest was reported by the author(s).

ORCID

Hakkı Taş http://orcid.org/0000-0003-3463-0804

References

Al-Sofari, Mutahar. "An Exceptional Case: Saudi Relations with Yemen's Islah Party." The Washington Institute Fikra Forum. July 26, 2021. Accessed March 2, 2022. https://www.washingtoninstitute.org/policy-analysis/exceptional-case-saudi-relations-yemens-islah-party.

Aydın, Mustafa. "Grand Strategizing in and for Turkish Foreign Policy: Lessons Learned from History, Geography and Practice." *Perceptions* 25 (2021): 203–226.

Aydıntaşbaş, Aslı, and Cinzia Bianco. "Useful Enemies: How the Turkey-UAE Rivalry Is Remaking the Middle East." *ECFR Policy Brief* 380 (2021): 1–22.

Ayyash, Abdelrahman. "The Turkish Future of Egypt's Muslim Brotherhood." *The Century Foundation*, August 17, 2020. Accessed September 1, 2021. https://tcf.org/content/report/turkish-future-egypts-muslim-brotherhood/?agreed=1&agreed=1.

Barnes-Dacey, Julien, and Hugh Lovatt. *Principled Pragmatism: Europe's Place in a Multipolar Middle East*. Berlin: ECFR, 2022.

Başkan, Birol, and Ömer Taşpınar. *The Nation or the Ummah – Islamism and Turkish Foreign Policy*. Albany NY: SUNY Press, 2021.

Berman, Chantal. "Islamist Mobilization during the Arab Uprisings." In *The Oxford Handbook of Politics in Muslim Societies*, edited by Melani Cammett and Pauline

Jones, January 2021. Accessed September 1, 2021. https://www.oxfordhandbooks.com/view/10.1093/oxfordhb/9780190931056.001.0001/oxfordhb-9780190931056-e-43.

Cagaptay, Soner. *Erdogan's Empire: Turkey and the Politics of the Middle East.* London: I.B. Tauris, 2020.

Çevik, Salim. "Erdogan's Endgame with Egypt." *The Cairo Review of Global Affairs*, August 6, 2021. Accessed 3 March 2022. https://www.thecairoreview.com/global-forum/erdogans-endgame-with-egypt/.

Cinkara, Gokhan. "Interpreting Turkey's Current Diplomatic Rapproachement Toward the Gulf." *The Arab Gulf States Institute in Washington.* March 22, 2022. Accessed April 1, 2022. https://agsiw.org/interpreting-turkeys-current-diplomatic-rapprochement-toward-the-gulf/.

Dalacoura, Katerina. "Turkish Foreign Policy in the Middle East: Power Projection and Post-Ideological Politics." *International Affairs* 97, no. 4 (2021): 1125–1142.

Darwich, May. "Foreign Policy Analysis and Armed Non-State Actors in World Politics: Lessons from the Middle East." *Foreign Policy Analysis* 17, no. 4 (2021): 1–11.

Duvar English. "CHP leader questions Erdoğan's mental wellbeing yet again." October 10, 2021. Accessed November 7, 2021. https://www.duvarenglish.com/chp-leader-questions-erdogans-mental-wellbeing-yet-again-news-59138., 2021.

El-Dessouki, Ayman, and Ola Rafik Mansour. "Small States and Strategic Hedging: The United Arab Emirates' Policy Towards Iran." *Review of Economics and Political Science* (2020): 1–14. DOI:10.1108/REPS-09-2019-0124.

Erdoğan, Tayyip. "President Erdoğan Meets Representatives of NGOs in Kayseri." TCCB, May 17, 2015. Accessed September 7, 2021. https://www.tccb.gov.tr/en/news/542/32391/cumhurbaskani-erdoganin-samsun-programi.

Fouad, Khaled. *Missing Influence – How MB Administers its Foreign Relations.* Cairo: Political Stimulus, 2022.

Fukuyama, Francis. Francis Fukuyama on the end of American hegemony." *The Economist.* November 8, 2021.

Gurpinar, Bulut. "Turkey and the Muslim Brotherhood: Crossing Roads in Syria." *Eurasian Journal of Social Sciences* 3, no. 4 (2015): 22–36.

Han, Ahmet K. "Paradise Lost: A Neoclassical Realist Analysis of Turkish Foreign Policy and the Case of Turkish-Syrian Relations." In *Turkey-Syria Relations: Between Enmity and Amity*, edited by Raymond A. Hinnebusch, and Özlem Tür, 55–70. Surrey: Ashgate, 2013.

Hinnebusch, Raymond. "Arap Ayaklanmaları ve Ortadoğu ve Kuzey Afrika Bölgesel Devletler Sistemi." *Uluslararası İlişkiler Dergisi* 11, no. 42 (2014): 7–27.

Hintz, Lisel. *Identity Politics Inside Out: National Identity Contestation and Foreign Policy in Turkey.* Oxford: Oxford University Press, 2018.

Honghui, Pan. "Prospects for Sino-Turkish Relations." *China Quarterly of International Strategic Studies* 02, no. 1 (2016): 101–117.

International Crisis Group. "Turkey Wades Into Libya's Troubled Waters." *Crisis Group Europe Report* 257 (2020): 1–31. Brussels: ICG.

Jabbour, Jana J, *After a Divorce. a Frosty Entente: Turkey's Rapprochement with the United Arab Emirates and Saudi Arabia. Strategic Necessity and Transactional Partnership in a Shifting World Order.* Paris: IFRI, 2022.

Kanat, Kılıç Buğra. "Theorizing the Transformation of Turkish Foreign Policy." *Insight Turkey* 16, no. 1 (2014): 65–84.

Kardaş, Şaban. "Revisionism and Resecuritization of Turkey's Middle East Policy: A Neoclassical Realist Explanation." *Journal of Balkan and Near Eastern Studies* 23, no. 3 (2021): 490–501.
Kitchen, Nicholas. "Systemic Pressures and Domestic Ideas: A Neoclassical Realist Model of Grand Strategy Formation." *Review of International Studies* 36, no. 1 (2010): 117–143.
Kubicek, Paul. "Structural Dynamics, Pragmatism, and Shared Grievances: Explaining Russian-Turkish Relations." *Turkish Studies* 23, no. 5 (2022): 1–31. Forthcoming. doi:10.1080/14683849.2022.2060637
Kutlay, Mustafa, and Ziya Öniş. "Turkish Foreign Policy in a Post-Western Order: Strategic Autonomy or new Forms of Dependence?" *International Affairs* 97, no. 4 (2021): 1085–1104.
Layne, Christopher. "This Time It's Real: The End of Unipolarity and the Pax Americana." *International Studies Quarterly* 56 (2012): 203–213.
Mashino, Ito. 2021 "The Bipolar Conflict in the Middle East over the Muslim Brotherhood." *Mitsui & Co. Monthly Report.* June 15, 2021. Accessed September 2, 2021. https://www.mitsui.com/mgssi/en/report/staff/1228935_10746.html.
Mutlu, Sefa. 2022 "Cumhurbaşkanı Erdoğan: Seçilmişlerin bulunduğu Meclis'in feshi Tunus halkının iradesine bir darbedir." *AA.* April 4, 2022. Accessed April 10, 2022. https://www.aa.com.tr/tr/gundem/cumhurbaskani-erdogan-secilmislerin-bulundugu-meclisin-feshi-tunus-halkinin-iradesine-bir-darbedir/2555000.
Nye, Joseph S. "The Rise and Fall of American Hegemony from Wilson to Trump." *International Affairs* 95, no. 1 (2019): 63–80.
Ovalı, Ali Şevket, and İlkim Özdikmenli. "Ideologies and the Western Question in Turkish Foreign Policy: A Neo-Classical Realist Perspective." *All Azimuth* 9, no. 1 (2020): 105–126.
Özkan, Behlül. "Relations Between Turkey and Syria in the 1980s and 1990s: Political Islam, Muslim Brotherhood and Intelligence Wars." *Uluslararası İlişkiler* 16, no. 62 (2019): 5–25.
Ramadan, Tariq. "Democratic Turkey Is the Template for Egypt's Muslim Brotherhood." *Huffington Post,* February 8, 2011. Accessed September 2, 2021. https://www.huffpost.com/entry/post_1690_b_820366.
Ripsman, Norrin, Jeffrey Taliaferro, and Steven Lobell. *Neoclassical Realist Theory of International Politics.* Oxford: Oxford University Press, 2016.
Şahin, Mehmet. "Theorizing the Change: A Neoclassical Realist Approach to Turkish Foreign Policy." *Contemporary Review of the Middle East* 7, no. 4 (2020): 483–500.
Schweller, Randall. "Unanswered Threats: A Neoclassical Realist Theory of Underbalancing." *International Security* 29, no. 2 (2004): 159–201.
Siri, Neset, et al. Turkey as a regional security actor in the Black Sea, the Mediterranean, and the Levant Region." *CMI Report* 2. Bergen: Chr. Michelsen Institute, 2021.
Stuenkel, Oliver. *Post-Western World: How Emerging Powers Are Remaking Global Order.* Cambridge: Polity Press, 2016.
Swinkels, Marij. "How Ideas Matter in Public Policy: A Review of Concepts, Mechanisms, and Methods." *International Review of Public Policy* 2, no. 3 (2020): 281–316.
T24. "Çandar: AK Parti, Müslüman Kardeşler'in bir şubesi niteliğinde." October 9, 2014. Accessed September 5, 2021. https://t24.com.tr/haber/kobane-dustu-dusuyor-demek-dussun-demektir,273281.

Taş, Hakkı. "AKP and the Muslim Brotherhood: Faithful Companions?," *Ahval.* April 28, 2021. Accessed September 5, 2021. http://ahval.co/en-116743.

Taş, Hakkı. "The Formulation and Implementation of Populist Foreign Policy: Turkey in the Eastern Mediterranean." *Mediterranean Politics* (2020): 1–25. DOI: 10.1080/13629395.2020.1833160.

Wohlforth, William. "The Stability of a Unipolar World." *International Security* 24, no. 1 (1999): 5–41.

Yaşar, Nebahat Tanrıverdi, and Hürcan Aslı Aksoy. "Making Sense of Turkey's Cautious Reaction to Power Shifts in Tunisia." *SWP Comment* 52 (2021): 1–4. Accessed December 1, 2021. https://www.swp-berlin.org/publications/products/comments/2021C52_TurkeyAndTunisia.pdf.

Yavuz, M. Hakan. "Erdoğan's Soft Power Arm: Mapping the Muslim Brotherhood's Networks of Influence in Turkey." *Center for Research & Intercommunication Knowledge Special Report* 187 (2020): 1–50. Accessed September 3, 2021. https://crik.sa/wp-content/uploads/2020/10/Erdogans-Soft-Power-Arm.pdf.

Yavuz, M. Hakan. "The Motives of Erdogan's Foreign Policy: Neo-Ottomanism and Strategic Autonomy." *Turkish Studies* 23, no. 5 (2022). forthcoming.

Yeşilyurt, Nuri. "Explaining Miscalculation and Maladaptation in Turkish Foreign Policy Towards the Middle East During the Arab Uprisings: A Neoclassical Realist Perspective." *All Azimuth* 6, no. 2 (2017): 65–83.

Yilmaz, Samet. "A Government Devoid of Strong Leadership: A Neoclassical Realist Explanation of Turkey's Iraq War Decision in 2003." *All Azimuth* 10, no. 2 (2021): 197–212.

Yüksel, Engin. "Turkey's Approach to Proxy war in the Middle East and North Africa." *Security and Defence Quarterly* 31, no. 4 (2020): 137–152.

Yüksel, Engin, and Haşim Tekineş. "Turkey's love-in with Qatar." *CRU Report* (2021). Accessed September 4, 2021. https://www.clingendael.org/publication/turkeys-love-qatar-marriage-convenience.

An examination of the underlying dynamics of Turkey-European Union relations through the lenses of international relations theory

Oya Dursun-Özkanca

ABSTRACT
This article analyzes contemporary Turkey-European Union (EU) relations through the lenses of international relations (IR) theory. After providing a brief overview of the history of Turkey-EU relations, it focuses on the underlying dynamics of Turkey-EU relations in the post-2016 period. It makes a case that realism is better suited to explain the latest episodes in Turkey-EU relations. It specifically argues that balancing and neoclassical realism provide a more nuanced explanatory value as to why Turkey and the EU are going through a particularly tense period in their relationship. It also outlines global/regional factors as well as intervening national/domestic factors behind the rising tensions in Turkey's relations with the EU.

Introduction

The short-lived enthusiasm about Turkey's European Union (EU) candidacy and accession negotiations has given way to a series of crises and disappointments in bilateral relations. In the post-2016 period, Turkey's already turbulent relations with the EU became more strained due to the stalemate in its EU accession negotiations, its drilling activities in the Eastern Mediterranean (EastMed), and the divergence of EU-Turkey interests on Syria, Libya, and Cyprus. This article examines the underlying dynamics of contemporary Turkey-EU relations through the lenses of international relations (IR) theory, asks what the main factors behind the contemporary strain in bilateral relations are, and seeks to contribute to the core objective of this Special Issue by producing a theory-informed analysis of contemporary Turkish foreign policy.

While there are numerous studies published on the EU-Turkey relationship, an overwhelming number adopt Europeanization and/or Constructivist approaches.[1] However, this genre of studies does not provide a good explanation as to why Turkey has derailed from Europeanization. There are problems with the 'top-down approach to the Europeanisation process,' and much of the existing literature 'overlooks the internal dynamics of European integration.'[2] Even the de-Europeanization literature that blossomed over the last few years does not offer a plausible explanation of the reasons behind changes in Turkish foreign policy. This is especially important given the dramatic changes observed in Turkey-EU relations under the rule of the Justice and Development Party (*Adalet ve Kalkınma Partisi*, AKP). If, in fact, ideology was the main culprit behind the deterioration in Turkey-EU relations, one would not observe considerable fluctuations in Turkey-EU relations under the AKP, which has consistently retained its an Islamist-oriented ideology throughout much of its tenure. Finally, even when ideology is used in a way to explain foreign policy, when one digs deeper, it is possible to locate pragmatic and interest-based explanations behind the use of ideology in foreign policymaking.

The analysis in this article builds on 'the framework of intra-alliance opposition,'[3] derived from the soft balancing literature, which distills different tools at the disposal of the secondary powers within alliances into three categories of intra-alliance opposition behavior: 'boundary testing,'[4] 'boundary challenging,'[5] and 'boundary breaking,'[6] delineating the motivations for engaging in different stages of intra-alliance opposition. While hard balancing involves military means, soft balancing is 'behavior designed to create a better range of outcomes for a state vis-à-vis another state or coalition of states by *adding* to the power assets at its disposal, in an attempt to offset or diminish the advantages enjoyed by that other state or coalition,'[7] and is often exercised through 'international institutions, concerted diplomacy via limited, informal ententes, and economic sanctions.'[8]

Soft balancing may transition into hard balancing when security competition becomes intense and a powerful state becomes threatening.[9] The leaders of weaker states may ignore the systemic constraints they face when they believe they possess an asymmetric strategy, i.e. a strategy that allows them to prevail quickly and cheaply in a conflict without facing the full military might of a vastly superior opponent.[10] Weaker powers might initiate hostilities to obtain limited objectives, such as breaking a deadlock in negotiations, or to highlight some perceived injustice in the status quo.[11] If a rising power thinks that 'the order is unlikely to be changed without violent challenge,' it may resort to conflict if the perceived costs are lower than the perceived benefits.[12] In this process, powerful constituencies and domestic factions may also demand a more immediate accommodation, especially if there are any perceived historical injustices.[13]

This article offers a systematic examination of Turkey's relations with the EU through the lenses of realism, considering in particular post-2016 developments in bilateral relations. It fills in an important gap in the literature by arguing that balancing and neoclassical realism provide a more nuanced explanation as to why Turkey and the EU are experiencing a particularly tense relationship. Neoclassical realism is 'a multilevel framework that combines both systemic incentives and mediating unit-level variables to arrive at conclusions about foreign policy choices.'[14] It places utmost emphasis on the country's place in the international system and its relative material power capabilities, followed by the intervening variables at the unit (state) level, such as domestic institutions, as well as political, economic, and social restraints (i.e. issues of leadership perception of the systemic stimuli and decisionmaking under the constraints of the domestic political and economic environments).[15] As such, it 'accounts for state behavior in a way that a more parsimonious systems-level theory is unable to achieve.'[16]

There are a few academic studies that seek to offer a more nuanced understanding of Turkish foreign policy by adopting neoclassical realism.[17] Nevertheless, none of these existing studies focus squarely on Turkey-EU relations. Therefore, this article addresses this gap in the literature. It first provides a very brief overview of the history of Turkey-EU relations and then focuses on the post-2016 period, before delving into an analysis of the factors behind rising bilateral tensions.

A brief historical overview of Turkey-EU relations

Turkey has been seeking membership in the European integration project for well over half a century. It submitted its application for associate membership in the European Economic Community (EEC) in 1959 and signed the Ankara Agreement in 1963. Turkey applied for full EEC membership in 1987 and signed a Customs Union (CU) Agreement in 1995, which came into force in January 1996, providing further trade integration between the EU and Turkey.

Turkey became an official EU candidate in December 1999. In October 2005, it started its accession negotiations with the EU. These have reached a stalemate over the past few years. In addition to its flawed record on human rights and rule of law, Turkey also failed to ratify and implement the 2004 Ankara Protocol (the Additional Protocol) and extend the CU Agreement to the Republic of Cyprus (RoC). Consequently, the European Council decided in December 2006 to suspend negotiations on eight key accession negotiation chapters. It further declared that no chapter would be closed until Turkey applies the Additional Protocol to the Ankara Agreement to the RoC. In 2007, France vetoed additional chapters (one of which intersects with the eight chapters blocked by the EU)[18] and the RoC also unilaterally vetoed six chapters.

Out of the 35 accession negotiation chapters, only 16 have been opened, and only one, Chapter 25 on Science and Research, has been provisionally closed.[19] Bilateral relations have been going through a particularly rocky period due to the lack of any real progress in accession negotiations. Even on security, the EU-Turkey relationship has failed to meet its full potential.[20] Since its EU accession was considered an open-ended rather than an automatic or guaranteed process, Turkey has approached the accession negotiations with skepticism.[21] Over time, Turkey has become 'less permeable to European pressure'[22] and less interested in EU membership.[23] Several commentators expressed that it was the EU that had 'turned away from Turkey'[24] by 'placing the bar too high'[25] for the country.

Post-2016 developments in EU-Turkey relations

As Turkey is a major refugee transit country, the EU-Turkey refugee deal signed on March 18, 2016, provided Turkey an opportunity to improve bilateral relations. This deal initially brought limited momentum into the EU-Turkey relations by reenergizing the stalled accession negotiations process and giving Turkey a commitment on visa liberalization and modernization of the CU, as well as financial support from the EU to help alleviate the costs of hosting Syrian refugees in Turkey,[26] Yet, it also made the relationship more complex by bringing into the limelight the 'blackmail power'[27] and the use of refugees as 'weapons of mass migration.'[28] Developments in February and March 2020, particularly the decision by Turkey to open its border with Greece to refugees, in order to put pressure on the EU on Syria, is a case in point. EU officials quickly indicated their support for Greece.[29]

Even though the relationship between Turkey and the EU has often been rocky, Turkey-EU relations drastically deteriorated following the coup attempt in Turkey on July 15, 2016. Turkish authorities frequently voiced Turkey's frustrations with what they perceived as the EU's lack of a strong condemnation of the coup attempt.[30] The EU, in return, has been repeatedly raising its disappointment with democratic backsliding and the deteriorating rule of law situation in Turkey. As such, especially since 2016, the relationship between Turkey and the EU has 'fallen far beyond the normative model, drifting to an interest-based relationship.'[31]

On November 24, 2016, the European Parliament (EP) voted to advise the EU to suspend accession negotiations with Turkey.[32] In response, Turkish leaders threatened to terminate the refugee deal.[33] In March 2017, the EU raised concerns regarding Turkey's switch into a presidential system due to weakened democratic checks and balances, erosion of judicial independence, and excessive executive power over the legislature.[34] Turkish authorities once again threatened to terminate the refugee deal.[35] In April 2017, following the constitutional referendum held under emergency rule in Turkey, the EU's Enlargement Commissioner Johannes Hahn highlighted that Turkey's EU accession process 'is not sustainable,' and recommended finding an alternative form of cooperation to replace the accession process.[36] In July 2017, the EP advised the EU to formally suspend Turkey's accession negotiations without delay upon the implementation of the Turkish Constitutional Reform package.

Furthermore, starting in 2018, Turkey has conducted several hydrocarbon drilling operations in the EastMed causing unwavering EU criticism, warnings, and sanctions against Turkey. In February 2018, when the Turkish military prevented 'a ship contracted by Italian oil company Eni from approaching an area off the coast of Cyprus to explore for natural gas,', tensions in the EastMed escalated.[37] In June 2018, the European Council acknowledged that 'Turkey has been moving further away' from the EU and declared that 'Turkey's accession negotiations have therefore effectively come to a standstill and no further chapters can be considered for opening or closing and no further work towards the modernization of the EU-Turkey Customs Union is foreseen.'[38] The General Affairs Council announced the accession negotiations with Turkey are 'effectively frozen'.[39] In March 2019, the EP once again voted to recommend the European Commission and the Council formally suspend accession negotiations with Turkey.[40] In July 2019, the European Council announced that the accession negotiation talks with Turkey are frozen and all high-level dialogue meetings would be suspended.[41] It stated:

> The Council deplores that, despite the European Union's repeated calls to cease its illegal activities in the Eastern Mediterranean, Turkey continued its drilling operations west of Cyprus and launched a second drilling operation northeast of Cyprus within Cypriot territorial waters. The Council reiterates the serious immediate negative impact that such illegal actions have across the range of EU-Turkey relations.[42]

The summer of 2020 was an especially difficult period in bilateral relations, as Turkey's increased drilling activities in the EastMed caused arguably one of the most serious crises between Turkey on the one hand and several EU member states – Greece, Cyprus, and France – on the other. There were skirmishes between Turkish and Greek militaries over maritime delimitation around the Greek islands,[43] and the naval involvement of France to support Greece.[44] In response to Turkey's drilling in the EastMed, the EU has adopted a 'sanctions regime' consisting of 'a travel ban to the EU and an asset freeze for persons and an asset freeze for entities.'[45] In November 2020, the Council decided to extend the 'existing framework for restrictive measures in response to Turkey's unauthorised drilling activities' in the EastMed 'until 12 November 2021,' maintaining 'its ability to impose targeted restrictive measures on persons or entities responsible.'[46] These are effective illustrations of the emphasis placed on hard power tools of statecraft employed on the part of both the EU and Turkey.

The disillusionment that the EU experiences with Turkey is mirrored in the way Turkey perceives the EU's treatment of its accession process and response to the developments in the EastMed, an issue also highlighted in Ioannis Grigoriadis's article in this Special Issue. Turkish authorities frequently criticize the inclusion of the 'inconsistent and biased Greek and Greek Cypriot arguments'[47] in EU declarations and add that it damages 'the EU's image as an honest broker.'[48] As illustrated here, the nature of the EU-Turkey relationship has taken a predominantly negative tone in the post-2016 period, adding to the crisis of trust. Drawing on neoclassical realism and the balancing literature, the next section identifies three factors behind the tensions in bilateral relations.

Contemporary Turkey-EU relations: a case for neoclassical realism and transitional soft balancing

This article argues that neoclassical realism, along with transitional soft balancing, provides the most nuanced explanation of the latest episodes in EU-Turkey relations. It maintains that 1) international systemic and regional sub-systemic factors, 2) irreconcilable interests between Turkey and the EU on the issues of Cyprus, Libya, Syria, and hydrocarbon explorations and the subsequent lack of trust, and 3) domestic economic and political factors have influenced the way the EU-Turkey relationship has evolved since 2016.[49] Here, it is important to underline the hierarchy between the systemic and unit-level variables. In neoclassical realism, as in neorealism —the latter adopted in several papers in this Special Issue—systemic factors come first and 'do the heavy-lifting'[50] when explaining state behavior.

International systemic and regional sub-systemic factors

Systemic and regional sub-systemic factors are the main factors affecting Turkish foreign policy toward the EU. Like neorealists,[51] neoclassical realists assume that states primarily respond to changes in relative power capabilities and the 'constraints and opportunities' that are presented by the international system, such as the condition of anarchy, self-help, the importance of security for national interest, and the difficulty of cooperation under anarchy due to concerns with relative gains.[52] The international system is currently transitioning from a unipolar system led by the US to a more multipolar one. This provides an inviting space for maneuvering and regional balancing on the part of rising powers at the global and regional levels.[53] Additionally, there are significant changes that are affecting both the EU and the West in general, including the EU's multiple crises (enlargement fatigue, the Eurozone crisis, the refugee crisis, rising anti-EU populism, and Brexit), the withdrawal of the US from Afghanistan, growing disinterest and disengagement from the problems of the Middle East, and pivoting of US foreign policy towards Asia.[54]

Given the assumption of anarchy and self-help in the international system and the growing regional power vacuum, Turkey, in line with realist expectations, has become more concerned about the relative distribution of capabilities. Turkey and the EU increasingly act as regional competitors in the Western Balkans,[55] and Turkey soft balanced against the EU in its veto of the security exchange between the EU and NATO.[56] Turkey sees itself as an independent player, desires to be treated as an equal partner of the West,[57] and wants to acquire a greater influence in the changing international and regional balance of power to carve out a regional sphere of influence.[58] Since 2016, Turkey has pursued a more independent and active foreign policy, and increasingly engages in boundary breaking against its European allies.[59] Furthermore, a more recent emphasis on hard power, along with an increase in security competition, indicates a potential transition in Turkish foreign policy from soft balancing to hard balancing against the EU. Therefore, *Realpolitik* principles of pragmatism, relative power, and interests seem to be at the helm.

Unlike neorealism, however, neoclassical realism argues that states' perception of the international environment is not always accurate. Leaders do not necessarily act like rational actors in response to systemic stimuli; threats and opportunities in the international system may not always present themselves clearly; and due to domestic constraints, states may not always mobilize the necessary domestic resources to respond to the international systemic stimuli.[60] This is where the following two sets of neoclassical realist unit-level variables factor in to provide a nuanced explanation of the current state of EU-Turkey relations.

Conflicting interests and the subsequent lack of trust

As noted earlier, perceptions play an important role in neoclassical realism. Diverging interests on contemporary developments in Turkey's immediate neighborhood, reciprocal biases, and mistrust between Turkey and the EU (with especially Greece, France, and the RoC) provide additional motivation behind Turkish foreign policy behavior vis-à-vis the EU. The EU accession stalemate, the unresolved Cyprus problem, EU support for Syrian Kurds at the expense of Turkey's key interests in the Middle East, differences on Libya, and the sanctions regime against Turkish actors are often presented as evidence of an anti-Turkish bias in the EU. This creates a feeling of resentment, a perception of Western hypocrisy and 'double standards,'[61] and intensifies the lack of trust towards the EU.

On the refugee crisis, the Cyprus problem, in Syria, Libya, as well as on the drilling in the EastMed, Turkish foreign policy attempts to leverage Turkey's importance as a regional actor and protect Turkish national interests, which are often perceived as diametrically divergent from the interests of several EU member states. For instance, the EU has been critical of the Turkish military interventions in Syria.[62] While the EU underlined the fight against the Islamic State (IS) terrorist organization, Turkey emphasized the fight against the Syrian Kurds' People's Protection Units (YPG), due to claims of 'organic ties' between the YPG and the terrorist organization, the Kurdistan Worker's Party (PKK).[63] In October 2019, the European Council condemned Turkey's Operation Peace Spring in northeast Syria and labeled it as a 'unilateral military action,' noting that it 'seriously undermines the stability and the security of the whole region, resulting in more civilians suffering' and 'undermines the progress achieved' on the fight against the IS.[64] In February 2020, to garner support for its next military operation in Idlib, Syria, and to put direct political pressure on the EU, Turkey opened its borders for the refugees to cross into Greece. This is a good indicator of Turkey's boundary-breaking foreign policy behavior against the EU. Using statecraft tools such as compellent threats, Turkey took advantage of its pivotal role in the refugee crisis as leverage against the EU.

Similarly, the EU's inability to reach a consensus on Libya created a window of opportunity for Turkey to balance against the EU. On November 27, 2019, Turkey signed a maritime agreement with the UN-backed Libyan Government of National Accord (GNA), engaging in maritime delimitation in the eastern part of the Mediterranean Sea. Turkey's deal with GNA served as a spoiler for the hydrocarbon exploration and transportation efforts in the EastMed, as it increased the risks involved in energy companies' investments in the region, and it was criticized by Greece, the RoC, and the US.[65]

Turkey's involvement in Libya has frequently put Turkey at odds with EU member states The EU launched Operation IRINI in March 2020 to enforce the UN sanctions against weapons smuggling to Libya. In June 2020, Turkey committed to helping the GNA in its advance to Sirte against rebel forces.[66] Turkey expressed skepticism about IRINI's objectivity, criticizing the lack of scrutiny of shipments to forces fighting the GNA.[67] In early June 2020, the Greek frigate *Spetsai,* operating under IRINI, was prevented from inspecting a Tanzania-flagged freighter escorted by the Turkish navy.[68] On June 10, 2020, Turkish warships allegedly flashed their radar lights at the French warship *Courbet,* operating in the NATO Sea Guardian Operation, following its attempts to inspect a suspected Turkish cargo ship for violating the UN-imposed arms embargo.[69] Turkish authorities denied the allegations.

NATO's investigation on the incident was 'inconclusive,' and its findings were not made public.[70] France withdrew from NATO's Sea Guardian following the incident and started working under IRINI.[71]

The opposing interests of Turkey and the EU on the unresolved Cyprus problem is yet another factor behind the EU-Turkey tensions. Since the resolution of the Cyprus conflict was not a precondition for the RoC's EU membership in 2004, Turkish policymakers acquired considerable skepticism about the EU's role as an honest broker in the conflict.[72] While the EU made it clear that Turkey would need to implement the Additional Protocol and open its ports and airports to Cypriot vessels and planes, Turkey continues its policy of non-recognition and increasingly supports a two-state solution in the island.[73] The two-state solution policy, along with the recent partial reopening of Varosha, represents a major break with Turkish foreign policy on the topic and received severe criticism from the EU. The EU 'strongly' condemned 'Turkey's unilateral steps' to reopen Varosha, reiterated its commitment 'to a comprehensive settlement of the Cyprus problem on the basis of a bi-zonal, bi-communal federation with political equality,'[74] and 'reaffirmed [its] determination ... to use the instruments and options at its disposal to defend its interests and those of its Member States as well as to uphold regional stability.'[75] This framing of the options available to the EU in case of escalation of conflict in the EastMed is in line with the hard balancing approach.

The differences of interest between Turkey and the EU on Syria, Libya, Cyprus, and energy issues in the EastMed have contributed to the lack of trust, leading to increasingly boundary-breaking foreign policy behavior. The European Commission's latest report on Turkey also highlighted that 'Turkey's increasingly assertive foreign policy continued to collide with EU priorities under the [Common Foreign and Security Policy],' and that 'Turkey maintained a very low alignment rate of around 14%.'[76] The Turkish Ministry of Foreign Affairs responded by blaming the EU for 'blocking ... high-level dialogue and cooperation mechanisms with Turkey.'[77]

Domestic factors

The changes in the international distribution of power and regional developments provided ample ground for the unit-level factors to gain more effectiveness in determining the outcome of EU-Turkey relations. Without such international systemic and regional sub-systemic factors, it would not be plausible to expect domestic variables to deliver much change in Turkish foreign policy, since 'systemic pressure must be translated through intervening unit-level variables.'[78] Domestic factors thus serve as intervening variables in explaining the increasing drive for a boundary-breaking behavior against the EU.

States may choose to balance against an external power when 'doing so helps them in the domestic power game.'[79] In the Turkish context, it is generally acknowledged that domestic political developments play an important role in the deteriorating EU-Turkey relations.[80] This is in line with the neoclassical realist assumptions, which emphasize that states 'navigate between systemic constraints and domestic political imperatives.'[81] Neoclassical realists draw attention to the adventurous foreign policies of elites in the face of domestic problems and constraints.[82]

In the context of Turkey-EU relations, internal variables, such as rising nationalism in Turkish public opinion, the electoral considerations of the Turkish political elites, the weakened checks and balances system in the Turkish presidential system, the shift of foreign policy-making power from a 'highly institutionalized foreign policy elite' to the AKP's political elites,[83] 'anti-Western populism,'[84] and the Turkish policymakers' perception of the international stimuli serve as intervening variables at the unit level. The European Commission recently restated that 'there are serious deficiencies in the functioning of Turkey's democratic institutions,' and noted that 'democratic backsliding continued' and 'structural deficiencies of the presidential system' remained in place.[85]

Pursuing a more adversarial foreign policy towards the EU seems to help divert the attention of the Turkish public opinion from domestic problems, such as the rising inflation and unemployment and the precipitous drop in the value of the Turkish lira. The harsh exchange of words in October 2021, when President Erdoğan threatened to declare ten Western Ambassadors – six of which are EU member states (Denmark, Germany, Finland, France, the Netherlands, and Sweden) – *persona non grata* over their criticism of the Osman Kavala case is a case in point.[86] Turkish opposition leaders 'accused Erdoğan of trying to create an artificial diplomatic crisis that he could then blame for the plunging value of the lira ahead of elections which are due to be held in 2023.'[87]

In the aftermath of the failed coup attempt in July 2016, President Erdoğan and other Turkish authorities have been depicting the EU and the US as major threats to Turkey's national interests, engaging in a series of visible disagreements on the world stage, and accusing the West of meddling in Turkish domestic affairs. Turkish voters also seem to favor a more independent and unilateralist foreign policy.[88] Turkey has also been investing in its indigenous defense sector. Perceptions of relative power, a neoclassical realist variable, play an important role here too. Turkey has accordingly been pursuing a more confrontational and competitive course in its foreign policy vis-à-vis the EU.

Conclusion

Turkey feels like its voice and national interests on important foreign policy and security issues is not heard or intentionally ignored by its European and Western allies, and that it is not perceived as an equal partner, which creates 'a dynamic of pushback.'[89] The frequency and intensity of Turkey-EU disagreements have sharply increased over time and led to major trust issues. The suspension of the accession negotiations, the lack of progress in its visa liberalization and the CU Agreement modernization talks, and the conflicting interests of the EU and Turkey on a number of foreign policy issues that Turkey deems central to its national security and sovereignty have further contributed to the crisis of trust between Turkey and the EU and led Turkey to pursue an increasingly independent foreign policy, eventually playing a spoiler role in its immediate neighborhood.

Moreover, the tools of statecraft which the parties have employed have gone through a transition over the last couple of years, with an increasing emphasis on hard power, such as the use of alternative alliances, economic sanctions, military exercises, defense agreements, pacts, etc. Turkey's increasingly militaristic foreign policy and significant grievances against the EU—highlighted as well by Paul Kubicek and Ioannis Grigoriadis in their contributions to this Special Issue—indicate that Turkey might set off on a hard balancing route against the EU. This article demonstrates that the risk of a shift from boundary breaking (which, albeit being a gray zone, is still classified mainly under soft balancing) to hard balancing increased after 2019.

In line with the realist school of thought, given the systemic changes and the power vacuum in its immediate neighborhood, relative power/regional power competition and distributional concerns have dominated contemporary Turkey-EU relations. Turkey is searching for a new place in the changing international and regional orders. It is increasingly perceived as 'a third country rather than an EU candidate country in EU circles.'[90] Turkish foreign policy is frequently portrayed as 'revisionist' and 'adventurist'[91] by the European and other Western allies and Turkey is more and more regarded as a security competitor by the EU, especially in the EastMed. Moreover, in line with the neoclassical realist expectations, domestic/internal variables serve as intervening variables in producing more tumultuous Turkey-EU relations.

Despite all fundamental problems, Turkey and the EU continue exchanging ideas on important issue areas, such as immigration and refugees, counterterrorism, energy, bilateral trade, and diplomatic relations.[92] Since the summer 2020 crises in the EastMed, there have been several attempts at de-escalating the crisis between Turkey and its EU counterparts. The EU proposed a 'forward-looking agenda' for Turkey, encouraging Turkey-

Greece dialogue as well as a constructive Turkey-EU relationship.[93] Nathalie Tocci states that 'the EU-Turkey relationship has taken a step back from the brink,' and that 'as Turkey de-escalated in the Eastern Mediterranean, supported a government of national unity in Libya, and signaled its willingness to mend ties with the EU, Europeans reciprocated with a restated readiness to improve relations, beginning with a modernized Customs Union.'[94] Amidst the de-escalation of tensions in the EastMed, the European Council in March 2021 and June 2021 'expressed readiness to engage with Turkey in a phased, proportionate and reversible manner in a number of areas of common interest.'[95] In June 2021, the Commission proposed allocating €3 billion to further assist the Syrian refugees and host communities in Turkey.[96] A high-level dialogue on climate between Turkey and the EU was held in September 2021.[97]

While it is possible to argue that boundary-testing behavior seems to be still applicable to Turkey-EU relations, especially against the background of the possibility of modernizing the CU Agreement and continued collaboration on the refugee issue, overall, on all contemporary foreign policy issues, boundary-breaking spilling into hard balancing seems to be the prevalent form of behavior. Nonetheless, the recent de-escalation in bilateral relations is a good indicator that the parties are not yet fully at peace with the idea of parting ways, especially on issues that are of mutual interest. They can still potentially revert to boundary testing and challenging, if they determine that their differences can or must be overcome, as the relationship is of strategic importance and therefore too important to lose.

According to the latest European Commission data, Turkey is the EU's 6th largest trade partner, and the EU is Turkey's largest trade partner and main source of investments.[98] About 33 percent of Turkey's imports came from the EU and 41 percent of the exports went to the EU, with total trade in goods amounting to €132.4 billion.[99] These economic considerations provide incentives for Turkey to maintain a working relationship with the EU. Turkey, therefore, engages in balancing against the EU 'without harming [its] economic ties' to it.[100]

It is widely accepted that Turkey and the trans-Atlantic actors have moved into a transactional period, 'without the flywheel of a long-term trajectory for cooperation' and partnership.[101] Illustrating this transactional relationship, the European Commission's 2021 Report on Turkey notably changes its critical tone when it comes to an evaluation of Turkey's migration and asylum policy. It states, 'The EU-Turkey Statement of March 2016 continued to deliver results and Turkey continued to play a key role in ensuring effective management of migratory flows along the eastern Mediterranean route.'[102] At the same time, however, Turkish officials accuse the EU of being willing 'to conduct 'give and take' relations ... only in areas of its own interests,' blame the EU for 'politicizing the process' of the modernization of the CU, and call on the EU to regard 'Turkey as a negotiating candidate country rather than as a partner to conduct 'give and take' relations with.'[103] While it might dilute strategic commitment,[104] transactionalism is consistent with realism's emphasis on interests-based relationships.

To mend the relationship, the two sides should refrain from further escalation of inflammatory rhetoric. Rekindling trust is central to navigating the ups and downs of bilateral relations. It is similarly important to keep the institutional ties between Turkey and the EU. On that front, there is some reason for optimism as about 56 percent of the Turkish public still support the country's EU membership.[105] Regardless of how realistic eventual Turkish accession to the EU is, it is in the EU's interest to motivate Turkey to keep it in line with the European stance on international issues. This becomes even more important against the background of the current nadir in Turkey-US relations and the 2022 Russian invasion of Ukraine.

The overarching question for the EU is how to manage relations given the hard balancing that is becoming more prevalent in Turkish foreign policy. Turkey's further alienation from the West and hedging its bet with additional moves toward Russia and China would significantly disturb common Euro-Atlantic strategic interests and impede the geopolitical strength of the Union in its immediate region. The future of Turkey's relations with the EU depends on a variety of conditions, such as the irreconcilability of the positions of the parties on key issues on their agendas, the political will of the parties to overcome their differences on important foreign policy issues, and the perceived value of the existing relationship for each party. As illustrated in this article, the developments since 2016 give one ample reason to adopt a skeptical attitude that genuine progress can be made.

Notes

1. Representative samples of this voluminous literature include Aydın and Açıkmeşe, "Europeanization Through EU"; Özcan, *Harmonizing Foreign Policy*; Öniş, "Turkey-EU Relations"; Öniş and Yılmaz, "Between Europeanization and Euro-Asianism"; Terzi, *The Influence of*; Börzel and Soyaltın, "Europeanization in Turkey"; Aydın-Düzgit, "Constructions of European"; Demirtaş, "Turkish Foreign Policy"; Nas and Özer, *Turkey and the European*, Hintz, *Identity Politics Inside Out*; and Aydın-Düzgit and Rumelili, "Constructivist Approaches"
2. Buhari, "Turkey-EU Relations", 96-97.
3. Dursun-Özkanca, *Turkey–West Relations*, 14-16.
4. Boundary testing allows the alliance members to understand the limits of the relationship and "which lines are not to be crossed" when dealing with other allies and entails active diplomacy, entangling diplomacy, cheap-talk diplomacy, and economic statecraft (Dursun-Özkanca, *Turkey–West Relations*, 35).

5. In boundary challenging, the challenging ally "seeks independence from within the allies," and uses interinstitutional balancing, cooperative balancing, strategic noncooperation, and costly signaling (Dursun-Özkanca, *Turkey–West Relations*, 35-36).
6. In boundary breaking, the ally "signals a growing dissatisfaction with membership in the alliance and an increasing willingness to transition into hard balancing" and seeks "independence from without" through compellent threats, territorial and asset denial, alternative alliances, hostage diplomacy, and blackmail (Dursun-Özkanca, *Turkey–West Relations*, 36).
7. Art, "Correspondence," 183-184 (italics in original).
8. Paul, *Restraining Great Powers*, 20. Representative samples of this voluminous literature include Joffe, "Defying History and Theory"; Paul, Wirtz, and Fortmann, *Balance of Power*; Paul, "Soft Balancing"; Pape, "Soft Balancing"; and Whitaker, "Soft Balancing."
9. Fortmann, Paul, and Wirtz, "Conclusions," 370; Pape, "Soft Balancing"; Paul, "The Accommodation of Rising Powers"; and Paul, "Introduction," 3.
10. Mearsheimer, *Conventional Deterrence*.
11. Paul, *Asymmetric Conflicts*.
12. Paul, "The Accommodation of Rising," 19.
13. Ibid.
14. Rose, "Neoclassical Realism and Theories," and quote from Foulon, "Neoclassical Realist Analyses."
15. Representative samples of this literature include Levy, "Diversionary Theory of War"; Rose, "Neoclassical Realism and Theories"; Schweller, "The Progressiveness of Neoclassical Realism"; and Ripsman, Taliaferro, and Lobell, *Neoclassical Realist Theory*.
16. Foulon, "Neoclassical Realist Analyses."
17. McLean, "Understanding Divergence"; Yeşilyurt, "Explaining Miscalculation"; Şahin, "Theorizing the Change."
18. Barysch, "Turkey and the EU."
19. European Commission, "Turkey: European Neighbourhood Policy."
20. Dursun-Özkanca, "Turkish Soft Balancing" and *Turkey–West Relations*.
21. Dursun-Özkanca, *Turkey–West Relations*, and Uğur, *The European Union and Turkey*.
22. Cornell, Knaus, and Scheich, "Dealing with a Rising Power," 11.
23. Pierini, "In Search of an EU Role."
24. Hale, *Turkish Foreign Policy Since 1774*, 257.
25. Tocci, "The Baffling Short-Sightedness," 6.
26. European Commission, "Meeting of Heads of State or Government."
27. Meerts, *Diplomatic Negotiation*, 29.
28. Greenhill, *Weapons of Mass Migration*.
29. Stamouli and Herszenhorn, "EU Leaders Deploy to Help."
30. Bozkır, Conference Remarks.
31. German Marshall Fund, "Turkish Perceptions of the European Union."
32. European Parliament, "Resolution of 24 November 2016."
33. Shaheen, Wintour, and Rankin, "Turkey Threatens to End Refugee Deal."
34. European Commission, "Joint Statement."
35. BBC News "Erdogan Threatens."
36. Beesley, "Brussels Pressed to Rethink Turkey."
37. Kambas, "Standoff in High Seas."

38. European Council, "Council Decisions on Enlargement."
39. European Commission, "Turkey: European Neighbourhood Policy."
40. European Parliament, "Resolution of 13 March 2019."
41. European Council, "Outcome of the Council Meeting."
42. Ibid., 10.
43. International Crisis Group, "Turkey-Greece."
44. At that point in time, Turkey was already alienated from the transatlantic alliance due to developments in Syria and its acquisition of S-400 missile defense systems from Russia. For a detailed discussion of Turkey's rapprochement with Russia and its foreign policies in Syria and Iraq and their impact on Turkey's relations with European allies, please see Dursun-Özkanca, *Turkey–West Relations*, Chapters 6 and 7, respectively.
45. European Council, "Sanctions Regime."
46. Ibid.
47. Turkish Ministry of Foreign Affairs, "Press Release."
48. Kalın, "Kalin: Interview with Mark Leonard."
49. Neoclassical realism holds explanatory power in the pre-2016 period of Turkey-EU relations as well. Turkey's quest for EU membership makes sense especially when considered against the background of the Cold War era and the bipolar international system under which it was initiated. Aside from the international systemic variables, at the unit-level, Turkish bureaucratic politics and the elites overwhelmingly aspired to be more closely associated with the Western and transatlantic institutions during that period, as Kemalism and Westernization dominated the discussion of Turkish foreign policy until 2002 (Turunc, "Post-Westernisation," and Şahin, "Theorizing the Change"). For example, Şahin, in "Theorizing the Change," argues that from the end of the Cold War until 2001, the Turkish bureaucratic elites chose to continue operating within the parameters of pro-Western security policies, despite the change of the international system from bipolarity to unipolarity.
50. The author thanks Reviewer #1 for this quote.
51. Waltz, *Theory of International Politics*.
52. Ripsman, "Neoclassical Realism"; Rathburn, "A Rose by Any Other Name"; and Frankel, "Restating the Realist Case."
53. Paul, "Soft Balancing" and "The Accommodation of Rising Powers."
54. This paper was finalized in the midst of Russia's invasion of Ukraine, which has galvanized the West and is sure to have significant regional and global implications in terms of the evolving multipolar international system.
55. Dursun-Özkanca, "Turkey and the European Union".
56. Dursun-Özkanca, "Turkish Soft Balancing."
57. Barysch, "Why the EU and Turkey."
58. Dursun-Özkanca, *Turkey–West Relations*.
59. Ibid.
60. Ripsman, "Neoclassical Realism."
61. Turkish Ministry of Foreign Affairs, "Press Release."
62. Dursun-Özkanca, *Turkey–West Relations*.
63. Al Jazeera, "NATO Countries."
64. European Council, "North East Syria."
65. Dursun-Özkanca, "Is the Atlantic Pact Sinking."
66. Blanchard, "Libya."

67. Ibid.
68. Petrangeli, "Operation IRINI".
69. Ogunkeye, "France Suspends Role."
70. Cook, "EU Sanctions Turkish Firm."
71. Irish, "After Turkish Incident."
72. Dursun-Özkanca, "Turkish Soft Balancing" and *Turkey–West Relations.*
73. Gümrükcü, "Turkey's Erdogan Says."
74. European Council, "Varosha."
75. European Commission, "Key Findings of the 2021 Report."
76. Ibid.
77. Turkish Ministry of Foreign Affairs, "Press Release."
78. Rose, "Neoclassical Realism and Theories", 147.
79. Whitaker, "Soft Balancing", 1124.
80. German Marshall Fund, "Turkish Perceptions of the European Union."
81. Ripsman, "Neoclassical Realism."
82. Levy, "Diversionary Theory of War"; Rose, "Neoclassical Realism and Theories"; Schweller, "The Progressiveness of Neoclassical Realism"
83. Şahin, "Theorizing the Change", 493.
84. Ibid., 497.
85. European Commission, "Key Findings of the 2021 Report."
86. Dursun-Özkanca, "Turkey-West Relations."
87. McKernan, "Turkey Backs Down."
88. Hoffman, Werz, and Halpin, "Turkey's 'New Nationalism'."
89. Dursun-Özkanca, *Turkey–West Relations*, 37.
90. German Marshall Fund, "Turkish Perceptions of the European Union."
91. Tziarras and Harchaoui, "What Erdogan Really Wants."
92. European Council, "Press Statement."
93. Berger, "Prospects for EU-Turkey Relations"; European Commission, "Key Findings."
94. Tocci, "Teetering on the Brink", 22.
95. European Commission, "Key Findings of the 2021 Report."
96. Ibid.
97. Directorate-General for Climate Action, "The EU and Turkey."
98. European Commission, "Trade."
99. Ibid.
100. Paul, "Soft Balancing", 70.
101. Lesser, "Turkey and the West."
102. European Commission, "Key Findings of the 2021 Report."
103. Turkish Ministry of Foreign Affairs, "Press Release."
104. Hamilton, "TTIP's Geostrategic Implications."
105. German Marshall Fund, "Turkish Perceptions of the European Union."

Acknowledgements

This article was written during the author's sabbatical at Harvard University, which was made possible through the APSA Spring Centennial Center Research Grant, the Center for Global Understanding and Peacemaking Grant and the two faculty grants received from Elizabethtown College. The author thanks Dr. Wayne Selcher, the editors of *Turkish Studies*, and two anonymous peer reviewers for their invaluable feedback on this article.

Disclosure statement

No potential conflict of interest was reported by the author(s).

Funding

This work was supported by American Political Science Association: [grant number Spring Centennial Center Research Grant]; Elizabethtown College: [grant number Faculty Research Grants].

ORCID

Oya Dursun-Özkanca http://orcid.org/0000-0001-5477-1028

Bibliography

Al Jazeera. NATO Countries Could Have Been More Frank." Video Interview with Turkish Defense Minister Fikri Işık, March 25, 2017. Available at: www.aljazeera.com/programmes/talktojazeera/2017/03/fikri-isik-nato-countries-frank-170323122127878.html (Accessed on October 30, 2021).

Arısan-Eralp, Nilgün. The Parlous State of Turkey-EU Relations: Searching for a Bridge over Troubled Waters." TEPAV Evaluation Note, 2019. Available at tinyurl.com/bdcmbjwt, accessed March 8, 2022.

Art, Robert J. "Correspondence: Striking the Balance." *International Security* 30, no. 3 (2005): 177–196.

Aydın-Düzgit, Senem. *Constructions of European Identity: Debates and Discourses on Turkey and the EU*. London: Palgrave, 2012.

Aydın-Düzgit, Senem, and Bahar Rumelili. "Constructivist Approaches to EU–Turkey Relations." In *EU-Turkey Relations: Theories, Institutions, and Policies*, edited by Wulf Reiners, and Ebru Turhan, 63–82. Cham Switzerland: Palgrave, 2021.

Aydın, Mustafa, and Sinem A. Açıkmeşe. "Europeanization Through EU Conditionality: Understanding The New Era In Turkish Foreign Policy." *Journal of Southern Europe and the Balkans* 9, no. 3 (2007): 263–274.

Barysch, Katinka. Turkey and the EU: Can Stalemate Be Avoided?" Centre for European Reform, Policy Brief, December 2010.

Barysch, Katinka. Why the EU and Turkey Need to Coordinate Their Foreign Policies." Carnegie Endowment for International Peace, August 31, 2011. Available at tinyurl.com/2a2kh7k3, accessed March 8, 2022.

BBC News. Erdogan Threatens to Scrap EU-Turkey Migrant Deal." March 16, 2017.

Beesley, Arthur. Brussels Pressed to Rethink Turkey Ties." *Financial Times*. April 24, 2017.

Berger, Miguel. Prospects for EU-Turkey Relations from a German Point of View." European Council on Foreign Relations, June 9, 2021. Available at: https://ecfr.eu/article/prospects-for-eu-turkey-relations-from-a-german-point-of-view/ (Accessed on October 29, 2021).

Blanchard, Christopher M. Libya: Conflict, Transition, and U.S. Policy," *Congressional Research Service*, RL33142, June 26, 2020.

Börzel, Tanja A., and Didem Soyaltın. Europeanization in Turkey: Stretching a Concept to its Limits?" *KFG Working Paper Series*, No. 36. Berlin: Freie Universität Berlin, 2012.

Bozkır, Volkan. Conference Remarks, Conference on Turkey, Middle East Institute. Washington DC, September 30, 2016.

Buhari, Didem. "Turkey-EU Relations: The Limitations of Europeanisation Studies." *Turkish Yearbook of International Relations* 40, no. 1 (2009): 91–121.

Cook, Lorne. EU Sanctions Turkish Firm over Libya Arms Embargo Violations," *The Washington Post*, September 21, 2020.

Cornell, Svante, Gerald Knaus, and Manfred Scheich. Dealing with a Rising Power: Turkey's Transformation and Its Implications for the EU." Centre for European Studies, Brussels, 2012. Available at: http://www.martenscentre.eu/sites/default/files/publication-files/livret-ces-turkey.pdf (Accessed on October 29, 2021).

Demirtaş, Birgül. "Turkish Foreign Policy Towards the Balkans: A Europeanized Foreign Policy in a De-Europeanized National Context?" *Journal of Balkan and Near Eastern Studies* 17, no. 2 (2015): 123–140.

Directorate-General for Climate Action. The EU and Turkey Discuss Climate Crisis and Future Cooperation." September 16, 2021. Available at tinyurl.com/yhdkk2vp, accessed March 8, 2022.

Dursun-Özkanca, Oya. Is the Atlantic Pact Sinking in the Deep Eastern Mediterranean?" Foreign Policy Research Institute and Heinrich Böll Foundation, Special Report, November 2020.

Dursun-Özkanca, Oya. Turkey-West Relations: The Escalating Crisis of Trust and Path Dependency," *Journal of Middle Eastern Politics & Policy*, published online, November 23, 2021. Available at tinyurl.com/bd3n44xk, accessed March 8, 2022.

Dursun-Özkanca, Oya. "Turkey and the European Union: Strategic Partners or Competitors in the Western Balkans?" *Journal of Regional Security* 11, no. 1 (2016): 33–54.

Dursun-Özkanca, Oya. "Turkish Soft Balancing Against the EU? An Analysis of the Prospects for Improved Transatlantic Security Relations." *Foreign Policy Analysis* 13, no. 4 (2017): 894–912.

Dursun-Özkanca, Oya. *Turkey-West Relations: The Politics of Intra-Alliance Opposition*. Cambridge: Cambridge University Press, 2019.

European Commission. "Meeting of Heads of State or Government with Turkey: EU-Turkey Statement." Brussels, November 29, 2015. Available at: http://europa.eu/

rapid/press-release_STATEMENT-15-6194_en.htm (Accessed on October 29, 2021).

European Commission. "Joint statement by High Representative/Vice-President Federica Mogherini and Commissioner Johannes Hahn on the Venice Commission's Opinion on the Amendments to the Constitution of Turkey and Recent Events." Brussels, March 13, 2017. Available at: http://europa.eu/rapid/press-release_STATEMENT-17-588_en.htm (Accessed on October 29, 2021).

European Commission. "Trade: Countries and Regions – Turkey," 2021. Available at: https://ec.europa.eu/trade/policy/countries-and-regions/countries/turkey/ (Accessed on October 29, 2021).

European Commission. "Turkey: European Neighbourhood Policy and Enlargement Negotiations," 2021. Available at: https://ec.europa.eu/neighbourhood-enlargement/countries/detailed-country-information/turkey_en (Accessed on October 29, 2021).

European Commission. "Key Findings of the 2021 Report on Turkey." October 19, 2021. Available at: https://ec.europa.eu/commission/presscorner/detail/en/qanda_21_5282 (Accessed on October 29, 2021).

European Council. "Council Decisions on Enlargement and Stabilisation and Association Process." Annex 10555/18, Brussels, June 26, 2018. Available at: https://www.consilium.europa.eu/media/35863/st10555-en18.pdf (Accessed on October 29, 2021).

European Council. Press Statement Following the 54th Meeting of the Association Council Between the European Union and Turkey," Brussels, March 15, 2019. Available at tinyurl.com/yc356kex, accessed March 8, 2022.

European Council. "Outcome of the Council Meeting: 3709th Council Meeting." Foreign Affairs. 11260/19. Brussels, July 15, 2019. Available at: https://www.consilium.europa.eu/media/41183/st11260-en19.pdf (Accessed on October 29, 2021).

European Council. North East Syria: Council Adopts Conclusions." Press Release, October 14, 2019. Available at tinyurl.com/2p8na5kj, accessed March 8, 2022.

European Council. Sanctions Regime against Illegal Drilling Activities in the Eastern Mediterranean Extended by One Year." Press Release, November 6, 2020. Available at tinyurl.com/mux644zb, accessed March 8, 2022.

European Council. Varosha: Declaration by the High Representative on Behalf of the European Union." Press Release, July 27, 2021. Available at tinyurl.com/mvu52h6, accessed March 8, 2022.

European Parliament. "European Parliament Resolution of 24 November 2016 on EU-Turkey Relations." Strasbourg, November 24, 2016. Available at: https://www.europarl.europa.eu/doceo/document/TA-8-2016-0450_EN.html (Accessed on October 29, 2021).

European Parliament. European Parliament Resolution of 13 March 2019 on the 2018 Commission Report on Turkey." Strasbourg, March 13, 2019. Available at tinyurl.com/2p8f73v2, accessed March 8, 2022.

Ferguson, Chaka. "The Strategic Use of Soft Balancing: The Normative Dimensions of the Chinese–Russian 'Strategic Partnership." *Journal of Strategic Studies* 35, no. 2 (2012): 197–222.

Fortmann, Michel, T. V. Paul, and James J. Wirtz. "Conclusions: Balance of Power at the Turn of the New Century." In *Balance of Power: Theory and Practice in the 21st Century*, edited by T. V. Paul, James J. Wirtz, and Michel Fortmann, 360–374. Stanford, CA: Stanford University Press, 2004.

Foulon, Michiel. "Neoclassical Realist Analyses of Foreign Policy." In *Oxford Research Encyclopedia of Politics*, 2017. Accessed 30 Mar. 2022. https://oxfordre.com/politics/view/10.1093/acrefore/9780190228637.001.0001/acrefore-9780190228637-e-387.

Frankel, Benjamin. "Restating the Realist Case: An Introduction." *Security Studies* 5, no. 3 (1996): 9–20.

German Marshall Fund. Turkish Perceptions of the European Union." April 29, 2021. Available at: https://www.gmfus.org/news/turkish-perceptions-european-union (Accessed on October 29, 2021).

Greenhill, Kelly M. *Weapons of Mass Migration: Forced Displacement, Coercion, and Foreign Policy*. Ithaca, NY: Cornell University Press, 2011.

Gümrükcü, Tuvan. Turkey's Erdogan Says Two-State Solution Only Option for Cyprus," *Reuters*, February 10, 2021.

Hale, William. *Turkish Foreign Policy Since 1774, 3rd Edition*. New York: Routledge, 2013.

Hamilton, Daniel S. TTIP's Geostrategic Implications Testimony" at the Hearing on National Security Benefits of Trade Agreements with Asia and Europe Subcommittee on Terrorism, Non-Proliferation and Trade Committee on Foreign Affairs U.S. House of Representatives, March 17, 2015. Available at tinyurl.com/9yjfuuxz, accessed March 8, 2022.

Hintz, Lisel. *Identity Politics Inside Out: National Identity Contestation and Foreign Policy in Turkey*. Oxford: Oxford University Press, 2018.

Hoffman, Max, Michael Werz, and John Halpin. "Turkey's 'New Nationalism' Amid Shifting Politics. *Center for American Progress*, February 11, 2018. Available at: https://www.americanprogress.org/issues/security/reports/2018/02/11/446164/turkeys-new-nationalism-amid-shifting-politics/ (Accessed October 29, 2021).

International Crisis Group. "Turkey and Greece: From Maritime Brinkmanship to Dialogue," Report No. 263, May 31, 2021. Available at: https://www.crisisgroup.org/europe-central-asia/western-europemediterranean/263-turkey-greece-maritime-brinkmanship-dialogue (Accessed October 29, 2021).

Irish, John. After Turkish Incident, France Suspends Role in NATO Naval Mission," *Reuters*, July 1, 2020.

Jenkins, Gareth, H. Conference Remarks, Conference on Turkey, Middle East Institute. Washington DC, September 30, 2016.

Joffe, Josef. "Defying History and Theory: The United States as the Last Remaining Superpower." In *America Unrivaled: The Future of Balance of Power*, edited by G. John Ikenberry, 155–180. Ithaca, NY: Cornell University Press, 2002.

Kalın, Ibrahim. Kalin, Interview with Mark Leonard," 2020. Available at: https://www.youtube.com/watch?v=P16Y93p2sHs (Accessed on October 29, 2021).

Kambas, Michele. Standoff in High Seas as Cyprus says Turkey Blocks Gas Drill Ship." *Reuters*. February 11, 2018.

Kutlay, Mustafa, and Ziya Öniş. "Turkish Foreign Policy in a Post-Western Order: Strategic Autonomy or New Forms of Dependence?" *International Affairs* 97, no. 4 (2021): 1085–1104.

Lesser, Ian. Turkey and the West: A Relationship Unmoored?" German Marshall Fund of the United States, May 15, 2017. Available at: http://www.gmfus.org/blog/2017/05/15/turkey-and-west-relationship-unmoored (Accessed on October 29, 2021).

Levy, Jack S. "Diversionary Theory of War: A Critique." In *Handbook of War Studies*, edited by Manus Midlarsky, 259–288. Boston: Unwin-Hyman, 1989.

McKernan, Bethan. Turkey Backs Down on Threat to Expel Foreign Ambassadors," *The Guardian*, October 25, 2021.

McLean, Wayne. "Understanding Divergence Between Public Discourse and Turkish Foreign Policy Practice: A Neoclassical Realist Analysis." *Turkish Studies* 16, no. 4 (2015): 449–464.

Mearsheimer, John J. *Conventional Deterrence*. Ithaca NY: Cornell University Press, 1983.

Meerts, Paul. *Diplomatic Negotiation: Essence and Evolution*. The Hague: Clingendael, 2015.

Nas, Çiğdem, and Yonca Özer. eds. *Turkey and the European Union: Processes of Europeanisation*. London: Routledge, 2016.

Ogunkeye, Erin. France Suspends Role in NATO Naval Mission over Tensions with Turkey," *France24*, July 1, 2020. Available at: https://www.france24.com/en/20200701-france-suspends-role-in-nato-naval-mission-over-turkish-warship-incident (Accessed on October 29, 2021).

Öniş, Ziya. "Turkey-EU Relations: Beyond the Current Stalemate." *Insight Turkey* 10, no. 4 (2008): 35–50.

Önis, Ziya, and Şuhnaz Yılmaz. "Between Europeanization and Euro-Asianism: Foreign Policy Activism in Turkey During the AKP Era." *Turkish Studies* 10, no. 1 (2009): 7–24.

Özcan, Mesut. *Harmonizing Foreign Policy: Turkey, the EU and the Middle East*. Aldershot: Ashgate, 2008.

Pape, Robert A. "Soft Balancing Against the United States." *International Security* 30, no. 1 (2005): 7–45.

Paul, T. V. *Asymmetric Conflicts: War Initiation by Weaker Powers*. New York: Cambridge University Press, 1994.

Paul, T. V. "Introduction." In *Balance of Power: Theory and Practice in the 21st Century*, edited by T.V. Paul, James J. Wirtz, and Michel Fortmann, 1–27. Stanford, CA: Stanford University Press, 2004.

Paul, T. V. "Soft Balancing in the Age of U.S. Primacy." *International Security* 30, no. 1 (2005): 46–71.

Paul, T. V. "The Accommodation of Rising Powers in World Politics." In *Accommodating Rising Powers: Past, Present, and Future*, edited by T. V. Paul, 3–32. Cambridge: Cambridge University Press, 2016.

Paul, T. V. *Restraining Great Powers*. New Haven: Yale University Press, 2018.

Paul, T. V., James J. Wirtz, and Michel Fortmann, eds. *Balance of Power: Theory and Practice in the 21st Century*. Stanford CA: Stanford University Press, 2004.

Petrangeli, Federico. Operation IRINI: Can a "No Longer Naïve" EU Tame the Libyan Conflict?" *Italian Institute for International Political Studies* (ISPI), July 31, 2020. Available at: https://www.ispionline.it/en/pubblicazione/operation-irini-can-no-longer-naive-eu-tame-libyan-conflict-27128 (Accessed on October 29, 2021).

Pierini, Marc. In Search of an EU Role in the Syrian Conflict." Carnegie Europe, August 18, 2016. Available at tinyurl.com/yfe7w83f, accessed March 8, 2022.

Rathbun, Brian C. "A Rose by Any Other Name: Neoclassical Realism as the Logical and Necessary Extension of Structural Realism." *Security Studies* 17, no. 2 (2008): 294–321.

Ripsman, Norrin M. "Neoclassical Realism," *International Studies: Oxford Research Encyclopedias* published online, 2017, doi:10.1093/acrefore/9780190846626.013.36.

Ripsman, Norrin M., Jeffrey W. Taliaferro, and Steven E. Lobell. *Neoclassical Realist Theory of International Politics.* Oxford: Oxford University Press, 2016.

Rose, Gideon. "Neoclassical Realism and Theories of Foreign Policy." *World Politics* 51, no. 1 (1998): 144–172.

Şahin, Mehmet. "Theorizing the Change: A Neoclassical Realist Approach to Turkish Foreign Policy." *Contemporary Review of the Middle East* 7, no. 4 (2020): 483–500.

Schweller, Randall. "The Progressiveness of Neoclassical Realism." In *Progress in International Relations Theory*, edited by Colin Elman, and Miriam Fendius Elman, 311–347. Cambridge, MA: MIT Press, 2003.

Shaheen, Kareem, Patrick Wintour, and Jennifer Rankin. Turkey Threatens to End Refugee Deal in Row over EU Accession." *The Guardian*, November 25, 2016.

Stamouli, Nektaria, and David Herszenhorn. EU Leaders Deploy to Help Greece Seal Turkish Border," *Politico*. March 3, 2020.

Terzi, Özlem. *The Influence of the European Union on Turkish Foreign Policy.* London: Routledge, 2010.

Tocci, Natalie. The Baffling Short-Sightedness in the EU-Turkey-Cyprus Triangle." *Istituto Affari Internazionali*, Document IAI 1021, October 2010.

Tocci, Nathalie. Teetering on the Brink: Turkey's Troubled Ties with the West," *Journal of Middle East Politics and Policy*. Harvard University Kennedy School, Fall 2021: 20-25.

Turkish Ministry of Foreign Affairs. Press Release Regarding the 2021 Country Report on Turkey by the European Commission," No: 351, October 19, 2021. Available at: https://www.mfa.gov.tr/no_-251_-avrupa-komisyonu-2021-turkiye-raporu-hk.en.mfa (Accessed on October 29, 2021).

Turunç, Hasan. "The Post-Westernisation of EU–Turkey Relations." *Journal of Contemporary European Studies* 19, no. 4 (2011): 535–546.

Tziarras, Zenonas, and Jalel Harchaoui. What Erdogan Really Wants in the Eastern Mediterranean." *Foreign Policy*, January 19, 2021.

Uğur, Mehmet. *The European Union and Turkey: An Anchor/Credibility Dilemma.* Aldershot: Ashgate, 1999.

Waltz, Kenneth N. *Theory of International Politics.* New York: McGraw Hill, 1979.

Whitaker, Beth Elise. "Soft Balancing among Weak States? Evidence from Africa." *International Affairs* 86, no. 5 (2010): 1109–1127.

Yeşilyurt, Nuri. "Explaining Miscalculation and Maladaptation in Turkish Foreign Policy Towards the Middle East During the Arab Uprisings: A Neoclassical Realist Perspective." *All Azimuth: A Journal of Foreign Policy and Peace* 6, no. 2 (2017): 65–83.

Constructing a realistic explanation of Turkish – US relations

Lenore Martin

ABSTRACT
U.S. support for the Syrian-Kurdish forces aligned with the PKK; U.S. declining to extradite Fethullah Gülen; Turkey's purchase of the Russian S-400 missile defense system; and Turkey's aggressive interference with natural gas exploration in the Mediterranean are four issues that have roiled U.S.-Turkish relations. This paper examines neorealist and constructivist explanations for these issues and determines that they provide a less than complete understanding of this troubled relationship. The paper then turns to middle level alliance theory and domestic factors favored by neoclassical realism to fill in the explanatory gaps.

Introduction

In his August 10, 2018 op-ed in *The New York Times*, President Recep Tayyip Erdoğan observed that there had been six decades of friendly relations between the United States (US) and Turkey and of Turkish support for the North Atlantic Treaty Organization (NATO). He declared that the US was jeopardizing this partnership by engaging in two 'unilateral actions' that threatened Turkish security. First, Washington was providing military assistance to the People's Defense Units (*Yekineyen Parastina Gel* [PYD]), the military wing of the Syrian Kurdish Democrat Union Party, (*Partiya Yekitiya Demokrat* [YPG]), which is an affiliate of the terrorist Kurdistan Workers' Party, (*Partiye Karkeren Kurdistan* [PKK]). Secondly, Washington refused to extradite Fethullah Gülen, who Erdoğan blames for the July 15, 2016 attempted coup. He warned that these unilateral actions 'will require us to start looking for new friends and allies.'[1]

What the Turkish President did not say in this editorial was that Turkey had already found new friends and 'allies' in Russia and Iran.[2] Moreover, a hypothetical response to this subtle threat would have declared that Washington was more likely to perceive Ankara ruled by Erdoğan's Justice and Development Party (*Adalet ve Kalkınma Partisi* [AKP]) government as a problematic and not entirely trustworthy ally. This is mainly because of two additional actions that Turkey was undertaking. First, it purchased and operationalized a Russian S-400 anti-aircraft and anti-missile system. Secondly, it had taken aggressive naval actions in the Mediterranean to confront the US and NATO allies, particularly Greece and France. Alignment with Russia and Iran, acquisition of a missile defense system that could shoot down NATO fighters, and attempts to block exploration by US allies for natural gas in the Eastern Mediterranean could all undermine NATO and the US leadership in it. These actions appear to be odd behavior by the Turkish Republic, a long-time NATO member who has joined in NATO's opposition to the Russian invasion of Ukraine and has militarily confronted Russian mercenaries in Libya as well as Iran's Hezbollah allies in Syria.

How can these developments be explained? What in particular is driving US-Turkish relations? In line with the overall theme of this Special Issue, the next two sections this paper will apply neorealist and constructivist grand theories to try to explain the areas of tension that, particularly since the 2016 coup attempt, have jeopardized US-Turkish relations. Each theory takes a radically different approach. Neorealists theorize at the systems level and treat state actors as undifferentiated units.[3] Their interactions differ according to system power structures classified as multipolar, bipolar, and unipolar. What matters to neorealists analyzing foreign policies is the relative material power and influence of a state in relation to the capabilities of other actors in the system. For neorealists, states pursue their national interests by competing for material power in an anarchic international system. For offensive neorealists, states gain material power by aggrandizement; for defensive neorealists, states protect themselves from threats of domination or extinction by balancing alignments.

In contrast, constructivists are more prone to theorize at the state level, where actors are motivated primarily by ideational conceptions and interests. Ideational interests include political identities, ideologies, perceptions, culture, history, and social norms.[4] The construction of political realities motivating foreign policies is influenced by factors such as regime typologies and forms of government (e.g. democratic or autocratic), as well as by societal cleavages and various domestic political parties and interest groups.

Dissatisfaction with the explanatory power of these two grand theories has led some international relations (IR) theorists to seek intervening variables or 'factors,' such as domestic politics and styles of leadership, that would fill the explanatory gaps.[5] This enterprise is known as neoclassical realism or NCR.[6] These variables are often drawn from 'middle level theories.'[7] The fourth section of the paper will therefore examine some recent attempts to augment the explanatory power of the grand theories with respect to the US-Turkish relationship using NCR and middle range theories. It will draw in particular on the work of Didem Buhari Gulmez[8] and Oya Dursun-Özkanca.[9] The conclusion will assess how successful these attempts have been.

Neorealist explanations of the tensions in US-Turkish relations

As Paul Kubicek notes in his introduction to this volume, Turkey can be described as a 'middle power.'[10] Because of its geographic location, it interacts with the US in several regions, including the Middle East, the Eastern Mediterranean, the Caucasus and the Black Sea. A neorealist analysis of the patterns of US and Turkish interactions in these regions at the systems level starts with the observation that there appear to be structural differences within these regions and considers the relative military capabilities of their major actors. According to this overview, the Black Sea/Caucasus regions have a more bipolar structure more reminiscent of the Cold War. In particular, the US and its NATO allies have opposed Russian efforts to destabilize or even absorb neighboring states such as Ukraine on the Black Sea and Georgia in the Caucasus. In responding to the 2022 Russian invasion of Ukraine, the US and its NATO allies have been building up a substantial force posture in Eastern Europe and at the Black Sea.

By contrast in the Middle East, the US has removed most of its ground forces from Iraq and keeps only a small ground force in Syria as part of its war on Islamist terrorists. However, it does maintain air and naval bases in Qatar, Bahrain, Kuwait and the UAE to defend its Gulf Cooperation Council (GCC) allies from Iran, while also providing substantial military assistance to Egypt and Israel. Manwhile, Turkey, Russia, Iran, Egypt, Israel, Saudi Arabia and the UAE have now become more actively involved in the Middle East and Eastern Mediterranean as a result of the apparent US relinquishment of its dominant role in the region. Bolstering this perception is the wariness among US regional allies as to the strength of the US commitment to defend them against Iranian aggression because the US (at least until Russia's attack on Ukraine) was most focused on containing China in the Far East.[11] Nor is the US any longer dependent on energy resources from the Middle East. Rather it is a net exporter of oil and a major exporter of liquified natural gas (LNG). All of these suspicions concerning a diminished role for the US in the Middle East have contributed to the perception that the region has become more of a multipolar system.

It is less clear how a neorealist would characterize the system of the Eastern Mediterranean.[12] It has been dominated by the US as a leader of NATO. Since its entry into the Syrian civil war, Russia has challenged this domination with bases in Syria and a toehold in Libya. Turkey also has been challenging some of its NATO partners in the region as well as Israel and Egypt. The region appears to be in transition towards a multipolar system.

Bipolarity in the Black Sea and Caucasus regions

With respect to the Black Sea and Caucasus regions, the bipolar structure suggests to neorealists that there should be a greater convergence of interests (*vide* friendlier relations) between Turkey and the US. Neorealists would expect in this structure that Turkey should be a loyal member of the NATO alliance for its protection against Russia and not 'balance' between the US and Russia in the region. This paper uses 'balancing' in the classical realist sense of maintaining an equilibrium between two more powerful states and not in the neorealist sense of opposing a hegemon.[13] From a neorealist perspective, if Turkey was not firmly bound into the NATO alliance, Ankara would face substantial threats to its national security. Among other things, from military bases in Crimea, Abkhazia and South Ossetia, Russia could theoretically threaten any city in Anatolia with its short-range missiles without even deploying ground, naval or air forces. From a neorealist perspective, Turkey needs NATO's Article 5 pledge to deter such threats and protect Turkey from Russian aggression, including nuclear blackmail. In particular, to defend against such missile threats as well as against a superior Russian air force, Turkey needs an effective anti-missile shield from NATO against Russian first and second-strike capabilities.

Ankara's decision to acquire the Russian S-400 missile defense system, therefore, appears from a neorealist perspective to be totally incompatible with a rational choice for providing Turkish national security with protection from Russian threats from the Black Sea and Caucasus regions. Turkey's apparent preference for playing a balancing role as between the US and Russia in these regions would not eliminate those threats.[14] Evidence of this balancing role include Ankara's willingness to provide military assistance to Ukraine to counter the Russian invasion.[15] However, actual Turkish military cooperation with Ukraine appears to be finely calibrated to avoid Russian military retaliation. Ankara's weapons sales to Kyiv have been limited to drones and communications technology that have annoyed Russia but not enough to provoke a rupture of the Kremlin's relations with Turkey. A similar balancing pattern is evident in Ankara's relatively low-level military cooperation with Romania, another one of its NATO Black Sea allies. It engages in US/NATO military exercises with Romania and has concluded a 'strategic partnership' with Romania without detailing how it would work militarily.[16]

In the Caucasus we find a similar pattern of Ankara balancing between Washington and Moscow. With respect to Georgia, Turkey and the US both oppose Russia extending its territorial toehold into South Ossetia and Abkhazia and take a positive approach towards Georgia's membership in NATO. Furthermore, there is an apparent convergence of the interests of Washington and Ankara in resolving the Nagorno-Karabakh dispute and promoting oil and gas pipelines from Central Asia into Europe that thwart Russia's monopolization of gas supplies to the EU. Still, Ankara provides negligible military cooperation to Tbilisi to avoid antagonizing Moscow. On the other hand, Turkey readily provided substantial military cooperation to Azerbaijan, while Russia was not totally committed to supporting Armenia in the 2020 war over Nagorno-Karabakh. Ankara's finely calibrated balancing act that assists Russia is evident in its proposal to form a 3 + 3 group with Russia and Iran to provide Caucasian security for Armenia, Azerbaijan, and Georgia. This new group would supplant the Minsk Group composed of France, Russia and the US.[17]

Multipolarity in the Middle East

From a neorealist perspective, Ankara's balancing act in the bipolar Black Sea and Caucasus regions appears to be incongruous with the way Turkey should interact with the US as leader of NATO. However, Ankara's balancing between the US and Russia and between the US and Iran is perfectly congruent with the behavior patterns neorealists expect to observe in a multipolar Middle East.

For balancing to work in a multipolar system, neorealists expect alignments to easily shift in order to more nimbly counter threats from other actors.[18] Where states compete for power and may need to oppose hegemony from a potentially predominant actor, creating a firm alliance with that actor risks losing the ability to bargain for a better deal to increase capabilities that other actors or competing alliances may offer. In the absence of a hegemonial actor, moreover, actors in a multipolar system need to maintain reasonably friendly diplomatic postures that do not antagonize potential allies. Otherwise, they risk being excluded from an alliance and becoming vulnerable to threats by potential enemies.[19]

From a neorealist perspective, the relinquishment of US dominance in the Middle East has given Turkey multiple opportunities to create fragile alliances and balance with the opposing factions jockeying for power. These factions include secular and monarchical regimes vs Islamist challengers; Sunni states vs. Shiite states and non-state actors such as ISIS; Israelis vs. Palestinians and their Arab supporters; as well as the US vs. Russia and Iran.

The Syrian civil war offers a major vantage point from which to observe Turkey balancing with the US. Turkey has a keen interest in maintaining 'safe zones' in Syria across the Turkish border. The zones form part of Ankara's campaign to deny the Syrian Kurds the type of autonomous region that Iraqi Kurds have achieved with the Kurdish Regional Government (KRG). In contrast to the KRG, however, the dominant Kurdish group in the Syrian civil war is the PYD and its military arm, the YPG, both of which are aligned with the PKK. Ankara sees the PYD/YPG and the PKK as terrorist groups to be forcefully suppressed. Washington, on the other hand, supports the Syrian Democratic Force (SDF) which is dominated by the YPG. The US deems the SDF/YPG as critical for its efforts to defeat ISIS in Syria.[20] In deference to that alignment, Washington has not labelled the YPG as a terrorist group, even though it labels the PKK as terrorists.

Notwithstanding its support for the SDF, three US administrations have waffled over four successive Turkish invasions of Syria and have permitted Ankara to establish and extend safe zones. While the US continues to maintain a token force in Syria, it does not interfere with Turkish military operations. At the same time, Turkey has worked out a tenuous *modus operandi* with Russia over Idlib and the Syrian border areas in opposition to the YPG. However, Ankara and Moscow are not in agreement over the longevity of the Assad regime. For one thing, Turkey's safe zones and support for Islamists in Idlib block the ability of Damascus and Moscow to end the civil war by military victory. Without the unconditional surrender or expulsion of anti-Assad forces in Idlib and the Turkish safe zones, Assad and Putin have little prospect of reuniting the country and restoring sovereign control over its pre-civil war borders.

This complex calibration of balancing between the US and Turkey can also be observed in their relations with Iran. Washington and Ankara have multifaceted interactions concerning Tehran. They involve a divergence of interests over Turkey's need for Iranian energy supplies, cross border trade, and Iranian cooperation with suppression of the PKK, whereas, the US has serious concerns over Iran's development of nuclear weapons and threats to US allies in the region. At the same time there is more of a convergence of interests between Washington and Ankara over reinstatement of the Joint Comprehensive Plan of Action (JCPOA), opposition to Iranian intervention in the Syrian civil war supporting the Assad regime and Tehran's support for Lebanon's Hezbollah as well as over Shiite Popular Mobilization Units in Iraq.

With respect to Turkey's need for Iranian oil and gas, the US has imposed sanctions on all Iranian export of oil and gas, including to Turkey. Turkey first objected and circumvented the sanctions including by using a state-owned Turkish bank. After the bank and a bank official were tried in US courts Turkey ultimately ended up complying with the sanctions.[21] Importing LNG from the US and elsewhere and the other steps Turkey has taken to diversify its supply of natural gas[22] have enhanced Ankara's ability to comply with the US sanctions.

To some extent Turkey's compliance with US sanctions against Iran provides leverage to Turkey in its complex balancing act with Iran. Tehran may not explicitly be 'playing a PKK card,' however, it is not cooperating with Turkey's attempt to eradicate PKK havens in the Qandil Mountains. The PKK leadership can easily cross over the border to find a haven in Iran. There are other clashes with Turkish forces in Iraq by Iraqi Shiite militias who receive Iranian support, as well as clashes with Turkish forces in Syria by Hezbollah combatants also supported by Iran. Moreover, Ankara and Tehran are on opposite sides of the Azerbaijan dispute with Armenia. On the other hand, Iran has a shared natural gas field and good relations with Qatar. When Saudi Arabia, Bahrain, the UAE and Egypt launched a boycott of Qatar to compel Doha to relinquish its support for Al Jazeera and cut ties with Iran, Ankara and Tehran worked in parallel to break the embargo. After the dispute with Qatar was resolved, Turkey, Iran and Qatar have entered into a deal for reducing shipping costs by exporting Turkish goods to Qatar through Iran.

With respect to Turkish interactions with US allies in the Middle East, it is far from clear that Ankara has been as careful to fine-tune its balancing with Washington. Ankara ruptured its relations with Cairo after the military coup that ousted Mohamed Morsi of the Muslim Brotherhood and brought President Al-Sisi to power. While Ankara has taken some tentative steps to repair that relationship, it is not clear how that will proceed while Turkey provides a haven for the leadership of the Egyptian Muslim Brotherhood.[23]

The disruption of Ankara's relations with Saudi Arabia and the UAE (plus Egypt and Bahrain) over Qatar included demands that Ankara remove its military base from Qatar. Even after the resolution of the Qatar boycott, however, that has not happened. Turkey maintains the base jointly with Qatari personnel and has a major military cooperation agreement with Qatar that serves as a deterrence to what are viewed as Saudi Arabian threats to take over Qatar. Nevertheless, in the past year Ankara has been working to restore closer diplomatic relations with Riyadh and the Saudi monarchy has renounced its informal boycott of Turkish goods. With Ankara continuing to balance its relations with Tehran, Riyadh's regional rival, and with Saudi Arabia concluding a military cooperation agreement with Greece,[24] Ankara's regional rival, it remains to be seen, however, how far the Saudi – Turkish rapprochement will be achieved.

The rift between Turkey and Israel is multifaceted. The rift has its origins in the 2009 personal denouncement of Israeli Prime Minister Peres by President Erdoğan at Davos and runs deep within the AKP government. Ankara is a strong backer of the Palestinian cause. In particular, it is a staunch supporter of the Hamas government in Gaza which is also aligned with the Muslim Brotherhood.[25] The rift may heal only slowly with priority given to improving security cooperation and trade and perhaps resolving the energy and pipeline issues in the Eastern Mediterranean.[26]

The Eastern Mediterranean system in transition

From a neorealist perspective, the relations between the US and Turkey and their NATO allies in the Eastern Mediterranean present a conundrum. As noted, to the extent that Russia may seek to establish in Libya the same type of military and economic foothold it has already established in Syria, this represents a geostrategic threat to NATO's 'soft underbelly.' It also represents an enhanced threat to Turkey as the gatekeeper of the Bosphorus through which the Black Sea navy of a potentially belligerent Russia needs to travel to reach its Mediterranean ports of call. Yet the AKP government appears to discount that threat. While it opposes Russia in Libya militarily, including through proxy forces in the Libyan civil war, instead of supporting NATO as a committed alliance partner, Ankara has engaged in disputes over natural gas exploration with its US allies in NATO plus Egypt and Israel.

There has been long-standing dissension in the ranks of NATO as between Turkey and Greece over their maritime boundaries.[27] However, these disputes have now been compounded by Turkey's demarcation of overlapping economic exclusion zones (EEZs) designed to protect its own rights to explore natural gas deposits in the Mediterranean.[28] The overlap is particularly problematic with respect to the gas fields discovered around Cyprus.[29] Other Eastern Mediterranean gas field discoveries have induced Israel and Egypt to make deals involving pipelines and LNG facilities that could service Europe's energy needs in competition with Turkish pipelines into Europe. This cooperation has expanded to include Cyprus, Greece, Italy, Palestine, and Jordan in the Eastern Mediterranean Gas Forum. The Forum excludes Turkey because of its unresolved disputes with Greece over Cyprus and the islands.

The US has sided with Turkey's rivals in these disputes, having been granted observer status to the Forum. Moreover, Washington has not hesitated to signal its displeasure with Turkey's attempts to interfere with Greek gas exploration by a strongly worded State Department condemnation and by sending a warship to standby off Crete. In further opposition to Turkey Washington has concluded military security arrangements with Greece for four more bases in Greece in addition to the naval bases on Crete and in northern Greece and its two air bases in central Greece. With respect to Cyprus, while the US had concluded a Statement of Intent on Security Cooperation with Cyprus in 2018, it has only led to dialogues between their respective Defense Departments. However, having lifted the arms embargo on Cyprus the prospect is raised of Washington bolstering the Greek Cypriot defense capability, to Ankara's great chagrin.[30]

On the other hand, the pragmatic turn by Ankara in its foreign policies in the larger Middle East in 2021 may indicate that Turkey's aggressive actions in the Eastern Mediterranean had the strategic goal of securing a place at the bargaining table in some future negotiations over Mediterranean gas extraction. Shared oil and gas fields in difficult to demarcate boundary regions such as on the Arabian Peninsula and in the Persian Gulf require agreements between neighbors.[31] Without such agreements any state can interfere with the oil and gas reserves of their neighbors. While one can fault Erdoğan for his tactics in securing Mediterranean gas. His strategic goals are at least logical for an energy-starved Turkey. Nevertheless, because of the historic conflict and continuing distrust between Turkey and Greece agreements over these issues have been elusive.

Constructivist explanations of the tensions in US-Turkish relations

For constructivists it matters that Turkey has an AKP government that has Islamist roots with an affinity for the Muslim Brotherhood and a nationalist ideology willing to forcefully suppress Kurdish cultural and political autonomy. With respect to the AKP government's relations with the US, constructivists attribute a palpable significance to Erdogan's populist anti-American sentiment, promotion of pan-Turkic or neo-Ottoman causes, and his aspiration to leadership of the Muslim world. It is similarly significant to constructivists that the Obama and Biden administrations operationalized different conceptions of American exceptionalism than did the Trump administration. The former demonstrated an affinity for liberal democracies, combatting corruption and promotion of world peace,[32] the latter an 'America first,' anti-globalist agenda. Constructivism offers fruitful explanations of many aspects of Turkish foreign policy such as the switch from its original Kemalist Western orientation to the Islamist and neo-Ottomanist orientation of the AKP.[33] It is less fruitful, however, to apply constructivism to explaining at least three of the four issues troubling Turkey's relations with the US in this paper.

Turkey – US differences over US support of the YPG

With respect to President Erdoğan's first complaint in his 2018 editorial criticizing US support for the YPG, there are strong elements of nationalist ideology and identity politics involved in this dispute. Among other things, the Turkish constitution does not recognize Kurds as a separate identity.

Opposition to separate Kurdish cultural and political rights has plagued Turkish domestic and foreign policy since the founding of the Republic.[34] Ankara views Washington as interfering with Turkey's need to suppress Kurdish autonomy, particularly given the close ties between the PYD/YPG and the PKK. Moreover, the AKP government has succeeded in creating a coalition of militant Islamist groups opposed to the Assad regime under the banner of the National Liberation Front (NLF) that would be as problematic to Washington as ISIS.[35] American support for the SDF/YPG might therefore prevent an NLF takeover of Syrian oil wells that could finance jihadi groups that might pose similar threats to US security as does ISIS.

On the other hand, it is difficult to ascribe any ideological affinity or identity politics behind Washington's support for the SDF, dominated by Kurdish nationalists with an admixture of opponents to the Assad regime.[36] The US interest in the SDF/YPG alignment appears to be purely pragmatic and short term. Washington uses them as a proxy to combat the remaining ISIS terrorists. Furthermore, while the AKP government professes solidarity with Sunni Islam in general and the Muslim Brotherhood in particular, its ideological bent does not restrain Ankara from making its own pragmatic deals with secularist and occasionally anti-Islamist Russia or with Iran. Iran represents an ideological opponent that supports Shiite Hezbollah and other Shiite militias to oppose Turkish interests in Syria and Iraq. These accommodations with Russia and Iran lead to further differences with Washington.

Turkey – US differences over US refusing to extradite Fethullah Gülen

It is more difficult to explain the dissension between Ankara and Washington over the extradition of Fethullah Gülen from a constructivist perspective. The political Islamist agenda/ideology of the AKP and Fethullah Gülen's *Hizmet* (service) movement may have somewhat different Islamic precedents, however, the dispute between them is not ideological. It is a clash over political power that arose well before Erdoğan accused Gülen of instigating the attempted coup of July 2016.[37] Moreover, there is no ideological affinity by US administrations with the Gülenists or any rational reason for Washington to support the *Hizmet* movement. The movement is essentially anti-democratic and led to the jailing and destruction of the lives and livelihoods of hundreds of secularist opponents and innocent people.[38] The long and tortuous legal process that the US Justice Department is required to follow is most likely the reason Gülen has not been extradited.[39] That may not be sufficient to convince Erdoğan. Nevertheless, as reminded by his 2018 editorial, the lack of extradition is useful for the AKP President to raise as a continuing grievance when seeking to negotiate over other issues with Washington.

Turkey – US differences over Ankara's aggressive behavior concerning Eastern Mediterranean gas

As noted, Ankara's aggressive attempts to interfere with natural gas exploration and building of gas pipelines in the Eastern Mediterranean has raised serious concerns in Washington and NATO as to Turkey's ultimate goals in this region. From a constructivist perspective, ideological and identity politics may be at stake in Ankara's bullish naval policies in the Eastern Mediterranean. In the first instance, constructivists can point to the doctrine of Blue Homeland that seeks to legitimize Turkish control over a broad swath of the Mediterranean off the Anatolian coast. The doctrine has been widely accepted in Turkey and has been 'adopted' by President Erdoğan.[40]

Secondly, there have been clear ideological clashes between the AKP government with its support for the Muslim Brotherhood and the Al-Sisi regime in Egypt that overthrew the Muslim Brotherhood government of Mohamed Morsi. Similarly, President Erdoğan and Israeli governments have clashed over Ankara's support for the Palestinian cause and for Hamas which is a branch of the Muslim Brotherhood. It may also be easier to explain from a constructivist perspective the interest in Saudi Arabia and the UAE, two other US allies, in concluding military cooperation agreements with Greece, a nation with little geostrategic connections with the Gulf monarchies. Riyadh and Abu Dhabi may have been stimulated to form this alignment with Greece in response to Ankara's continuing military support for Qatar, which supports the Muslim Brotherhood. Given Turkey's pragmatic interest in repairing relations with Saudi Arabia and the UAE, it remains to be seen whether this will be perceived as a retraction of the AKP's ideological foundations and lead to a modification of these anti-Turkish policies in the Eastern Mediterranean.

Turkey – US differences over Ankara's acquisition of the S-400 system

It is difficult for constructivism to explain the rationale behind Turkey's acquisition of Russian S-400 anti-aircraft and anti-missile system. To some extent, purchasing the system may reflect the sovereigntist bent in Turkish foreign policy under the AKP.[41] Still, acquiring an S-400 system does nothing to advance the AKP government's ideological preference for supporting Muslim Brotherhood causes in the Middle East or for pursuing political programs designed to give Erdoğan a leadership role in the Muslim world or increase his domestic popularity in suppressing Kurdish autonomy in the cause of identity politics. It is not even clear that the S-400 system contributes to Erdoğan's desire to benefit politically from the growth in popular antipathy towards the US[42] Admittedly, a majority of the people polled consider the US hostile and an untrustworthy ally.[43] On the other hand, such polls are also reflection of the fact that the electorate is manipulated by Erdoğan and the AKP with respect to supporting any policy decision that the President and his party advocates.[44]

Alternative explanations for the tensions in US – Turkish relations

Alliance theory

Didem Buhari Gulmez seeks to explain the disjunctions in US-Turkish relations from two perspectives. One is the result of divergent threat perceptions – a concept derived from neorealism's concerns with the balance of threats in a system. The other is the result of divergent world views – a concept derived from constructivism. In particular, Gulmez applies neorealist middle range alliance theory to demonstrate that the AKP government's push for 'strategic autonomy' creates a security dilemma for Turkey. In balancing its dealings with the US, Russia and Iran, Ankara is caught between a 'fear of abandonment' were NATO/US to decline to protect Turkey against an aggressive Russia and Iran, and 'fear of entrapment' were NATO/US to trigger a war against Russia and Iran that would impact Turkey, a frontline state. Underscoring the dilemma is Turkey's distrust of the West and decline in the credibility of the US/NATO alliance. For Gulmez, the 'resilience' of the US/NATO alliance can be attributed to an admixture from alliance theory of the 'transactional' concern that Turkey needs the US as a hedge against Russia and Iran and the 'ontological' benefit that Turkey obtains from legitimating its status as a rising middle power straddling between East and West.

Gulmez underscores what we have learned from neorealism concerning the tension created by US support for the YPG/PYD. The tension results from the difference in threat perceptions. However, while noting the tensions over the extradition of Gülen and the purchase of the S400, Gulmez's approach does nothing to further our explanation of them.[45]

Intra-alliance opposition theory

Oya Dursun-Özkanca, another contributor to this Special Issue, details Turkey's pursuit of opposition strategies within the Western alliance, including NATO/US.[46] She applies 'soft balancing' techniques derived from neorealist alliance theory which are designed to increase the influence of a lesser powerful ally within an asymmetrical alliance dominated by a more powerful ally. While acknowledging that there are irreconcilable differences of interests between the US and Turkey, such as over the YPG/PYD, she also enhances her explanations of US-Turkish tensions by bringing into focus domestic factors, as favored by neoclassical realism. The factors consist of nationalist sentiment stoked by the AKP that contributes to its consolidation of control over the government, as well as diversionary theory that blames the West for the government's poor economic performance. Dursun-Özkanca posits that these domestic factors explain the extensive 'distrust' between Turkey and the US, exemplified by the relatively widespread antipathy to the West and US within the Turkish population. She also notes that the submission of the Turkish military to civilian rule, particularly after the purging of pro-Western officers following the attempted coup of 2016, has increased the AKP's ability to make deals with Russia in opposition to NATO. She points to Erdoğan's use of the US refusal to extradite Gülen to promote an anti-Western conspiracy theory that victimizes Turkey. She makes no comment on Turkey's aggressive anti-NATO member actions in the Eastern Mediterranean. However, with respect to Turkey's persistence in acquiring the S-400 system, she principally cites the AKP justifications for it. These include resentment for NATO's lack of objection for Greece's acquisition of a Russian S-300 system; the US offering too high a price for the Patriot system and refusing to permit technology transfers to enable Turkey to develop its own anti-missile system; and NATO leaving 70 percent of Turkey exposed to regional missile attacks. Interestingly, she does not cite another domestic level explanation for the S-400 system: Erdoğan's desiring a defense against his NATO trained and equipped air force, some members of which were implicated in the July 2016 attempted coup.[47]

Conclusions

This paper has explored the ability of neorealism and constructivism to explain areas of tension in the relations between the US and Turkey in the Middle East, Eastern Mediterranean, Black Sea and Caucasus regions. In particular, we have examined two issues raised by President Erdoğan in his 2018 *New York Times* op-ed, US support for the YPG/PYD in Syria and Washington's refusal to extradite Gülen to Turkey, and two other matters that have raised Washington's ire with Ankara, Turkey's aggressive actions seeking to block gas exploration in the Mediterranean and its purchase of a Russian S-400 anti-missile system.

Neorealism was helpful in explaining the tension between Ankara and Washington over US support for the YPG/PYD in northern Syria, as a clash over their respective national security interests. Ankara sees the YPG/PYD as an extension of the PKK which poses an existential threat to the territorial integrity of the Republic were it ever to succeed in carving out an autonomous Kurdistan as the KRG has done in northern Iraq. Washington sees the YPG/PYD as its proxy boots on the ground combatting the ISIS enemy that poses extraterritorial terrorist threats to the US and the West. However, Turkey's aggressive actions against NATO and US allies in the Eastern Mediterranean are incongruous with neorealist expectations concerning the Turkish-American alliance. Ankara appears to underestimate the potential threats to the Republic posed by a belligerent Moscow in the Black Sea/Caucasus region and to overestimate the willingness of Turkeys' NATO allies and the US to overlook Ankara's own belligerence in the Eastern Mediterranean. Neorealism offers no explanation as to the rift between Ankara and Washington over the extradition of Fethullah Gülen. Moreover, the AKP purchase of the S-400 system also makes no sense to a neorealist analysis of the American-Turkish partnership. The costs to Turkey in terms of economic sanctions and denial of access to US military technology outweigh any benefit to Turkey from pursuing 'strategic independence.'

Constructivism's foreign policy level analysis was helpful in explaining how ideational and identity politics have created the clash of US and Turkish interests in Syria and to some extent the tensions in the Eastern Mediterranean. Turkey's unwillingness to resolve its own 'Kurdish issue' and single-minded desire to crush the PKK and its Syrian-Kurdish affiliates have heightened the tensions between Washington and Ankara. Moreover, the AKP's affinity for the Muslim Brotherhood cause in the Middle East have complicated attempts to reduce tensions in the Eastern Mediterranean with Israel, Egypt, Saudi Arabia and the UAE. Washington's refusal to facilitate the extradition of Gülen may also reflect the liberal democratic opposition to the autocratic tendencies of Erdoğan's leadership. However, constructivism is hard-pressed to provide any explanation for the tension caused by Turkey's purchase of the S-400 system.

The incongruities and incompleteness within the neorealist and constructivist explanations of the four thorns in the foundation of the US-Turkish relationship led to our consideration of alternative explanations provided by middle level alliance theories as well as domestic factors drawn from the NCR approach. These theories and factors help to fill in gaps and fill out the rationales for the four tensions and their implications for US-Turkey relations. The picture they draw for us is of a complex mix of Ankara's pragmatism and Erdoğan's domestic political strategies that have allowed Ankara room for maneuverability in the disparate regional systems within which Turkey operates. Whether or not this remains tolerable to the US and its other allies remains open to speculation, with the most difficult sticking point being Turkey's unwillingness to give up the S-400 system.

Notes

1. Erdoğan, "Erdogan: How Turkey."
2. Turkey has also developed a friendship with China, which is beyond the scope of this paper.
3. Waltz, *Theory of International Politics*.
4. Wendt, *Social Theory*, and Katzenstein, *The Culture*.
5. Other approaches not explored here include the attempt to combine realism and constructivism without using intervening variables (see Barkin, "Realist Constructivism," and "Constructivists and Neoclassical Realisms." 2020). There are also attempts to make grand theories compatible with each other through "integrative pluralism" (see Banta and Kaufman, "Integrative Pluralism.")
6. See Meibauer et al., "Forum"; Smith and Smith, "Can Neoclassical Realism"; and Götz, "Neoclassical Realist Theories." For an application of NCR to Turkish foreign policy generally see Sönmez, *A Neoclassical Realist Approach*.
7. See Brooks, "Distinguishing."
8. Gulmez, "The Resilience."
9. Dursun-Özkanca, *Turkey-West Relations*.
10. See Kubicek, "Introduction."
11. The Abraham Accords of August 13, 2020 among Israel, the UAE and the US and the normalization agreement between Bahrain and Israel are considered a consequence of the lessening of US influence in the Arab Middle East.
12. Because of its civil war this paper excludes Syria as a major player in the Eastern Mediterranean together with Lebanon, Gaza, and the North African states of Morocco, Tunisia, Libya and Algeria which are not sufficiently "major" players.
13. See Toledo, "Classic Realism." For theories of "balancing" see Nexon, "The Balance of Power," 344–47, and Bock and Henneberg, "Why Balancing Fails," 10–17.
14. For a neorealist explanation of the AKP government's relations with Russia, see Kubicek, "Structural Dynamics" in this special issue of *Turkish Studies*.
15. The AKP government has also expressed concern for the "Crimean Turks" under Russian occupation. See Ereker and Özer, "Crimea," 372.
16. Bayar, "Turkey Hails."
17. The Minsk Group had unsuccessfully tried to resolve the dispute over Nagorno-Karabakh since 1992.
18. Walt, *The Origins of Alliances*, 27 and 172–76.
19. This is reminiscent of the prisoner's dilemma used in game theory and occasionally built into systems theory in international politics. See Kaplan, *System and Process*. It is also reminiscent of the social theory of cross-cutting cleavages that reinforce moderation in groups that compete against each other in one arena but need to cooperate with the competitors in another. See Wallace, "Alliance Polarization."
20. See Biden, "Letter."
21. International Energy Agency (IEA), "Turkey 2021," 116.
22. Kahlesar, "More US LNG Exports."
23. Tastekin, "Muslim Brotherhood."
24. Iddon, "How Significant."
25. President Erdoğan did not help the reconciliation process by making anti-Semitic remarks in May 2021 that stimulated a sharp rebuke from the Biden

White House. See Reuters, "US condemns Erdogan comments." See also the anti-Semitic trope of Nureddin Nebati, the AKP Treasury and Finance Minister who claimed that "The United States central bank does not belong to the public. It is in the hands of five families." See *Ahval*, "Turkish Finance Minister."

26. "Turkey-Israel Pipeline."
27. See International Crisis Group, "Turkey-Greece."
28. Stanicek, "Turkey: Remodelling."
29. Andrei, "The Cyprus Issue."
30. Reuters, "US to Lift."
31. See Martin, *The Unstable Gulf*, 31–73.
32. See White House "Washington Declaration."
33. See Kubicek, "Introduction," 7–8.
34. Martin, "A New Track."
35. Yüksel, "Strategies of Turkish Proxy Warfare," 8–12.
36. Holmes, "SDF's Arab Majority."
37. Tol, "The Clash."
38. Reynolds, "Damaging Democracy."
39. Werz and Hoffman, "The Process."
40. Denizeau, "Mavi Vatan." *Mavi vatan* was also designated as the name for the large-scale naval exercise in February-March 2021. See also Candar, "Turkey's Blue Homeland Doctrine."
41. See Alles and Badie, "Sovereigntism."
42. Grigoriadis, "Friends No More?"
43. Aydin, "Public Perceptions."
44. Kalaycioğlu, "Public Opinion."
45. Moreover, Gulmez's comment on the tensions over Eastern Mediterranean gas exploration as reinforcing Turkey's fear of abandonment is hard to fathom.
46. See Dursun-Özkanca, "An Examination." A fuller development of her argument can be found in Dursun-Özkanca, *Turkey-West Relations*.
47. Stewart, "US Officials Wonder."

Disclosure statement

No potential conflict of interest was reported by the author(s).

ORCID

Lenore Martin http://orcid.org/0000-0002-4924-3551

Bibliography

"Turkey-Israel Pipeline on Table as Europe's Alternative to Russian Gas," *Daily Sabah*, March 29, 2022.
Ahval. "Turkish Finance Minister Berated For Claiming US Fed Run by 5 Families," December 30, 2021.
Alles, Delphine, and Bertrand Badie. "Sovereigntism in the Internationalsystem: From Change to Split." *ERIS – European Review of International Studies* 3, no. 2 (2016): 5–19.
Andrei, Roxana. "The Cyprus Issue and Natural Gas in the Eastern Mediterranean." *Geopolitical Monitor*, September 2, 2019.
Aydin, Mustafa. "Public Perceptions on Turkish Foreign Policy." *Kadir Has Perceptions Survey – 2021*, Kadir Has University, June 15, 2021.
Banta, Benjamin, and Stuart J. Kaufman. "Integrative Pluralism and Security Studies: The Implications for International Relations Theory." *European Journal of International Security*. Published on-line March 8, 2022. doi:10.1017/eis.2022.6.
Barkin, J. Samuel. "Realist Constructivism." *International Studies Review* 5, no. 3 (2003): 325–342.
Barkin, J. Samuel. "Constructivist and Neoclassical Realisms." In *The Social Construction of State Power: Applying Realist Constructivism*, edited by J. Samuel Barkin, 47–72. Bristol: Bristol University Press, 2020.
Bayar, Gozde. "Turkey Hails Strategic Partnership with Romania." *Anadolu Agency*, April 22, 2021.
Biden, Joseph R. "Letter to the Speaker of the House of Representatives and the President of the Senate on the Continuation of the National Emergency with Respect to the Situation in and in Relation to Syria," October 7, 2021.
Bock, Andreas M., and Ingo Henneberg. "Why Balancing Fails." *AIPA* (Working Paper, University of Cologne) no. 2 (2013): 1–38. https://jaeger.uni-koeln.de/fileadmin/templates/publikationen/aipa/AIPA_2_2013.pdf.
Brooks, Stephen G. "Distinguishing a Minimalist Role for Grand Theorizing." *International Relations* 31, no. 1 (2017): 85–89.
Candar, Cengiz. "Turkey's Blue Homeland Doctrine: Signaling Perpetual Conflict in the Mediterranean and Rough Waters Ahead." *Turkey Analyst*, August 26, 2020.
Denizeau, Aurélien. "Mavi Vatan, the "Blue Homeland": the Origins, Influences and Limits of an Ambitious Doctrine for Turkey." *Etudes de l'Ifri* (French Institute of Internatioanl Relations), April 2021. https://www.ifri.org/en/publications/etudes-de-lifri/mavi-vatan-blue-homeland-origins-influences-and-limits-ambitious
Dursun-Özkanca, Oya. *Turkey-West Relations: The Politics of Intra-Alliance Opposition*. Cambridge: Cambridge University Press, 2019.
Dursun-Özkanca, Oya. "An Examination of the Underlying Dynamics of Turkey-European Union Relations Through the Lenses of International Relations Theory," *Turkish Studies* 23, no. 5 (2022): 1–22, forthcoming. Available on-line at doi:10.1080/14683849.2022.2060083.
Erdoğan, R. T. "Erdogan: How Turkey Sees the Crisis with the US." *The New York Times*, August 10, 2018.
Ereker, Fulya, and Utku Özer. "Crimea in Turkish-Russian Relations: Identity, Discourse, or Interdependence?" *Athens Journal of Social Sciences* 5, no. 4 (2018): 371–388.
Götz, Elias. "Neoclassical Realist Theories, Intervening Variables, and Paradigmatic Boundaries." *Foreign Policy Analysis*, 17 no. 2 (2021), online. doi:10.1093/fpa/oraa026

Grigoriadis, Ioannis N. "Friends No More? The Rise of Anti-American Nationalism in Turkey." *The Middle East Journal* 64, no. 1 (2010): 51–66.

Gulmez, Didem B. "The Resilience of the US-Turkey Alliance: Divergent Threat Perceptions and Worldviews." *Contemporary Politics* 26, no. 4 (2020): 475–492.

Holmes, Amy A. "SDF's Arab Majority Rank Turkey as the Biggest Threat to NE Syria." Wilson Center Occasional Paper Series, 2019. https://www.wilsoncenter.org/publication/sdfs-arab-majority-rank-turkey-the-biggest-threat-to-ne-syria-survey-data-americas

Iddon, Paul. "How Significant is Greece's Growing Military Cooperation With The UAE And Saudi Arabia." *Forbes*, May 31, 2021.

International Crisis Group. "Turkey-Greece: From Maritime Brinkmanship to Dialogue," Report no. 263, May 31, 2021.

International Energy Agency (IEA). "Turkey 2021: Energy Policy Review," March 11, 2021.

Kahlesar, Omid S. "More US LNG Exports to Turkey, Less Dependency on Iran and Russia's Gas." *Daily Sabah*, July 10, 2020.

Kalaycıoğlu, Ersin. "Public Opinion and Foreign Affairs in the National Elections of June 24, 2018 in Turkey." In *Elections and Public Opinion in Turkey: Through the Prism of the 2018 Elections*, edited by Ali Carkoglu, and Ersin Kalycioglu. Milton Park: Routledge, 2022.

Kaplan, Morton A. *System and Process in International Politics*. New York: Wiley, 1957.

Katzenstein, Peter. *The Culture of National Security: Norms and Identity in World Politics*. New York: Columbia University Press, 1996.

Kubicek, Paul. "Introduction: Contrasting Theoretical Approaches to Turkish Foreign Policy." *Turkish Studies* 23, no. 5 (2022), forthcoming.

Kubicek, Paul. "Structural Dynamics, Pragmatism, and Shared Grievances: Explaining Russian-Turkish Relations." *Turkish Studies* 23, no. 5 (2022): 1–18. doi:10.1080/14683849.2022.2060637.

Martin, Lenore G. *The Unstable Gulf: Threats from Within*. Lexington, MA: Lexington Books, 1984.

Martin, Lenore G. "A New Track Towards Resolving Turkey's Kurdish Issue." *Asian Journal of Middle Eastern and Islamic Studies* 11, no. 2 (2017): 1–13.

Meibauer, Gustav, Linde Desmaele, Tudor Onea, Michiel Foulon, Alexander Reishwein, and Jennifer Sterling-Folker. "Forum: Rethinking Neoclassical Realism at Theory's End." *International Studies Review* 23 (2021): 268–295.

NATO. "Environment, Climate Change and Security." December 3, 2021. https://www.nato.int/cps/en/natohq/topics_91048.htm

NATO. "Boosting NATO's Presence in the East and Southeast." January 7, 2022.

Nexon, Daniel H. "The Balance of Power in the Balance." *World Politics* 61, no. 2 (2009): 330–359.

Reuters. "US Condemns Erdogan Comments on Jewish People as Anti-Semitic." May 18, 2021.

Reuters. "US to Lift 33-Year Arms Embargo on Cyprus, Angering Turkey." *Reuters*, September 15, 2020.

Reynolds, Michael A. "Damaging Democracy: The US, Fethullah Gülen, and Turkey's Upheaval." *Foreign Policy Research Institute*, September 26, 2016. https://www.fpri.org/article/2016/09/damaging-democracy-u-s-fethullah-gulen-turkeys-upheaval/

Smith, Nicholas Ross. "Can Neoclassical Realism Become a Genuine Theory of International Relations? *Squandered Opportunity: Neoclassical Realism and Iranian Foreign Policy.* By Thomas Juneau. Stanford, CA: Stanford University Press, 2015. *EU and NATO Relations with Russia: After the Collapse of the Soviet Union.* By Glenn Diesen. Abingdon: Routledge, 2016. *Neoclassical Realist Theory of International Politics.* By Norrin M. Ripsman, Jeffrey W. Taliaferro, and Steven E. Lobell. Oxford: Oxford University Press, 2016." *The Journal of Politics* 80, no. 2 (2018): 742–749.

Sönmez, Göktuğ. *A Neoclassical Realist Approach to Turkey under JDP Rule.* Cambridge: Cambridge University Press, 2020.

Stanicek, Branislav. "Turkey: Remodelling the Eastern Mediterranean: Conflicting Exploration of Natural Gas Reserves." European Parliamentary Research Service, September 2020. https://www.europarl.europa.eu/thinktank/en/document/EPRS_BRI(2020)652048

Stewart, Phil. "US Officials Wonder: Did Turkish Leader's Coup Memories Drive Russia Arms Deal?" *Reuters*, July 18, 2019.

Tastekin, Fehim. "Muslim Brotherhood Exiles in Turkey Face Uncertain Future." *Al-Monitor*, November 10, 2021.

Tol, Gönül. "The Clash of Former Allies: The AKP Versus the Gulen Movement." *Middle East Eye*, March 7, 2014. https://www.mei.edu/publications/clash-former-allies-akp-versus-gulen-movement

Toledo, Peter. "Classic Realism and the Balance of Power Theory." *Glendon Journal of International Studies* 4 (2005): 52–63.

Wallace, Michael D. "Alliance Polarization: Cross-Cutting, and International War, 1815-1964: A Measurement Procedure and Some Preliminary Evidence." *Journal of Conflict Resolution* 17, no. 4 (1973): 574–604.

Walt, Stephen M. *The Origins of Alliances.* Ithaca, NY: Cornell University Press, 1987.

Walt, Stephen M. "International Relations: One World, Many Theories." *Foreign Policy* 110 (1998): 29–46.

Waltz, Kenneth N. *Theory of International Politics.* Reading: Addison-Wesley, 1979.

Wendt, Alexander. *Social Theory of International Politics.* New York: Cambridge University Press, 1999.

Werz, Michael, and Max Hoffman. "The Process Behind Turkey's Proposed Extradition of Fethullah Gülen." *CAP Report*, September 7, 2016.

White House. "Washington Declaration," July 16, 2021.

Yüksel, Engin. "Strategies of Turkish Proxy Warfare in Northern Syria," Clingendael (Netherlands Institute for International Affairs), November 2019. https://www.clingendael.org/pub/2019/strategies-of-turkish-proxy-warfare-in-northern-syria/

Structural dynamics, pragmatism, and shared grievances: explaining Russian-Turkish relations

Paul Kubicek

ABSTRACT
In recent years, closer Turkish-Russian relations have captured the attention of both academics and policymakers, but also seem rather paradoxical as the two countries find themselves on opposite sides of conflicts in Syria, Libya, and the Caucuses. This paper evaluates how effective neo-realist (structural) and ideational (constructivist) theories of international relations are in explaining the Turkish-Russian relationship. Ultimately, this paper finds more merit in accounts grounded in neo-realism that can capture aspects of both cooperation and conflict/competition in the relationship.

Introduction

Turkish-Russian relations offer a paradox. For the past decade, Ankara and Moscow have been on opposite sides of the Syrian conflict, arguably Turkey's greatest security crisis. In 2015, Turkish planes shot down a Russian aircraft along its border with Syria—prompting Russia to temporarily impose harsh economic sanctions on Turkey—and Russian-supplied Syrian forces have killed Turkish soldiers in northern Syria. Turkey and Russia also oppose each other in Libya, and a renewal of fighting between Armenia and Azerbaijan in 2020 prompted fears that the two countries could become involved in a more direct conflict with each other. Given these developments—as well as animosity and conflict between Turkey and Russia dating back to the days of the Ottomans and Romanovs and continuing through the Cold War—one might expect contemporary Turkish-Russian relations to be hostile and belligerent. However, today[1] there are numerous areas of intense cooperation, including a robust trading relationship, investments in energy infrastructure, including construction of Turkey's first nuclear power plant, and even Turkish purchase of Russian military equipment over the objection of the former's NATO allies. Since the failed military coup in

2016, Turkish President Recep T. Erdoğan and Vladimir Putin, his Russian counterpart, have met numerous times, praising both each other and what they have dubbed a strategic partnership between their two countries.[2] Numerous academic observers have commented on these developments, although some also highlight the contradictions, ambiguity, and mutual suspicions that exist within this 'partnership'.[3]

This paper attempts to account for the mixture of conflict and cooperation in Turkish-Russian relations and assess their future prospects. Consistent with the aims of this special issue, it draws upon theories of international relations and foreign policy, in particular neo-realism (often called structural realism) and constructivism, which represent two contrasting paradigms.[4] Within the natural limits of a single case-study, it seeks to develop hypotheses to assess the explanatory power of these approaches. The goal, shared by all papers in this special issue, is to contribute a more theoretically-informed analysis of contemporary Turkish foreign policy.

Neorealist expectations and outcomes in Turkish-Russian relations

Neorealism occupies a prominent place in the study of world politics. Like realism, it emphasizes states' pursuit of power and how power (or lack thereof) enables or constrains various forms of state behavior. Its chief insight is that the power distribution in the international system among great powers provides an overarching structure to the system and conditions the behavior of states.[5]

As suggested in the framework paper of this special issue, neo-realist perspectives tended to look favorably on the stabilizing features of bipolarity during the Cold War. For a middle power like Turkey, ensconced in NATO, one of the two main alliance structures, bipolarity was in many ways constraining, as Turkey was generally compelled to adhere to the positions of its Western powers and eschew adoption of a more independent foreign policy. This was particularly true of relations with the then-Soviet Union, NATO's primary adversary. While functional (mainly economic) cooperation did develop between Turkey and the Soviet Union in the 1970s and 1980s, this did not alter the fundamental direction of Turkish foreign policy, and, Soviet hopes notwithstanding, there was no prospect of Turkey and the Soviet Union developing a strategic partnership.[6]

The end of the Cold War brought an end to bipolarity, ushering in a brief period of American hegemony that has, in most accounts, now given way to a multipolarity.[7] Alliance structures may now be more fluid, and global dynamics are not determined by competition among two superpowers. Certainly, today one can talk about the emergence of various 'rising powers' (e.g. the BRICs) as well as regional powers such as Turkey that now have more freedom to pursue a more activist and independent foreign policy. This fundamental shift in the structure of the international system gives rise to a number of hypotheses. The most basic one would posit the end of the Cold War as opening up possibilities for new directions in Turkish foreign policy, including better relations with Russia.

This most general, simple hypothesis does capture part of the story. Certainly, under the leadership of President Turgut Özal (1989-1993) in the immediate post-Cold War period, there was a burst of activism in Turkish foreign policy. This included overtures to numerous post-Soviet states in the Caucuses and Central Asia, as well greater activism in the Middle East and the broader Muslim world. Much of this was done with Western/American encouragement. In the 2000s, under the Justice and Development Party (*Adalet ve Kalkınma Partisi*, AKP), Turkish foreign policy became even more focused on the Middle East, and Turkey sought to use its status as a 'rising power' to play a larger and often more independent role on the global stage.

However, this most general hypothesis does not adequately explain Turkish-Russian relations, which in the immediate post-Cold War period suffered numerous problems. Several of these, including Turkish overtures in the post-Soviet space such as support for Azerbaijan in its conflict with Armenia and expressions of sympathy to Chechen separatists, were a direct result of Turkish foreign policy activism and Turkey's desire to support Turkic peoples, a cultural element that does not fit well with neo-realism. By the late 1990s, observers characterized Russian-Turkish relations as a 'cold peace' and 'schizophrenic'.[8] In short, the end of bipolarity may have been necessary to open up new possibilities for Turkish foreign policy, but insufficient to explain what foreign policy options would be realized.

A more particular neo-realist hypothesis would focus on relative power and perception of threat between Turkey and Russia. One simple prediction would be that as the two sides became closer in power—meaning Russia became relatively weaker compared to a rising Turkey—that relations would improve. Aktürk, in a review of Russian-Turkish relations in the first decade after the Cold War, emphasized this point by assessing each side's relative power.[9] In a similar vein, resolving or working around various security issues (e.g. ending Turkish backing of Chechens and Russian support for Kurdish separatists, 'freezing' the Nagorno-Karabakh conflict) could also be seen as a prerequisite to better relations. Sezer argues that the removal of Russia in the 1990s as an 'existential security threat' to Turkey opened up new possibilities for cooperation, particularly in the economic and energy spheres.[10]

While this hypothesis, like the first one, might be invoked as necessary to explain any Turkish-Russian entente or partnership, one might ask if it is sufficient. Diminishing threat perceptions do not necessarily produce common interests, let alone a strategic partnership. Sezer, for example, noted that the decrease in threat perceptions had produced by the early 2000s only 'managed competition,' with Turkey's position in NATO and its support for oil and gas pipelines from the Caspian Basin that would bypass Russia as two chief impediments to better relations.[11] More seriously, perhaps, the rise of a more assertive Russia under President Putin in the late 2000s-early 2010s and, by the mid-2010s, Russian military intervention in Syria, where Russia and Turkey have diametrically-opposed political aims, would, by this logic, lead to a worsening relationship. Indeed, Aktürk finds this to be the case[12], and, as noted, a clash in 2015 between Turkish and Russian forces in Syria seriously damaged Turkish-Russian relations. However, the two sides have managed to overcome both this crisis and their geostrategic and military confrontation in both Libya and (in 2020) in the Caucasus.

More nuanced neo-realist hypotheses might give one more purchase to analyze the admittedly complex, 'serpentine' nature of Turkish-Russian relations.[13] In particular, we might want to consider how Turkey's position within the Western bloc as well as actions by the United States, still the world's leading power, might affect its relations with Russia. Put in more neo-realist terms, we might want to consider whether and how alignment with Western states bolsters Turkey's power and security. If these ties are no longer as valuable or useful as they once were, and considering, as noted, that multipolarity opens up other options for Turkey, this re-assessment might help explain Turkey's apparent tilt toward Russia. It is thus worth noting that there is little question that Turkey's relations with the West have worsened, particularly in the 2010s. There are a host of reasons for this, ranging from Turkey's 'authoritarian turn' (especially in the wake of the 2013 Gezi Park protests), disappointments with Western failure to support Turkey's position in Syria and its bid to join the European Union (EU), suggestions that Western countries helped organize or tacitly supported the 2016 coup attempt and the subsequent American refusal to extradite the alleged coup mastermind, Fethullah Gülen, to Turkey, and Washington's support for the Syrian Kurds in the campaign against the Islamic State, even though Turkey considers Syrian-Kurdish forces terrorists that threaten Turkey's security.[14] Some commentators suggested that Turkey and United States had become 'frenemies.'[15] Put in the language of neo-realism, the estrangement between Turkey and its Western partners could lead the former to pursue 'soft-balancing' or even what Dursun-Özkanca calls 'boundary-breaking' behavior, looking for other options to advance its own power and gain security.[16]

This argument is both straight-forward and offers some insight into several features of Turkish foreign policy, including its turn to Russia. For example, if Sezer's earlier analysis[17] is correct—namely that Turkey's position in NATO was a key stumbling block to a stronger Turkish-Russian relationship in the 1990s and early 2000s—then Turkey's estrangement from the West should lead to improved relations with Moscow. This argument partially hinges, however, on some factors that go beyond the formal confines of neo-realism's concern with power and power distribution and assumption that all states pursue similar goals. Notably, one element driving the new directions in Turkish foreign policy is Turkey's self-perception as a 'rising power,'[18] one that is both able and perhaps even entitled to exercise a greater role in world affairs, and one that may not 'need' its Western partners as much as it did in the past. However, there is more in play here than purely objective measures of power, because power dynamics by themselves do not explain the attraction of Russia—which has its own disagreements and historical rivalry with Turkey—although one might simply argue that due to geographic proximity and Russia's own power, it might present the most obvious alternative.

Grievance, in particular, is a crucial element that helps fill out this explanation. Both Russia and Turkey are not only rising powers but, to varying degrees, revisionist powers, seeking fundamental change in global and regional affairs.[19] Russia's status as a revisionist power is rather clear; for Turkey, it is manifested in various ways, including calls to reform the UN and other international organizations, criticism of the 'Eurocentric' world order, support for various 'outsider' groups in the Middle East (Hamas, the Muslim Brotherhood), support for Turkish co-ethnics in neighboring states and suggestions that the 1923 Lausanne Treaty be revised, as well as more general imperial nostalgia for a time when Turkey (the Ottoman Empire) was a great power. Using different terms, Öniş and Kutlay describe Turkey as an 'emerging middle power,' with 'emerging' noting that Turkey has a certain ambivalence and critical perspective regarding the international order dominated by liberal Western powers and may seek to undermine or change it.[20] Given these conditions, Russia, which openly rejects Western values while embracing a more statist-oriented development path, emerges as a possible partner, one, which shares with Turkey a longstanding status as a competitor or outsider/peripheral country vis-à-vis the West.[21] Notably, relative Turkish isolation or friction with the West has historically driven Ankara closer to Moscow in the twentieth century.[22] In more recent years, as both countries have grown alienated from the West, they have grown closer together, Already by the mid-2000s, Hill and Taşpınar called them part of the 'axis of the excluded',[23] although, to be sure, the two countries have not always see eye-to-eye on key issues (e.g. Syria) and elements of each's 'grand strategy' clashed with the other's.[24]

There are, however, objections and shortcomings to this quasi-structural account rooted in shared grievances or revisionist intentions. Most obviously, this explanation bleeds into a non-structuralist, more constructivist one that is rooted in identity, insofar as aggrievement or revisionism becomes a feature of Turkish identity that drives it away from the West (the source of its grievance) and towards Russia, which shares some of Turkey's anti-Western orientations. Put differently, it is not simply power *per se* but Turkish perceptions and notions of right/wrong or 'justice' that animate Turkish policy. In this sense, Turkish ambitions and orientations may be driven by particular ideational factors, such as imperial nostalgia (neo-Ottomanism) or greater ambivalence toward the West from the governing AKP, which has been unafraid to challenge existing norms or practices in both domestic and foreign policy in its bid to create a 'New Turkey'. In short, *who* has political power, as well as their values and ideas, matters. In this respect, we may need to augment structural explanations with ideational or constructivist ones—considered below—to give us a more complete picture of Turkish foreign policy in general as well as the Turkish-Russian relationship. In addition, however, this argument, rooted in grievance, fails to take into account the fact that in other cases, mostly clearly in Syria, Turkey has a profound grievance against Russia. In other words, if Turkey is upset with the West or sees less value in its ties to Western countries, this does not fully explain why it would turn to Russia, which stands against Turkey in numerous instances. However, despite past clashes between Turkish and Russian forces in Syria and the potential for greater conflict between them both in Syria and on other fronts, the Turkish-Russian relationship, at present, appears to be quite robust.

One final neo-realist oriented hypothesis might therefore be advanced, one that can account for what by 2018 had become—and at present continues to be—Turkish-Russian cooperation in Syria. The fundamental consideration here is that Russia has become the main power broker in Syria. Its forces provide crucial support to the Assad government, and Turkey lacks the will and means to challenge Russian military superiority. Given the fact that the US, Turkey's ostensible ally, was supporting the Syrian Kurds (viewed by Turkey as a top security threat) in its battle with the Islamic State and, since 2019, has largely withdrawn from Syria, Turkey has been compelled to work with Russia if it wants to have any influence on developments in Syria. Why Russia has been willing to work with Turkey in northern Syria is, of course, an important element as well, one that stretches a bit beyond the confines of this article.[25] The key point here, from a neo-realist perspective, is that Turkey has been compelled to work with the regionally-dominant power in an effort to balance and counter what it viewed as a more threatening development, namely the creation of a Kurdish-statelet on its southern border. Cooperation with Russia in Syria can thus be seen as a pragmatic concession to the power realities on the ground and the lack of support Turkey received from its ostensible ally, the US, in addressing its own security concerns.

A similar sort of cost–benefit logic can be applied to other aspects of Turkish-Russian relations. Due to both economic endowments and geography—the United States is far away and cannot build gas pipelines to Turkey—Russia emerges as an attractive partner. And as with Syria, Ankara's apparent 'turn' to Moscow reflects neglect or disengagement from Washington and other Western capitals. Turkey long lobbied Western states to assist it in construction of a nuclear power plant; they refused, and Russia offered to do so, although a Russian company will own and operate the Akkuyu plant, scheduled to go on-line in late 2023. Turkey asked NATO for Patriot missiles to protect its southern border, but these were removed in 2015, and thus it turned to Russia and purchased (with generous financing from Moscow) the latter's S-400 air defense system. Thus, to the extent that Turkey can no longer realize some of its key security and developmental goals through its Western partners, it needs to look for alternatives. Russia, which has the resources and will to assist Turkey, thus makes sense as a partner.

Constructivist expectations and outcomes in Turkish-Russian relations

Neo-realism is a popular and often useful means for analyzing international relations, but it is hardly the only theory or paradigm. Kenneth Waltz, perhaps the most well-known neo-realist scholar, conceded that states' actions are not determined solely by structure, but that structures 'shape and shove.'[26] As suggested above, neo-realism may identify necessary conditions, but they may not be sufficient, as states' policies can be 'shaped' and 'shoved' in various possible directions. Put differently, power considerations may present a 'menu' to states, but they are still able to make their selections from the menu.

What determines their choice? There are some obvious considerations. One is who is making the choice and what their own values, identities, orientations, and priorities are. Another is whether these decision-makers are subject to the influence of others or need to appeal to other actors or constituencies to gain support for their policies or otherwise remain in power. These considerations force us to consider domestic political and ideational factors, meaning we may need to look at another set of factors and another level of analysis to understand the dynamics of Turkish-Russian relations.

As noted in the framework paper in this special issue, ideational/constructivist perspectives as well as domestic political factors may offer some explanatory power or at least fill in some of the holes in purely structuralist accounts. Foreign policy is often, even if only rhetorically, linked to some grander idea or value than power. Moreover, what sort of power one seeks, the means one employs to gain or maintain power, and over whom one wishes to exercise power may be determined by cultural, ideological or political considerations. To the extent that one might be able to identify a shift in Turkish foreign policy under the AKP, this could be linked to the particular orientation and values of the party. In other words, one needs to consider what the AKP actively brings to the foreign policy table, as Turkish decisionmakers may not be simply reacting to or being forced to respond to structural imperatives.

What ideologies, identities, or values might animate Turkish foreign policy in general and, more specifically, Turkey's relations with Russia? Some of the more popular constructivist explanations of contemporary Turkish foreign policy—those that invoke neo-Ottomanism and Islamism[27]—while perhaps useful in other contexts (as noted in other contributions to this issue), do not fit well with growing Turkish-Russian ties. True, both might be considered manifestations of anti-Westernism, but on their own terms they would not predict Turkey turning to Moscow. Russia was, after all, the chief rival of the Ottoman Empire, thus precluding construction of a narrative within neo-Ottomanism emphasizing Turkey's historical friendship with Russia. Furthermore, Russia remains a competitor to Turkey in the primary areas of interest—the Balkans and the Middle East—envisioned by Turkish neo-Ottomanists. To the extent that Russia and Turkey made have found a *modus vivendi* in these regions, it would be hard to argue that this is due to neo-Ottomanist considerations. Similarly, Islamism does not get one very far in analyzing Russian-Turkish relations. Russia is not an Islamic country and generally takes a dim view of Islamic-oriented groups (e.g. Egypt's Muslim Brotherhood and its affiliates elsewhere, rebellious Chechens) that Turkey had/has supported. Islamism, pan-Islamism, Islamic solidarity, or Turkey's ambitions concerning the global Sunni *umma*, to the extent they may animate Turkish foreign policy, would predict more confrontation, not rapprochement, with Russia.

Perhaps one could argue that a broader discourse and orientation around 'nationalism' has taken root and is driving Turkish foreign policy. This, however, is also problematic, albeit for different reasons. Nationalism is a rather ambiguous concept that can bleed into others (e.g. neo-Ottomanism). 'Nationalist' explanations can become veritable tautologies by leaving key notions undefined, e.g. a foreign policy is 'nationalist' because it is following the 'national interest'. Ultimately, perhaps, 'nationalism' might be used as a stand-in for assertiveness or growing militarization[28], as well as anti-Westernism in general. While it is a fair question to ask what animates anti-Westernism—possible answers include historical and contemporary grievances (as noted above), a newly developed quest for 'strategic autonomy'[29], the inheritance of anti-Western elements of the National Outlook Movement (*Millî Görüş*) on the AKP, as well as neo-Ottomanism and Islamism—why 'nationalism' *per se* would include a turn toward Russia is rather unclear. Indeed, the more 'nationalist' party in the current ruling coalition, the Nationalist Action Party, is hardly pro-Russia, as it has expressed criticism over Russian treatment of (Turkic) Tatars in Crimea, Russian backing of Armenia in the Nagorno-Karabakh conflict, and Russian support for Syrian military forces that have killed Turkish soldiers. Moreover, public opinion surveys that have identified 'rising nationalism' link it to a desire for a more independent or 'go-it-alone' foreign policy, not closer ties with Moscow.[30] As suggested above, however, Turkey lacks the means to accomplish key foreign policy goals (e.g. securing energy supplies, securing its border with Syria) on its own. Geographic proximity along with Russia's own power and resources makes it a useful partner and does much to explain the transactional (as opposed to affective) elements of the Turkish-Russian relationship.

To the extent there may be a pro-Russian ideology that could account for Turkey's closer ties with Russia, it is (neo)Eurasianism which (unlike neo-Ottomanism or Islamism) emphasizes Turkey's common interests with Eurasian powers such as Russia, China, and Iran. Eurasianism has a venerable history in Turkey, often associated with the anti-American political left, but it was long confined to the political fringe and/or repressed by the state and could not gain much traction given Turkey's role in NATO. In recent years, however, as relations with Turkey's Western allies have soured, it has gained more prominence and attention.[31] Analysts point to the 'rise' of Eurasianists, particularly in academia, think tanks, the bureaucracy, and the security sector, especially in light of purges that took place after the failed July 2016 coup attempt. Gurcan, for example, contends that the Eurasianist perspective has 'gained intellectual and institutional depth', and Erşen documents how various Turkish officials and academicians have made overtures to Alexander Dugin, the most well-known of Russia's 'Eurasianists' and who has softened his own past criticism of Turkey and by some accounts has helped facilitate the improvement in Turkish-Russian relations.[32]

While one can certainly point to an 'Eurasianist' tilt in Turkish foreign policy, it is uncertain how much this is due to the rise of 'Eurasianist' voices or construction of a pro-Russian 'Eurasianist' ideology. Erşen notes that the political party most associated with pro-Russian Eurasianism, the *Vatan* (Fatherland) Party (formerly the Workers' [*Işçi*] Party), led by Doğu Perinçek, has not gained much political support, and that in foreign policy and security circles the 'Eurasianist' perspective is but one of several (including nationalist, neo-Ottomanist, Turkist) that has gained prominence in advocating for a more security-oriented and autonomous Turkish foreign policy. Whereas one might be able to find Eurasianist 'fingerprints' on some foreign policy decisions (e.g. purchase of the S-400 defense system), other actions (e.g. arming Azerbaijan prior to its 2020 offensive against Armenian forces, development of a more assertive 'Blue Homeland Doctrine' that helps guide Turkey's policy in Libya) run counter to expectation of a pro-Russian 'Eurasianist' perspective. Erşen and Balci, acknowledging the greater prominence of 'Eurasianism' in Turkish foreign policy and even its 'emotional attractiveness,' nonetheless suggest that it is best understood as an umbrella ideology of anti-Westernism, that common Russian-Turkish Eurasianist affinities remain fragile (particularly given uncertainties in Syria), and that Turkish Eurasianism's trajectory is significantly shaped by Turkey's (recently troubled) relations with the US and European Union.[33] Put differently, the apparent 'rise' of Eurasianism may be less a cause of the change in Turkish foreign policy and more the effect of shifts in global and regional dynamics and Turkey's relations with the West, factors discussed above that fit in better with a structural explanation of Turkish foreign policy. Furthermore, as discussed in conclusion of this article, any 'Eurasianist alliance' between Ankara and Moscow is being sorely and perhaps fatally tested by the February 2022 Russian invasion of Ukraine.

Finally, among ideational factors, one might entertain the idea that common political values might help explain growing Turkish-Russian ties. This may be reflected at various levels of analysis. In (more journalistic) accounts, growing Turkish-Russian ties are often put in personal terms, hinging on alleged bonhomie between Putin and Erdoğan, which became particularly marked after the 2016 coup attempt, after which Putin, in contrast to many Western leaders, offered Erdoğan his strong support.[34] Both, notably, have refrained from criticizing each other over repressive actions or violations of human rights and lavish praise on each other when they (frequently) meet. One might ask, however, how much of this is diplomatic affectation as opposed to genuine affection and if their alleged personal bonds are deep enough to build and sustain a genuine 'strategic partnership'.[35] One should recall that Putin and Erdoğan vilified each other in 2015 after the downing of the Russian aircraft, and Putin has also acted in a manner to humiliate his ostensible 'partner'.[36] A more significant point, however, may be that this is not a relationship of equals—Putin holds many cards (energy, Syria, Russian media presence in the Turkish market) that he could use against Erdoğan should he wish to do so. Putin has proven himself to be a mercurial leader who could throw Erdoğan 'under the bus' or seek to make him his 'puppet'.[37] While Putin may find Erdoğan a useful or convenient partner and to date they have been able to weather several crises, it would be hard to argue that whatever affective ties there are between are more important drivers than the transactional value each, at present, receives from stronger Turkish-Russian ties.

On a more ideational level, as suggested above, one could consider Turkey's turn toward Russia as part a 'deliberate choice' reflecting Turkish leaders' frustration with the West and Western values and embrace of more illiberal, statist approaches.[38] Indeed, it is on this point where constructivism may be most helpful in explaining how a shared identity is helping shape Turkish-Russian relations. However, while one can identity aspects of overarching anti-Western elements in Russian and Turkish foreign policy, the particular elements of each do differ. Both appeal heavily to nationalism and religion, which present very different views of civilizational or cultural identity (e.g. Orthodoxy vs. Islam). Aleksandr Khramchikhin, deputy director of Russia's Institute of Political and Military Analysis, notes that even though Russia and Turkey have both rejected Western-style democracy, that the 'natural' position of Turkey is that of a 'systemic' rival to Russia, and that Erdoğan's pro-Sunni and 'neo-Ottoman' ambitions in the Middle East conflict with those of Moscow. He argues that this 'cannot be compensated with gas, wheat, and tomatoes, as [geo]politics was, is, and always will be more important than economics,' and that it is likely that today's 'artificial (*iskusstvennaia*) friendship' will devolve into 'natural (*yestyestvennaia*) confrontation'.[39] More generally, one might also mention that sharing illiberal or authoritarian attributes is hardly sufficient to form an alliance or even generate good relations (see, for example, Turkey's current relationship with Egypt and Saudi Arabia).

Conclusion

As this article has suggested, there are various theories, approaches, and hypotheses that one might advance to account for developments in Turkish-Russian relations. While one can certainly make a case that a complete picture of the relationship would draw on insights from multiple perspectives, it seems clear that neo-realist or structural explanations provide greater explanatory power, particularly in terms of supplying the necessary conditions for improved Russian-Turkish relations. Global power shifts have facilitated both Turkey's foreign policy ambitions and its multi-directional nature, and Turkey is less tethered to Western states and institutions than before. With respect to the latter, 'grievance' stands out as a factor, and although one can put a constructivist gloss on it by presenting it as an ideational factor, it can also be construed as a more-or-less natural development arising from Turkey's 'rising power' power status and its inability to fulfill key objectives through relations with Western countries. While Russia, in some respects, remains a rival, it also presents an opportunity, including in Syria, where Russia is now the key military player and where working with Moscow, despite Ankara's hostility to the Russian-backed Syrian government, helps Turkey resolve a crucial security issue. Thus, while the rise of 'Eurasianism' within Turkey provides a voice or a political constituency for a more pro-Russian foreign policy, one can argue that this development is more an effect of the changing geopolitical environment and disillusionment with the West than a primary cause or mover in the Turkish-Russian relationship.

One should also address more fully the economic dimension of the Turkish-Russian relationship and how it fits into the broader theory-informed discussion. A fundamental consideration in this respect is how (inter)dependence undergirds the relationship. Notably, when Russia imposed sanctions on Turkey in 2015-2016, it did not suspend natural gas shipments (which would have been crippling for Turkey but also costly for Russia) or permanently cancel plans to build additional pipelines to Turkey or the Akkuyu nuclear power plant. More recently, in wake of Russia's invasion of Ukraine and the imposition of harsh sanctions against Moscow by most Western countries, Turkey has tried to balance its interests, condemning Russian actions but, for economic reasons, refusing to impose sanctions on Russia.[40] Notably, explanations suggesting interdependence helps promote more cooperative or peaceful relations derive not from neo-realist or ideational paradigms but from liberal-internationalist perspectives in international relations, and they include the rise of pragmatic-oriented trade 'lobbies' (as opposed to the more geopolitical or ideologically-oriented 'Eurasianists') that directly benefit from healthy Turkish-Russian ties.[41]

There are limits, however, to how far one should take this interdependence argument. First of all, while economic ties may provide a floor under Russian-Turkish relations so they do not completely collapse (e.g. during the 2015–2016 crisis period), it is harder to claim that it drives the relationship itself. The highest year of total Turkish-Russian trade, for example, was in 2008 ($37.8 billion, of which $31.4 was Russian exports to Turkey), and total trade in 2014 (a full sanctions-free year) was actually higher than in 2019 (the last COVID-free year).[42] The recent (post-2016) blossoming of Turkish-Russian ties has thus not been accompanied by a substantial take-off in economic ties.[43] As for the oft-repeated rhetoric by Erdoğan and Putin that they seek to grow overall trade ties to over $100 billion, this is, in the words of one pair of analysts, 'artificial,' reflecting more political aspirations than the 'not promising' reality of the Russian market for Turkish exports, whose highest value, in 2013, was only $7.3 billion.[44] Furthermore, aside from energy, the EU remains a far more important trade and investment partner for Turkey, although this has not stopped Erdoğan from making statements or taking actions to annoy his EU partners.[45] To be sure, there are significant Russian investments in Turkey, particularly in the energy sector. However, these projects—in particular the Turkstream gas pipeline and the Akkuyu nuclear power plant —have been driven by geopolitical considerations, reflecting both states turn away from or disappointment in the West.[46] They also underscore the asymmetric nature of the economic relationship, one in which Turkey is heavily dependent on Russian energy supplies.

With respect to this last point, we need to return to a more (neo)realist focus on power, as Russia holds more cards both in the economic relationship and in military theater that most threatens Turkey (Syria). This helps explain Erdoğan's eventual apology to Putin for the 2015 incident, which ended most of Russia's costly sanctions against Turkey and helped spur the two sides to work together to prevent future attacks on each other's forces, even as Russia continued to aid the Syrian government to push Turkish-backed rebels out of many of their positions. It also explains Turkey's reticence for join the sanctions regime against Russia in wake of the war in Ukraine, as Turkey cannot easily break its dependence upon Russia.

However, the Russian invasion of Ukraine may fundamentally transform Turkish-Russian relations and can provide an additional 'test' of competing theoretical explanations. Without question, it has changed the international environment, revealing Russia as a clear threat and unifying the Western alliance against it. To the extent this creates a more of a bipolar structure (with China aligning with Russia), Turkey will be compelled to choose a side. While Turkey, for numerous reasons elaborated in this article, does not want to completely alienate Russia, there is little doubt that Turkey's NATO membership has now become a much more valuable commodity. Notably, one does not hear—as of this writing—prominent voices in Turkey calling for 'partnership' or 'alliance' with Russia, as one might have expected if there was a deep-rooted affinity or common identity between the two countries or even a strong bond between Putin and Erdoğan. On the contrary, even prior to the Russian invasion, there was evidence of Turkey balancing against Russia, most clearly illustrated by Erdoğan's visit to Kyiv in early February 2022 to sign a deal to produce Turkish-designed military drones in Ukraine.[47] Indeed, the supply of Turkish drones to Ukraine has become, from Moscow's point of view, a major irritant in bilateral relations.[48] Moreover, as Russia forces focused on Ukraine, Azerbaijan, Turkey's ally, moved into contested territory in Nagorno-Karabakh. Such actions are in-line with (neo)realist expectations about aligning and balancing against threats. Whether these developments signal a broader (re)turn to NATO and embrace of a containment (as opposed to engagement) strategy toward Russia in Turkish foreign policy—including, perhaps, moves to reduce dependence on Russia—remains as the war in Ukraine will likely prove to be consequential on a number of foreign policy and security issues. The analysis in this article, however, would suggest that Russian aggression (as well as its potential to become a pariah state) as well as greater Western unity will create a change in the international system that will likely compel Turkey to re-assess the benefits of its erstwhile 'partnership' with Russia.

Notes

1. The final draft of this article was completed in late March 2022, a month after Russian forces invaded Ukraine. This development has global implications, including on the Turkish-Russian relationship. These are discussed more fully in this article's conclusion.
2. For an accessible review of main developments in both Russian-Turkish ties and the Putin-Erdogan relationship, see *The Economist*, "The odd couple." For a more scholarly review, see Balta, "From Geopolitical Competition."
3. See Özcan, Balta, and Beşgül, *Türkiye ve Rusya*, and Baev, "Turkey's ambiguous."
4. Liberal approaches in international relations, which often emphasize economic ties and interdependence, can also give one some purchase on Russian-Turkish relations, but, as noted later in the paper, I argue that their utility may be limited. For an approach that relies more heavily on "complex interdependence" between Russia and Turkey, see Kelkitli, *Turkish-Russian Relations* as well as Öniş and Yılmaz. "Turkey and Russia."
5. The *locus classicus* for neo-realism remains Waltz, *Theory of International Politics*.
6. For a review of Soviet-Turkish relations, see Kubicek, "Turkey's Relationship."
7. One can debate when the "unipolar moment" ended, but certainly the opposition to the American invasion of Iraq, which eventually became a significant drain on US power, is an important event. Mearsheimer, "Bound to Fail," suggests 2016, with Brexit and the election of Donald Trump, as marking the end of unipolarity.
8. Bilge, "An Analysis," 92, and Trenin, "A Cure," 57.
9. Aktürk, "Turkish-Russian Relations."
10. Sezer, "Turkish–Russian Relations."
11. Ibid.
12. Aktürk, "A Realist Reassessment."
13. Baev and Kirişci, "An ambiguous partnership."
14. For a useful review of complications in Turkish-Western relations, see Kirişci, *Turkey and the West*.
15. See, for example, Steven Cook, "Turkey: Friend or frenemy? A tangled relationship keeps getting worse," *Salon.com*, November 12, 2017.
16. Dursun-Özkanca, *Turkey-West Relations*.
17. Sezer, "Turkish–Russian Relations."
18. This was a common topic in analyses of Turkish foreign policy, particularly in the 2010s. See, for example, Kubicek, Dal, and Oğuzlu, *Turkey's Rise*.
19. Kubicek, "Strictly Pragmatism?" and Candar, *Turkey's Neo-Ottomanist Moment*.
20. Öniş and Kutlay, "The dynamics."
21. Zarakol, *After Defeat*.
22. Kubicek, "Turkey's Relationship."
23. Hill and Taşpınar, "Turkey and Russia."
24. For the latter, see Aktürk, "A Realist Reassessment" and "Turkey's Grand Strategy." In particular, Turkey aims to keep rival powers out of its immediate neighborhood, an ambition that clashes with Russia's greater assertiveness in the post-Soviet space and Middle East.
25. One could hypothesize, of course, that the costs of working with Turkey (perhaps temporarily) are low and the potential gains in both pacifying

parts of Syria and driving a wedge between Turkey and its NATO partners are worthwhile. The endgame in Syria is yet to be known, and Russia, with its military advantage, may be able to press forward against Turkey, although that could be a risk Moscow wishes to avoid.

26. Waltz, "Evaluating Theories," 915.
27. Both of these terms have been widely used in academic and policy-oriented writings on Turkey, often linked with the "Strategic Depth" doctrine of former Foreign Minister and Prime Minister Ahmet Davutoğlu. However, not all observers agree on their usefulness both as clear analytical concepts and in capturing the empirical reality of Turkish foreign policy. For extended treatment of these topics, see Yavuz, *Nostalgia for the Empire*; Murinson, *Turkish Foreign Policy*; Hintz, *Identity Politics*; Candar, *Turkey's Neo-Ottomanist Moment*; and Ozkan, "Turkey, Davutoglu."
28. Öztürk, "Turkey's Post-2016."
29. Kutlay and Öniş. "Turkish foreign policy."
30. Hoffman, Werz, and Halpin, "Turkey's 'New Nationalism'."
31. A useful review of Eurasianism can be found in Aktürk, "The Fourth Style."
32. Gurcan, "The Rise," and Erşen, "The Return."
33. Erşen, "The Return," 43-44, and Balci, "L'eurasisme."
34. Erdoğan himself acknowledged this in the aftermath of the coup attempt, stating that support from his "dear friend" [Putin] has been a "strong psychological factor" for restoration of an "axis of friendship between Moscow and Ankara". See "Erdogan praises 'dear friend' Vladimir Putin in Russian-Turkish détente," *The Telegraph*, August 9, 2016,
35. For a skeptical view, see Baev, "Turkey's ambiguous."
36. For example, in March 2020, after dozens of Turkish soldiers were killed in Syria by Russian-supplied Syrian forces, Erdoğan was summoned to Moscow to meet with Putin, but was left awkwardly waiting in an antechamber prior to his meeting. The episode was filmed by Russian state television and included a timer in the corner of the screen to show how long Erdoğan had been kept waiting. See Williams, "The Uneasy Alliance."
37. Anna Borshchevskaya, "Is Erdogan a Russian Ally or Putin's Puppet?" *Forbes* (on-line), January 27, 2017, available at https://www.forbes.com/sites/annaborshchevskaya/2017/01/27/is-erdogan-a-russian-ally-or-putins-puppet/#6c50084f1596
38. Erşen and Köstem, "Introduction," 8.
39. Aleksandr Khramchikin, 'Kem v deystvitel'nosti yavliaetsia Turtsiia dlia Rossii,' *Nezavisimaia gazeta*, April 14, 2017.
40. Zaman, "Will Turkey?".
41. An application of these concepts to Russian-Turkish relations can be found in Kelkitli, *Turkish-Russian Relations*.
42. Data from the United Nation's Comtrade database, available at comtrade.un.org.
43. Similarly, Aktürk ("A Realist Assessment") downplays the liberal/interdependence argument but noting that trade ties grew in the late 2000s-early 2010s even as overall ties worsened.
44. Özel and Uçar, "The Economics," p. 25. Figures from UN Comtrade database. In 2018, Russia ranked 12th among Turkish exports markets.
45. Özel and Uçar, ("The Economics"), for example, note that Turkish exports to the EU are ten times the value of exports to Russia and overall foreign direct

investment (FDI), at least from 2007-2016, amounted to under 3 percent of FDI stock in Turkey and less than 1 percent of FDI in Russia.
46. The Russian choice to promote the Turkstream pipeline occurred after Moscow, in a spat with the EU, scuttled plans for a South Stream pipeline that would have transported gas directly to the EU through Bulgaria, and Turkey's choice of Russia to construct a nuclear power plant occurred after numerous other countries, including the United States, France, and Japan, had declined to work with Turkey on such a project.
47. "Erdogan seals pact with Ukraine over trade and drones," *Financial Times*, February 3, 2022.
48. "Why drones pose a threat to Russia-Turkey relations as Ukraine crisis develops," *Financial Times*, February 17, 2022,

Acknowledgements

The author would like to thank Sener Aktürk, Emre Erşen, and anonymous reviewers for helpful comments on the initial draft of this paper.

Disclosure statement

No potential conflict of interest was reported by the author(s).

Bibliography

Aktürk, Sener. "A Realist Assessment of Turkish-Russian Relations, 2002-2012: From the Peak to the Dip?" Caspian Strategy Institute, Istanbul, January 2013.
Aktürk, Şener. "Turkish-Russian Relations After the Cold War (1992-2002)." *Turkish Studies* 7, no. 3 (2006): 337–364.
Aktürk, Sener. "The Fourth Style of Politics: Eurasianism as a Pro-Russian Rethinking of Turkey's Geopolitical Identity." *Turkish Studies* 16, no. 1 (2015): 54–79.
Aktürk, Sener. "Turkey's Grand Strategy." *Insight Turkey* 23, no. 4 (2021): 95–118.
Baev, Pavel. "Turkey's Ambiguous Strategic Rapprochement with Russia." In *Turkey's Pivot to Eurasia: Geopolitics and Foreign Policy in a Changing World Order*, edited by Emre Erşen, and Seçkin Köstem, 48–63. London: Routledge, 2019.
Baev, Pavel, and Kemal Kirişci. "An ambiguous partnership: The serpentine trajectory of Turkish-Russian relations in the era of Erdoğan and Putin." Brookings Institution, *Turkey Policy Paper* no. 13, September 2017.
Balci, Bayram. "L'eurasisme et le Rapprochement Entre la Turquie et la Russie." *Revue Internationale et Stratégique* N°116, no. 4 (2019): 134–145.

Balta, Evren. "From Geopolitical Competition to Strategic Partnership: Turkey and Russia After The Cold War." *Uluslararasi İliskiler* 16, no. 63 (2019): 69–86.

Bilge, Suat A. "An Analysis of Turkish-Russian Relations." *Perceptions* 2, no. 2 (1997): 66–92.

Candar, Cengiz. *Turkey's Neo-Ottomanist Moment: An Eurasianist Odyssey.* London: Transnational Publisher, 2021.

Dursun-Özkanca, Oya. *Turkey-West Relations: The Politics of Intra-Alliance Opposition.* Cambridge: Cambridge University Press, 2019.

The Economist. "The odd couple: Putin and Erdogan have formed a brotherhood of hard power," February 27, 2021.

Erşen, Emre. "The Return of Eurasianism in Turkey: Relations with Russia and Beyond." In *Turkey's Pivot to Eurasia: Geopolitics and Foreign Policy in a Changing World Order*, edited by Emre Erşen, and Seçkin Köstem, 31–47. London: Routledge, 2019.

Erşen, Emre, and Seçkin Köstem. "Introduction: Understanding the Dynamics of Turkey's Pivot to Eurasia." In *Turkey's Pivot to Eurasia: Geopolitics and Foreign Policy in a Changing World Order*, edited by Erşen and Köstem, 1–14. London: Routledge, 2019.

Gurcan, Metin. "The Rise of the Eurasianist vision in Turkey." *Al-Monitor*, May 17, 2017, available at https://www.al-monitor.com/pulse/originals/2017/05/turkey-rise-of-euroasianist-vision.html (accessed September 21, 2021), 2017.

Hill, Fiona, and Ömer Taşpınar. "Turkey and Russia: Axis of the Excluded?" *Survival* 48, no. 1 (2006): 81–92.

Hintz, Lisel. *Identity Politics Inside Out: National Identity Contestation and Foreign Policy in Turkey.* Oxford: Oxford University Press, 2018.

Hoffman, Max, Michael Werz, and John Halpin. "Turkey's 'New Nationalism' Amid Shifting Politics," Center for American Progress, February 11, 2018, available at https://www.americanprogress.org/issues/security/reports/2018/02/11/446164/turkeys-new-nationalism-amid-shifting-politics/.

Kelkitli, Fatma A. *Turkish-Russian Relations: Competition and Cooperation in Eurasia.* London: Routledge, 2017.

Kirişçi, Kemal. *Turkey and the West: Fault Lines in a Troubled Alliance.* Washington: Brookings Institution Press, 2018.

Kubicek, Paul. "Strictly Pragmatism?: Prospects for a Russian-Turkish Partnership." *Journal of Balkan and Near Eastern Studies* 23 (2021): 233–250.

Kubicek, Paul. "Turkey's Relationship with the Soviet Union and Russia." In *A Companion to Modern Turkey's Centennial: Political, Sociological, Economic and Institutional Transformations Since 1923*, edited by A. Erdi Özturk, and Alpaslan Ozerdem. Edinburgh: Edinburgh University Press, 2023 (forthcoming).

Kubicek, Paul, Emel Parlar Dal, and H. Tarik Oğuzlu, eds. *Turkey's Rise as an Emerging Power.* London: Routledge, 2015.

Kutlay, Mustafa, and Ziya Öniş. "Turkish Foreign Policy in a Post-Western Order: Strategic Autonomy or new Forms of Dependence?" *International Affairs* 97, no. 4 (2021): 1085–1104.

Mearsheimer, John. "Bound to Fail: The Rise and Fall of the Liberal International Order." *International Security* 43, no. 4 (2019): 7–50.

Murinson, Alxander. *Turkish Foreign Policy in the 21st Century: Neo-Ottomanism and the Strategic Depth Doctrine.* London: IB Tauris, 2020.

Öniş, Ziya, and Mustafa Kutlay. "The Dynamics of Emerging Middle-Power Influence in Regional and Global Governance: The Paradoxical Case of Turkey." *Australian Journal of International Affairs* 71, no. 2 (2017): 164–183.

Öniş, Ziya, and Şuhnaz Yılmaz. "Turkey and Russia in a Shifting Global Order: Cooperation, Conflict and Asymmetric Interdependence in a Turbulent Region." *Third World Quarterly* 37, no. 1 (2016): 71–95.

Özcan, Gencer, Evren Balta, and Burç Beşgül, eds. *Türkiye ve Rusya İlişkilerinde Değişen Dinamikler: Kuşku ile Komşuluk*. Istanbulk: Iletişim, 2017.

Özel, Soli, and Gökçe Uçar. "The Economics of Turkey-Russia Relations." Centre for Economics and Foreign Policy Studies (EDAM), Istanbul, July 2019.

Ozkan, Behlül. "Turkey, Davutoglu, and the Idea of Pan-Islamism." *Survival* 56, no. 4 (2014): 119–140.

Öztürk, Ahmet E. "Turkey's Post-2016 Foreign Policy Drivers: Militarisation, Islam, Civilisation and Power," Working Paper, Hellenic Foundation for European and Security Policy (Athens), 2021.

Sezer, Duygu Bazoğlu. "Turkish–Russian Relations a Decade Later: From Adversity to Managed Competition." *Perceptions* 6, no. 1 (2001): 79–99.

Trenin, Dmitri. "Russia and Turkey: A Cure for Schizophrenia." *Perceptions* 2, no. 2 (1997): 57–65.

Waltz, Kenneth. *Theory of International Politics*. Reading MA: Addison-Wesley, 1979.

Waltz, Kenneth. "Evaluating Theories." *American Political Science Review* 91, no. 4 (1997): 913–917.

Williams, Stuart. "The Uneasy Alliance Between Putin and Erdogan." *Newslines*, March 11, 2021, available at https://newlinesmag.com/essays/the-uneasy-alliance-between-putin-and-erdogan/ (accessed September 21, 2021).

Yavuz, M. Hakan. *Nostalgia for the Empire: The Politics of Neo-Ottomanism*. Oxford: Oxford University Press, 2020.

Zaman, Amberin. "Will Turkey Become as Haven for Sanctioned Russians?". *Al-Monitor*, March 24, 2022.

Zarakol, Ayşe. *After Defeat: How the East Learned to Live with the West*. Cambridge: Cambridge University Press, 2010.

Between escalation and détente: Greek-Turkish relations in the aftermath of the Eastern Mediterranean crisis

Ioannis N. Grigoriadis

ABSTRACT
This paper aims to evaluate the state of Greek-Turkish relations in light of recent developments in the reconfiguration of Turkish foreign policy. Following twenty years of détente and relative calm in bilateral relations, the year 2020 witnessed two escalations in Greek-Turkish relations, one in March involving refugees and immigrants on the Greek-Turkish land border and another in August involving military vessels of the two countries. The refugee crisis and potential military conflict regarding energy exploration in the Eastern Mediterranean have raised tensions at a moment the political and institutional tools for the promotion of conflict resolution between Greece and Turkey linked to Turkey's EU membership perspective appear to be obsolete. This paper seeks an answer to the question of whether structural or ideational factors played the most prominent role in the recent escalation of the Greek-Turkish disputes.

Introduction

Recent rising tensions in Greek-Turkish relations have attracted attention to a long-standing dispute that had ceased to produce news for almost two decades. The invisibility of the Greek-Turkish disputes was linked to a détente produced by a seminal decision at the end of the last century. Under Prime Minister Konstantinos Simitis and Foreign Minister George Papandreou, the Greek government decided to lift the Greek veto against the improvement of European Union (EU)-Turkey relations before the resolution of Greek-Turkish disputes and the Cyprus problem. Following the December 1999 decision of the European Council to grant Turkey EU candidate status, Greece moved, in Couloumbis' words, from 'a policy of conditional sanctions to that of conditional rewards.'[1] Greece's strategic goal to become EU's bulwark against Turkey changed, as now Greece understood that closer relations between the EU and Turkey boosted the chances to resolve its bilateral disputes with Turkey and the Cyprus problem on the basis of international law and UN Security Council resolutions.[2] However, historic opportunities were missed during the heyday of EU-Turkey relations: In April 2004, when Greek Cypriots rejected the Annan Plan, scuttling prospects for the resolution of the Cyprus problem. Additionally, in December 2004 the Greek government failed to press Turkey for the referral of the outstanding maritime zone delimitation disputes to the International Court of Justice (ICJ) in the Hague. Nevertheless, economic and civil society ties between Ankara and Athens grew stronger, and a new paradigm of cooperation challenged zero-sum game-based approaches.

On the other hand, Turkey's fading chances of EU membership, as well as missing the 2004 opportunity to resolve the Cyprus problem and bilateral disputes, meant that the role of the EU as a catalyst for Greek-Turkish relations would become weaker over time. Alternatives to full EU membership, such as cooperation in managing the refugee crisis, the update of the customs union agreement, visa liberalization, and a 'privileged partnership' agreement failed to provide a viable alternative. The Cyprus problem continued complicating Turkey's relations with the EU, and the EU itself was no longer a third party, due to the membership of both Cyprus and Greece.[3]

Yet there was no relapse to the pre-1999 state of affairs. Turkey's fading chances of EU membership in view of enlargement fatigue and immigration concerns in key EU member states (among other concerns) were matched by diminishing commitment on the side of Turkey. Turkey's remarkable economic success in the late 2000s and the EU sovereign debt crisis lent credibility to views that Turkey's EU membership is more important for the EU than for Turkey itself. In this line of thought, Turkey coyld thrive with or without EU membership, as one of the world's emerging powers.[4] The outbreak in 2011 of the Arab Uprisings coincided with an ambitious Turkish diplomatic opening towards the global South and a new strategic vision for Turkish foreign policy.[5] Sub-Saharan Africa, Latin America and Southeast Asia became new focal points of Turkish diplomatic and economic activity, with strategic autonomy becoming a chief goal.[6] Under these circumstances, the relative significance of Greek-Turkish relations decreased in Turkey. This became all evident following the outbreak of the Greek economic crisis. Had Turkey been preoccupied with its disputes with Greece, one could expect that Turkey would have tried to take advantage of Greece's economic and diplomatic woes to advance its positions.[7] Such moves were nevertheless not observed; the Syrian and later the Libyan civil war, and relations with the United States, Russia and China emerged as key priorities for Turkish foreign policy. The scope and ambition of Turkish foreign policy went far beyond its relations with neighboring states. Turkey attempted to fill the gap created by the declining involvement of the international community, especially the United States, in several regions, including the Middle East.

Deterioration of Greek-Turkish relations occurred following the peak of the Greek economic crisis. The collapse of the Kurdish peace process in 2015 also allowed new recriminations about Greek support for Kurdish militants who had received asylum protection in Greece. This became even stronger following the failed coup of 15 July 2016. The flight of numerous Turkish dissidents to Greece and the refusal of Greek courts to extradite eight fugitive officers allegedly involved in the failed coup was interpreted in Turkey as Greek government support for the coup plotters.[8] It also fitted a Turkish government narrative linking the failed coup with foreign powers seeking to remove President Recep Tayyip Erdoğan from power.

Meanwhile, Turkey's rapprochement with Russia and unilateralist tendencies have not only alienated it from key Western allies. They have also provided Greece with the opportunity to emerge as the West's credible regional partner, promote its strategic cooperation with the United States, and sign a defense pact with France. The nature of EU-Turkey relations shifted from a more normative to a more pragmatic one, with focus on security problems.[9] Both sides recognized the existence of essential interests necessitating collaboration even though there existed fundamental differences on several fronts and Turkish membership prospects faded. In particular the EU tried to turn Turkey into a buffer zone as far as the refugee/migrant crisis was concerned. This common understanding weakened any transformative power that the relationship would have on the Turkish polity. Giving up on the idea of promoting democratization in Turkey also left Turkey's pro-democracy forces exposed. The less realistic the prospect of Turkey's EU membership became, the more difficult was to raise the urgency of resolving the Greek-Turkish bilateral disputes within the Turkish political elite. Inertia again rose the dominant feature of Greek-Turkish disputes. The foreign ministries of both countries sought ways to improve the level of communication and prevent escalations without addressing the root causes of the tension and taking steps for their resolution of bilateral disputes. Managing the *status quo* appeared as the preferred solution on both sides. The resumption of the exploratory talks between the two sides was hailed as an important step in the normalization of relations following the August 2020 crisis and the fleet standoff in the Eastern Mediterranean. Yet this also pointed at the new lower equilibrium point in the bilateral relations. Nobody expected that the exploratory talks would produce an agreement on the maritime zone delimitation dispute. Yet they constituted a vital channel of communication that prevented further deterioration of relations.

What could then explain the reescalation of Greek-Turkish disputes in the late 2010s? This article argues that this is due to a combination of structural factors, namely the lack of resolution in the Cyprus problem and regional cooperation efforts in the Eastern Mediterranean excluding Turkey, as well as ideational factors, namely the official adoption of the 'Blue Homeland' (*Mavi Vatan*) vision and identification with the Muslim Brotherhood (MB) in Libya, leading to Turkey's intervention in the Libyan civil war and the signature of the November 2019 Libyan-Turkish memorandum on the delimitation of maritime zones. Therefore, neo-realist as well as constructivist accounts could help explain the negative shift of developments in the bilateral relationship, in light of the recent tectonic shifts in Turkish foreign policy and Turkey's relations with the EU and the West.

The ubiquitous Cyprus problem

It is hard to overstate the significance of the Cyprus problem as a root cause of Greek-Turkish tension and competition. While the Cyprus problem is not *stricto sensu* a Greek-Turkish but an international dispute, with one of the longest-standing involvements of the United Nations (UN), it projects a tormented history to date.[10] Greek-Turkish nationalist competition, which dominated bilateral relations in the early twentieth century but receded following the 1929–1930 bilateral agreements, was revived on the island of Cyprus. The outbreak of the Cyprus problem in the 1950s eventually led to a sharp deterioration of bilateral relations. The Cyprus problem acted as trigger for a number of bilateral disputes, ranging from minority rights to the delimitation of maritime and airspace zones and energy exploration activities. While the problem *per se* may no more be a priority for Greek or Turkish public opinion, it can still trigger nationalist sentiment in both countries.

After missing the opportunity of April 2004, another opportunity for the Cyprus peace negotiations emerged in the 2010s. The discovery of sizeable natural gas reserves in the Eastern Mediterranean[11] was hoped to become a catalyst for conflict resolution, given that the monetization of hydrocarbon reserves would be possible through regional cooperation, including Turkey.[12] The election of Nicos Anastasiades in the Republic of Cyprus and Mustafa Akıncı in the internationally unrecognized 'Turkish Republic of Northern Cyprus (TRNC)' also strengthened optimistic views, due to the moderate record of both leaders. Nevertheless, the failure of the Cyprus peace conference at Crans Montana (Switzerland) in August 2017 not only was a major disappointment for the international community, but it also increased the risk of crisis spillover in the region. Turkey's reaction against the Cypriot energy monetization program in the Eastern Mediterranean in the aftermath of the failed 2017 Crans Montana conference eventually morphed into a confrontation against Greece in the Eastern Mediterranean in August 2020. The Turkish government considered that the Greek and Cypriot policies in the Eastern Mediterranean were fully coordinated and therefore introduced a uniform policy against both. There was also a real threat that the Cyprus problem could be instrumentalized on the Turkish domestic political front ahead of the Turkish presidential elections which would be held by June 2023 at the latest. Delaying the resumption of the UN-facilitated peace process in Cyprus could lead to a negative spiral. Considering that Turkey and the 'TRNC' have relapsed to hardline positions rejecting a bizonal, bicommunal federal solution, a possible referendum for the annexation of the 'TRNC' to Turkey would have disastrous consequences not only to Greek-Turkish relations but to EU-Turkey relations as a whole.

The emergence of East Med trilateral diplomacy

A second reason for the deterioration of Greek-Turkish relations could be found in the changing regional dynamics in the Eastern Mediterranean. While Greece's focus on the Eastern Mediterranean had been rather limited since the 1990s, a new interest emerged in the 2010s. This was linked to the discovery hydrocarbon reserves under the seabed of the Eastern Mediterranean but was also understood as Greece's renewed interest in a region where it held major economic and strategic interests. Greek-Turkish energy cooperation that had already involved the construction of overland natural gas pipeline could have been boosted when sizeable natural gas reserves were discovered in the Eastern Mediterranean. This discovery introduced the Eastern Mediterranean as a prospective natural gas supplier to the European energy market.[13] The most efficient way to transport the natural gas to the European market would be via pipeline to Turkey and Greece. This could further bolster the role of both countries as energy security assets for the EU.[14]

On the other hand, the absence of conflict resolution in Cyprus posed a real risk to such projects. While it was hoped that energy discoveries could provide a crucial incentive to achieve conflict resolution, they instead rekindled Greek-Turkish confrontation over maritime zones in the Aegean and the Eastern Mediterranean. They also strengthened Greek and Cypriot interests in pursuing multilateral cooperation schemes and building strategic partnerships in the region, in particular with the two strongest countries in the Levant, Egypt and Israel. Both countries used to enjoy cordial relations with Turkey, which were interrupted as Turkey's involvement in Middle East affairs grew stronger. Despite the strong economic and strategic ties between the two states, Turkey's identification with the Palestinian cause and its support for Hamas in the Gaza Strip had led to a confrontation with Israel, and Israeli-Turkish relations completely collapsed following the 2009 Mavi Marmara incident.[15] In the case of Egypt, the Justice and Development Party (*Adalet ve Kalkınma Partisi*-AKP) government fully supported the MB-led government of Mohamed Morsi, which emerged following the Arab Uprisings.[16] However, Turkey's subsequent refusal to recognize the government of General Abdelfattah al-Sisi, which toppled Morsi's government in a coup in July 2013, meant that bilateral relations would be reduced to a minimum.

Benefiting from the crisis in Turkey's relations with Egypt and Israel, Greece succeeded in advancing its relations with both. The organization of regular trilateral meetings with Cyprus, Egypt and Greece on the one hand, and Cyprus, Greece and Israel on the other boosted Greek self-confidence as they heralded advanced cooperation in one of the world's least interconnected regions. Efforts to achieve a common understanding among Cyprus, Greece, Egypt and Israel on issues of natural gas maritime exploration and monetization culminated in the establishment of the East Mediterranean Gas Forum, a multilateral initiative eventually rising to the status of international organization in March 2021. Its foundation pointed at an attempt to develop an institutional framework of cooperation spanning across the Eastern Mediterranean. This was the first regional organization to be founded in many years in a region normally hampered by regional conflicts. As Turkey was not involved in the process that led to the establishment of the Forum, it remained suspicious of its motives, as this initiative was viewed as reminiscent of efforts to isolate or bypass Turkey in the 1990s.[17]

The EastMed pipeline emerged as a flagship project of these regional cooperation initiatives. The construction of an undersea natural gas pipeline connecting Egypt, Israel, Cyprus and Greece was hailed as a gamechanger in regional geopolitics.[18] This pipeline was not only meant to improve EU energy security by transporting Eastern Mediterranean natural gas essential for EU energy security. It was also expected to forge a strategic relationship among Egypt, Greece, Israel and Cyprus in the absence or even despite Turkey. Greece and the European natural gas market would acquire access to sizeable reserves recently discovered in the Eastern Mediterranean. This would reduce EU dependency on Russian natural gas imports, a topic that has become even more significant in the wake of Russia's 2022 invasion of Ukraine. However, the East Med pipeline was anything but a simple project.[19] The technical challenges of constructing a pipeline deep in the Mediterranean were significant. The economic feasibility of the project remained debatable, as the construction cost was projected to be high, and the unit price of the natural gas to be transported through the pipeline did not appear to be more attractive than existing alternative options.

The continuation of the Cyprus problem also posed a formidable challenge against the feasibility of the project, as it defined the interests of Turkey as antithetical to those of the project partners. While the resolution of the Cyprus problem could have brought about the inclusion of Turkey and Turkish Cypriots to the project, the failure of the Crans Montana talks meant that energy exploration and monetization efforts would proceed without any change aiming to engage Turkey and Turkish Cypriots. On its part, Turkey challenged the right of the Republic of Cyprus to conduct natural gas exploration drillings on two grounds. First, it cited the rights of Turkish Cypriots, who were not involved in the decision-making process in the Republic of Cyprus.[20] Second, it put forward its own claims on the delineation of the maritime zones in the Eastern Mediterranean, which fully disregarded the exclusive economic zone (EEZ) rights of the Republic of Cyprus, despite that fact that Cyprus had signed EEZ agreements with Egypt, Israel and Lebanon. This move eventually dragged Greece into the confrontation, as there is no delimitation between the EEZs of Greece and Turkey in the Aegean and the Eastern Mediterranean. The political and economic dividend of Greek-Turkish energy cooperation appeared too weak to influence the terms of competition in the Eastern Mediterranean, as sovereignty questions were also involved. The monetization of the reserves remained dependent upon global energy prices and diplomatic relations between the regional actors. It remained up to the various countries' leaders to present energy as a catalyst for peace in the region or become yet another issue which would eventually foment further confrontation. In the end, Turkey increased the political risk of an already hard project further complicating its feasibility.

The acute character of Turkish reactions was linked to the reemergence of atavistic encirclement fears that had haunted Turkey since the 1930s. The fear that Turkey could be 'imprisoned' to Anatolia if Cyprus, Greece, Egypt and Israel further proceeded with their cooperation triggered a retaliatory response.[21] Ignoring Turkey and its interests and bypassing it in regional energy monetization plans was interpreted as a 'provocation' that required a firm response. Turkey's rising self-confidence as an 'order-setting' power in the region could not tolerate any exclusionary policies by other neighbors. Turkey's decision to acquire vessels and other equipment suitable for energy exploration activities and launch its own exploration program was seen as evidence of Turkey's determination to 'spoil the game' (*oyunu bozmak*) of its adversaries.

Disrupting the East Med pipeline project thus became a priority for the Turkish government. This could materialize either by harassing the exploration activities of energy companies, which had acquired licenses from the Cypriot government, or by conducting own exploratory activities within the Cypriot EEZ. Sometimes the Turkish authorities stated that they obtained permission from the authorities of the 'TRNC' to conduct seismic research. Sometimes it claimed that the Turkish survey vessels operated within the Turkish EEZ. While Turkish exploration activities were suspended following EU pressure, Greece's trilateral diplomatic initiatives continued without securing the financial and diplomatic means necessary for the construction of the East Med pipeline. The outbreak of the pandemic and the declining prospects of the hydrocarbon industry in view of the climate crisis and transition to renewable energy further weakened the viability of the East Med pipeline project. A white paper of the US Embassy to Athens in January 2022 pointed at the need to abandon pharaonic hydrocarbon projects and promote renewable energy projects. However, Russia's invasion of Ukraine and the EU's desire to reduce or eliminate its imports of Russian natural gas might help revive prospects for the pipeline.

Imagining Turkey as a maritime state-the Blue Homeland (*Mavi Vatan*) doctrine

Applying ideational elements on the formation of Turkish foreign policy has become an increasingly common feature since the outbreak of the Arab Uprisings and emergence of what many have dubbed a 'neo-Ottoman' approach to foreign policy, a topic taken up by Hakan Yavuz's contribution to this Special Issue.[22] One development that has greatly impaired Greek-Turkish relations is the emergence of a vision of Turkey as a 'maritime state' through the official adoption of the 'Blue Homeland' (*Mavi Vatan*) doctrine.[23] Imagining Turkey as a maritime country and a naval power[24] used to be popular within a marginal group of naval officers who viewed Turkey's future not in the EU but in Eurasia and saw Greece and Cyprus as the biggest obstacles to the development of Turkey's maritime potential.[25] These views coincided with opposition against key features of international maritime law and emphasis on systematic naval armaments. The development of the international law in the Third United Nations Conference on the Law of the Sea culminated with the signature of the United Convention on the Law of the Sea (OS)[26] in Montego Bay (Jamaica) in 1982, which in principle confirmed the rights of islands, as far as the delimitation of maritime zones was concerned. While the vast majority of states ratified the UNCLOS, Turkey maintained its dissent. Turkey refused to sign the UNCLOS due to its provisions concerning the rights of islands regarding territorial waters, the continental shelf, and EEZs. Moreover, to challenge Greek control over the majority of the Aegean Sea, Turkey disputed the sovereignty of Greek islands, islets and rocks across the Aegean. This raised the stakes of Turkey's disputes with Greece as far as their mutual claims over the Aegean continental shelf was concerned, resulting in the Imia/Kardak crisis of January 1996. Such views, however, lost political clout with the advent of the Greek-Turkish rapprochement and the improvement of EU-Turkey relations. They further lost appeal with the 2002 rise of the AKP administration with which this group of officers had deep political differences. As the AKP government eventually clashed with the secularist military elites, key 'Blue Homeland' advocates were accused of conspiring to overthrow the government. In the *Ergenekon* and Balyoz investigations, the leading figures of the movement were arrested and sentenced to long prison terms.

The outbreak of the conflict between the AKP and the Gülen movement, culminating in the attempted coup of July 2016, had a profound effect on civil–military relations as well as on those who had previously convicted of conspiring against the government. Following the failed coup, a purge in the Turkish military led to the rehabilitation of the 'Blue Homeland' officers who had been previously. Emerging as new allies of the Erdoğan administration in his anti-Gülenist purge, they were able to have the *Mavi Vatan* doctrine legitimized.[27] This was followed by a renewed challenge against the UNCLOS principles regarding the rights of islands. As seen in Figure 1, the *Mavi Vatan* doctrine would extend Turkish jurisdiction over a wide swathe of the Eastern Mediterranean and the Aegean Sea, in many cases surrounding Greek islands with 'Turkish' water.

Figure 1. Turkey's 'Blue Homeland' claims. (Source: Wikipedia https://commons.wikimedia.org/wiki/File:Mavi_Vatan.jpg)

The 'Blue Homeland' vision coincided with the AKP's views about Turkey, its position in the Mediterranean, and a more assertive military and defense strategy.[28] As Hakki Taş notes in his article in this Special Issue, aspiring for Turkish leadership in the Middle East through MB mobilization across the Arab Middle East appeared to be a preferred option.[29] This attitude locked Turkey into support for MB-affiliated groups throughout the Middle East, most importantly in Libya and Syria. Turkish support for the MB, while grounded in material interests, also turned to an identity question for the Islamist-oriented AKP government. Notably, identification of the AKP with the Tripoli-based Government of National Accord (GNA) in Libya matched the emergence of that government as the sole international actor that could lend some credibility to the *Mavi Vatan* doctrine. The Libyan-Turkish memorandum of 27 November 2019 regarding their claims to parts of the Mediterranean heralded a new era in the Greek-Turkish dispute over the delimitation of their respective maritime zones.[30] For Turkey and Libya to have a common EEZ border, the EEZs of the islands of Crete, Karpathos, Kasos and Rhodes had been reduced zero. This precluded any possibility of reaching common ground between Greece and Turkey as far as the delimitation of maritime zones was concerned.[31]

Erdoğan's new allies also had an agenda that would inevitably escalate relations with Greece. This became clear in summer 2020 when the dispatch of the Turkish survey vessel *Oruç Reis* to the waters of the Eastern Mediterranean, which both Greece and Turkey consider a part of their EEZ, led to an escalation unprecedented since the beginning of the rapprochement process. Greece responded by sending its own military vessels in the area, and a standoff between the Greek and the Turkish navy ensued. A reported accident involving the Greek frigate *Lemnos* and the Turkish frigate *Kemal Reis* on 12 August 2020 showed how close the two sides had come to military confrontation. It was further feared that the consolidation of 'Blue Homeland' as a feature of Turkish foreign policy strategy would produce very destabilizing effects not only for Greek-Turkish relations but for the whole region as well.[32] Partially in response to Turkey's actions, Greece responded by signing EEZ agreements with Egypt[33] and Italy.[34] These agreements were based on the principles of UNCLOS, while the Greek government at times showed flexibility when it came to the recognition of full EEZ rights to some islands, islets and rocks. In particular the EEZ agreement with Egypt contravened the Libyan-Turkey memorandum, thereby creating an international dispute.[35] Persistent Turkish efforts to seek common understanding with Egypt and Israel regarding claims in the Eastern Mediterranean have failed so far to produce any breakthrough.[36]

The migration crisis and its civilizational twist

A second ideational factor that facilitated the escalation of Greek-Turkish disputes was the migration crisis and its instrumentalization in a comparison of Western and Islamic civilizations. The moral superiority of the Islamic civilization against the Western one has been a favorite trope of Islamist thinkers since the Tanzimat reform.[37] They admitted that the West had acquired a technological edge and had converted it into a power instrument. Nonetheless, conceding the technological superiority of the West was not tantamount with the abandonment of Islamic moral values. On the contrary, importing technological innovations from the West was hoped to reinforce Islamic civilization. This discourse was introduced in the vocabulary of Republican Turkish politics by Necmettin Erbakan. In his 'just order' (*adil düzen*) political program, the founding father of republican-era political Islam reformulated this argument in line with the needs of republican Turkish politics. The moral superiority of the Islamic civilization would be reflected in the 'just order' Turkish Islamists figures aspired to establish in Turkey. While Erbakan became a leader of a coalition government for less than a year in 1996–1997, Erdoğan has managed to consolidate his position in the helm of the Turkish state. While he initially avoided employing Islamist vocabulary in his political statements, this changed with the decline of the democratization process and the realignment of the AKP political alliances. The Arab Uprisings and the decline of Turkey's relations with the West created an opportunity for the use of Islam as a soft power instrument in Turkish foreign policy, a development considered in more detail in the article by Özturk and Baser in this Special Issue.[38]

The 2015–2016 refugee crisis provided Erdoğan an opportunity to demonstrate the superiority of the Islamic civilization, in line with Occidentalist views of far-right Islamist thinkers such as Necip Fazıl Kısakürek.[39] Turkey and the Aegean Sea emerged as one of the key migratory routes for Afghan, Syrian, and other refugees and migrants to Europe. The number of asylum seekers skyrocketed in 2015, when the EU received 1.5 million official asylum applications and 2.4 million non-EU migrants arrived in the EU.[40] This humanitarian crisis became a crisis of governance, as the EU's asylum system performed quite poorly and anti-immigrant views became more pronounced in several countries, threatening both the position of governments as well as the powers and unity of the EU.

On 18 March 2016, Turkey and the EU signed a controversial statement.[41] According to it, Turkey agreed to re-accommodate Syrian refugees who had failed to apply for asylum in Greece or whose application had been otherwise rejected. In return, the EU accepted that Syrian refugees who returned to Turkey from Greece would be resettled in the EU, with a maximum of 72.000 people.[42] The EU also committed to accelerating Turkish citizens' free-visa eligibility and payment of €3 billion to help offset the cost of maintaining displaced persons in Turkey.[43] This agreement succeeded in curbing refugee flows from Turkey to Greece across the Aegean Sea and strongly reducing refugee casualties. However, it tacitly rendered Syrian immigrants a bargaining chip and a burden to be avoided, thus condoning their weaponization against the EU.[44]

In 2019, President Erdoğan himself stated that Turkey came to see refugees as a 'burden', a statement driven in part by the AKP's defeat in several local elections. In these elections, the AKP lost mayorships in several of the biggest cities of the country, including Ankara and Istanbul. In particular, the message taken by the 2019 Istanbul elections was that the refugee crisis rose to a matter of unrest against the AKP in areas where it had previously enjoyed strong support.[45] Crucially, Istanbul's conservative Fatih district was was won by the opposition Republican People's Party's candidate Ekrem İmamoğlu. Fatih, for many years, had been a veritable fortress for the AKP, with its more religiously-oriented population and historical connotations dating to the conquest of Constantinople. Fatih residents reacted to the failure of AKP's refugee policy, as Syrian and Afghan refugees were massively settling in their district. Such election results showed that the perception that the Turkish government took greater care of refugees over its own citizens could be very detrimental to the AKP.[46] Contrary to the initial AKP discourse about traditional Turkish hospitality vis-à-vis refugees, it was also clear that xenophobic sentiment was on the rise.

Additionally, the refugee crisis emerged as a challenge to the EU asylum system and the EU itself. The refugee influx triggered populist and Euroskeptical discourse, which hampered European unity.[47] On 23 June 2016, one year after the peak of the refugee flows to the EU, the Brexit referendum drew on Eurosceptical and anti-immigrant discourses, demonstrating how profitable refugee-bashing could be for European political parties. Furthermore, Turkey also found itself a topic in Brexit campaign, as its democratic backsliding and perceived role as a potential refugee distributor played a great role in boosting xenophobic and Eurosceptic voices.[48]

Pointing at the numbers of refugees that Turkey has hosted, the anti-refugee backlash in many European countries, and the determination of European governments to define migration as a security issue[49], President Erdoğan argued that the hospitality that Turkey had shown to the refuges juxtaposed with the unfriendly attitude of European states and this revealed the superiority of Turkish culture. In early 2020, facing a crisis because of a Russian airstrike against Turkish armed forces in northern Syria, the Turkish government decided to shift public attention to the refugees by orchestrating a crisis on the Greek-Turkish land border.[50] This followed a statement of President Erdoğan in which he declared that Turkey would no longer prevent refugees and immigrants from entering Greece.

What did we say months ago? 'If this goes on like this, we will have no choice but to open the doors.' They were disturbed. They did not believe in what we said. Well, what we did yesterday? We opened the doors.[51]

In late February and early March 2020, thousands of refugees and immigrants were transported to the Greek-Turkish border and were encouraged to cross. Clashes ensued with Greek security forces. This unprecedented development was described as the 'weaponization' of the refugee crisis[52] or 'hybrid warfare' and brought bilateral tensions to a new high and raised concerns about the future of Greek-Turkish relations. Apart from the apparent wish to deflect public opinion's attention from developments in the Syrian civil war, the response of Greek authorities was presented as evidence for the hypocrisy and the moral decline of Western civilization.[53] Western states may be affluent and strong but lack compassion and conscience. These anti-Western attitudes were congruent with the views of the new Eurasianist allies of the Erdoğan administration.[54]

Conclusion

Following twenty years of relative calm and missed opportunities for conflict resolution, Greek-Turkish relations are now more unsettled due to a set of structural and ideational factors. Since Turkey's EU membership ceased to be an instrument for the resolution of Greek-Turkish bilateral disputes, the strategic choices of both countries were bound to influence the future of their relations. Turkey's drifting away from Western institutions[55] and search for strategic autonomy weakened the influence of socialization mechanisms on Turkey which Greece had considered as essential to promote its vision of bilateral partnership. This inevitably changed the nature of bilateral relations. Greece's ability to rebound from its recent political and economic crisis and project itself as the only reliable Western ally in the region also influenced the way bilateral disputes were viewed in Western capitals. As the normative element of the relations between Turkey and the West has declined and as emphasis on the transactional side of EU-Turkey relations grew with emphasis on migration and security affairs – a point also made by Oya Dursun-Özkanca in her article in this Special Issue,[56] Greek-Turkish relations became increasingly vulnerable on shocks emanating from the strategic shifts in the Eastern Mediterranean as well as domestic political factors.

Notes

1. Couloumbis, "Strategic Consensus."
2. Tsakonas, *The Incomplete Breakthrough*, 52–81, and Ker-Lindsay, "The Policies of Greece and Cyprus," 72-74.
3. Öniş and Yılmaz, "Greek-Turkish Rapprochement," 135-140.

4. Kubicek, Parlar Dal, and Oğuzlu, *Turkey's Rise*; Erşen and Köstem, *Turkey's Pivot to Eurasia*; and Öniş and Kutlay, "The Dynamics."
5. Oğuzlu, "Turkish Foreign Policy," 133-135.
6. Kardas, "Quest for Strategic Autonomy," 1-4.
7. Grigoriadis, "Greek-Turkish Relations," 622-626.
8. See Shaheen and Smith, "Greek Court Turns Down Extradition Request for Eight Turkish Officers," and Pamuk, "Greece Harbors Terrorists, Including PKK".
9. Kujawa, "Security Challenges," 102-108.
10. Özkırımlı and Sofos, *Tormented by History*.
11. Roberts, "Gas in the Eastern Mediterranean," 76.
12. Grigoriadis, "Energy Discoveries," and Adamides and Christou, "Can Resolving."
13. Tagliapietra, *Towards a New Eastern Mediterranean Energy Corridor?* 24-27.
14. Grigoriadis, "Energy Discoveries," 127-33, and Tsakiris, "The Importance of East Mediterranean Gas."
15. Ulusoy, "Turkey and Israel," 421-422.
16. Turkey's overall relationship with the Muslim Brotherhood is an important issue in Turkish foreign policy, one taken up in Hakki Taş's contribution to this Special Issue. See Taş, "Erdoğan and the Muslim Brotherhood."
17. İpek and Gür, "Turkey's Isolation," 14-17.
18. See Tziampiris, "The New Eastern Mediterranean," and *The Emergence*.
19. Ellinas, Tzimitras, and Roberts, *Hydrocarbon Developments*, 24.
20. Cubukcuoglu, "Turkey's Muted Response," and Hadjicostis, "Cyprus Blasts 'Pirate State' Turkey's New Gas Drilling Bid".
21. Demiryol, "Between Security and Prosperity."
22. See also Yavuz, *Nostalgia for the Empire*, as well as Hintz, *Identity Politics Inside Out*.
23. Denizeau, "Mavi Vatan."
24. On this see, Yaycı, "Doğu Akdeniz'de Yetki Alanlarının Paylaşılması," and "Doğu Akdeniz'de deniz yetki alanlarının sınırlandırılmasında"; Başeren, *Doğu Akdeniz'de Hukuk*; and Öztürk and Başeren, "The exclusive economic zone debates."
25. Çandar, *Turkey's Blue Homeland Doctrine*.
26. United Nations, *United Nations Convention on the Law of the Sea (UNCLOS)*.
27. Tol and Taspinar, "Erdogan's Turn."
28. Yeşiltaş, "Deciphering."
29. Taş, "Erdoğan and the Muslim Brotherhood."
30. Kancı, "Mavi Vatan'ı savunmak."
31. Cubukcuoglu, "A Maritime Dispute."
32. Gingeras, "Blue Homeland, " and Erdemir and Kowalski, "'Blue Homeland'".
33. Hellenic Parliament, *Agreement between the Government of the Hellenic Republic and the Government of the Arab Republic of Egypt*.
34. Hellenic Parliament, *Agreement between the Government of the Hellenic Republic and the Government of the Italian Republic*.
35. Grigoriadis and Belke, "UNCLOS."
36. Bassist, "Emekli Türk amiralin."
37. Erbakan, *Milli Görüş*, Uzer, "Conservative narrative.": and Uzer, "Glorification of the Past."
38. See also Ozturk, "Islam and Foreign Policy."

39. Duran and Aydın, "Competing Occidentalisms," 485–491.
40. UNHCR, *Syria Regional Refugee Response*.
41. European Council, "EU-Turkey Statement."
42. Gatti, "The EU-Turkey Statement."
43. The Facility for Refugees in Turkey is a fund to coordinate and administer the aid for the refugees resettled in Turkey by the EU.
44. Himmrich, "A 'Hybrid Threat'?" 6.
45. Meanwhile, Turkish opposition writers tried to place the Syrian refugees on the securitization agenda. See, for example, Zileli, "Türkiye'nin en acil beka sorunu: Suriyeliler!..".
46. Esen and Gumuscu, "Killing Competitive Authoritarianism," 321–327.
47. Scipioni, "Failing Forward."
48. Kaya, "Right-wing populism," 16–18.
49. Adamson, "Crossing Borders."
50. Gürsel, "Why Ankara's,".
51. "Son dakika haberleri! Erdoğan, "'Kapatmayacağız' deyip ekledi: Bugün 30 bini bulabilir!".
52. Greenhill, *Weapons of Mass Migration*, and Greenhill, "Migration as a Weapon."
53. Aydin, "Between Occidentalism and the Global Left."
54. Çolakoğlu, "The Rise of Eurasianism."
55. Dursun-Özkanca, *Turkey-West Relations*.
56. Dursun-Özkanca, "An Examination."

Disclosure statement

No potential conflict of interest was reported by the author(s).

ORCID

Ioannis N. Grigoriadis http://orcid.org/0000-0003-0882-6125

Bibliography

Adamides, C., and O. Christou. "Can Resolving Cyprus Hold the Key to Regional Energy Cooperation." *Turkish Policy Quarterly* 15, no. 2 (2016): 85–94.
Adamson, F. B. "Crossing Borders: International Migration and National Security." *International Security* 31, no. 1 (2006): 165–199.
Aydin, C. "Between Occidentalism and the Global Left: Islamist Critiques of the West in Turkey." *Comparative Studies of South Asia, Africa and the Middle East* 26, no. 3 (2006): 446–461.
Başeren, S. H. *Doğu Akdeniz'de Hukuk ve Siyaset*. Ankara: Ankara Üniversitesi Siyasal Bilgiler Fakültesi Yayınları, 2013.
Bassist, R. "Emekli Türk amiralin İsrail'de yayınlanan makalesi ne anlama geliyor?" *Al-Monitor*, December 8, 2020.
Çandar, C. "Turkey's Blue Homeland Doctrine: Signaling Perpetual Conflict in the Mediterranean and Rough Waters Ahead." *The Turkey Analyst* (Stockholm), August 26, 2020.
Çolakoğlu, S. "The rise of Eurasianism in Turkish foreign policy: Can Turkey change its pro-Western orientation." Washington: Middle East Institute, 2019.
Couloumbis, T. "Strategic Consensus in Greek Domestic and Foreign Policy Since 1974." In *Greece and The New Balkans. Challenges and Opportunities*, edited by V. Coufoudakis, H. J. Psomiades, and A. Gerolymatos, 407–422. New York: Pella, 1999.
Cubukcuoglu, S. S. "Turkey's Muted Response to Cyprus' Offshore Drilling Reflects a New Diplomatic Reality." Washington: Atlantic Council, January 2022.
Cubukcuoglu, S. S. "A Maritime Dispute in the Mediterranean: Assessing the Greece-Turkey Relationship Through the Lens of Neorealism." *Fletcher Forum of World Affairs* 45 (2021): 65–74.
Demiryol, T. "Between Security and Prosperity: Turkey and the Prospect of Energy Cooperation in the Eastern Mediterranean." *Turkish Studies* 20, no. 3 (2019): 442–464.
Denizeau, A. "Mavi Vatan, the 'Blue Homeland': The Origins, Influences and Limits of an Ambitious Doctrine for Turkey." *Études de l'IFRI*. Paris: IFRI, April 2021.
Duran, B., and C. Aydın. "Competing Occidentalisms of Modern Islamist Thought: Necip Fazıl Kısakürek and Nurettin Topçu on Christianity, the West and Modernity." *The Muslim World* 103, no. 4 (2013): 479–500.
Dursun-Özkanca, O. *Turkey-West Relations: The Politics of Intra-Alliance Opposition*. Cambridge: Cambridge University Press, 2019.
Dursun-Özkanca, O. "An Examination of the Underlying Dynamics of Turkey-European Union Relations Through the Lenses of International Relations Theory." *Turkish Studies* 23, no. 5 (2022). forthcoming.
Ellinas, C., H. Tzimitras, and J. Roberts. *Hydrocarbon Developments in the Eastern Mediterranean: The Case for Pragmatism*. Washington, DC: Atlantic Council, 2016.
Erbakan, N. *Milli Görüş*. Istanbul: Dergâh Yayınları, 1975.
Erdemir, A., and P. Kowalski. "'Blue Homeland' and the Irredentist Future of Turkish Foreign Policy." *War on the Rocks*, September 30, 2020. https://warontherocks.com/2020/09/blue-homeland-and-the-irredentist-future-of-turkish-foreign-policy/.
Erdoğan, C. "'Kapatmayacağız' deyip ekledi: Bugün 30 bini bulabilir!" *Milliyet*, February 29, 2020.

Erşen, E. and S. Köstem, eds., *Turkey's Pivot to Eurasia: Geopolitics and Foreign Policy in a Changing World Order*. Abingdon: Routledge, 2019.

Esen, B., and S. Gumuscu. "Killing Competitive Authoritarianism Softly: The 2019 Local Elections in Turkey." *South European Society and Politics* 24, no. 3 (2019): 317–342.

European Council. "*EU-Turkey statement, 18 March* 2016." Press Release, March 18, 2016. https://www.consilium.europa.eu/en/press/press-releases/2016/03/18/eu-turkey-statement/.

Gatti, M. "The EU-Turkey Statement: A Treaty That Violates Democracy (Part 1 of 2)," *EJIL:Talk!* (Blog of the European Journal of International Law), April 18 2016. https://www.ejiltalk.org/the-eu-turkey-statement-a-treaty-that-violates-democracy-part-1-of-2/.

Gingeras, R. "Blue Homeland: The Heated Politics Behind Turkey's New Maritime Strategy." *War on the Rocks*, June 2, 2020. https://warontherocks.com/2020/06/blue-homeland-the-heated-politics-behind-turkeys-new-maritime-strategy/.

Greenhill, K. M. *Weapons of Mass Migration: Forced Displacement, Coercion, and Foreign Policy*. Ithaca, NY: Cornell University Press, 2010.

Greenhill, K. "Migration as a Weapon in Theory and in Practice." *Military Review* 96, no. 6 (2016): 23–36.

Grigoriadis, I. N. "The Unripe Fruits of Rapprochement: Greek-Turkish Relations in the Post-Helsinki Era." *International Journal* 67, no. 1 (2012): 119–313.

Grigoriadis, I. N. "Energy Discoveries in the Eastern Mediterranean: Conflict or Cooperation?" *Middle East Policy* 21, no. 3 (2014): 124–133.

Grigoriadis, I. N. "Greek-Turkish Relations." In *The Oxford Handbook of Modern Greek Politics*, edited by K. Featherstone, and D.A. Sotiropoulos, 613–628. Oxford: Oxford University Press, 2020.

Grigoriadis, I. N., and L. T. Belke. "UNCLOS and the Delimitation of Maritime Zones in the Eastern Mediterranean." *ELIAMEP Policy Brief* (Athens) no. 131 (2020).

Gürsel, K. "Why Ankara's Syrian Refugee Threat Has Lost Its Impact." *Al-Monitor*, March 19, 2020.

Hadjicostis, M. "Cyprus Blasts 'Pirate State' Turkey's New Gas Drilling Bid." *AP News*, January 19, 2020. https://apnews.com/article/5caea09c1fdaeb2f0212cdfd8d8d402d.

Hellenic Parliament. *Agreement Between the Government of the Hellenic Republic and the Government of the Arab Republic of Egypt of the Delineation of the Exclusive Economic Zone of the Two States (in Greek and English)*. Athens, 2020.

Hellenic Parliament. *Agreement Between the Government of the Hellenic Republic and the Government of the Italian Republic on the Delineation of their Respective Maritime Zones (in Greek and English)*. Athens, 2020.

Himmrich, J. "A 'Hybrid Threat'? European Militaries and Migration." Paper Presented at the LSE Ideas, Dahrendorf Forum Working Paper, 2018.

Hintz, L. *Identity Politics Inside Out: National Identity Contestation and Foreign Policy in Turkey*. Oxford: Oxford University Press, 2018.

İpek, P., and V. T. Gür. "Turkey's Isolation from the Eastern Mediterranean Gas Forum: Ideational Mechanisms and Material Interests in Energy Politics." *Turkish Studies* 23, no. 1 (2022): 1–30.

Kancı, M. A. "Mavi Vatan'ı savunmak." *Anadolu Ajansı*, November 26, 2019. https:/www.aa.com.tr/tr/analiz/mavi-vatan-i-savunmak/1655862.

Kardas, S. "Quest for Strategic Autonomy Continues, or How to Make Sense of Turkey's New Wave." *On Turkey*. Washington DC: German Marshall Fund of the United States, November 28, 2011. http://www.gmfus.org/wpcontent/blogs.dir/1/files_mf/1323287254_magicfields_attachment__1_1.pdf.

Kaya, A. "Right-wing Populism and Islamophobism in Europe and Their Impact on Turkey–EU Relations." *Turkish Studies* 21, no. 1 (2020): 1–28.

Ker-Lindsay, J. "The Policies of Greece and Cyprus Towards Turkey's EU Accession." *Turkish Studies* 8, no. 1 (2007): 71–83.

Kubicek, P., E. Parlar Dal, and H. T. Oğuzlu, eds., *Turkey's Rise as an Emerging Power* London: Routledge, 2015.

Kujawa, K. "Security Challenges in Relations Between Turkey and the European Union." *European Research Studies* 24 (2021): 98–111.

Oğuzlu, H. T. "Turkish Foreign Policy in a Changing World Order." *All Azimuth: A Journal of Foreign Policy and Peace* 9, no. 1 (2020): 127–139.

Öniş, Z., and M. Kutlay. "The Dynamics of Emerging Middle-Power Influence in Regional and Global Governance: The Paradoxical Case of Turkey." *Australian Journal of International Affairs* 71, no. 2 (2017): 164–183.

Öniş, Z., and Ş Yılmaz. "Greek-Turkish Rapprochement: Rhetoric or Reality?" *Political Science Quarterly* 123, no. 1 (2008): 123–149.

Özkırımlı, U., and S. A. Sofos. *Tormented by History: Nationalism in Greece and Turkey*. London: Hurst, 2008.

Ozturk, A. E. "Islam and Foreign Policy: Turkey's Ambivalent Religious Soft Power in the Authoritarian Turn." *Religions* 12, no. 1 (2021): 38. https://www.mdpi.com/2077-1444/12/1/38.

Öztürk, B., and S. H. Başeren. "The Exclusive Economic Zone Debates in the Eastern Mediterranean Sea and Fisheries." *Journal of Black Sea/Mediterranean Environment* 14, no. 2 (2008): 77–83.

Pamuk, D. "Greece Harbors Terrorists, Including PKK: Turkey." *Anadolu Agency*, April 10, 2021. https://www.aa.com.tr/en/europe/greece-harbors-terrorists-including-pkk-turkey/2204045.

Roberts, J. "Gas in the Eastern Mediterranean: Great Promise but no Early Answers." *European Energy Journal* 4 (2014): 71.

Scipioni, M. "Failing Forward in EU Migration Policy? EU Integration After the 2015 Asylum and Migration Crisis." *Journal of European Public Policy* 25, no. 9 (2018): 1357–1375.

Shaheen, K., and H. Smith. "Greek Court Turns Down Extradition Request for Eight Turkish Officers." *The Guardian*. January 26, 2017.

Tagliapietra, S. *Towards a new Eastern Mediterranean Energy Corridor? Natural gas Developments Between Market Opportunities and Geopolitical Risks*. Milan: Fondazione ENI Enrico Mattei, 2013.

Taş, H. "Erdoğan and the Muslim Brotherhood: An Outside-In Approach to Turkish Foreign Policy in the Middle East." *Turkish Studies* 23, no. 5 (2022). forthcoming.

Tol, G., and O. Taspinar. "Erdogan's Turn to the Kemalists: How It Will Shape Turkish Foreign Policy." *Foreign Affairs*, October 27, 2016. https://www.foreignaffairs.com/articles/turkey/2016-10-27/erdogans-turn-kemalists.

Tsakiris, T. "The Importance of East Mediterranean gas for EU Energy Security: The Role of Cyprus, Israel and Egypt." *Cyprus Review* 30, no. 1 (2018): 25–50.

Tsakonas, P. *The Incomplete Breakthrough in Greek-Turkish Relations: Grasping Greece's Socialization Strategy*. Basingstoke: Palgrave Macmillan, 2010.

Tziampiris, A. *The Emergence of Israeli-Greek Cooperation*. Cham: Springer, 2014.

Tziampiris, A. "The New Eastern Mediterranean as a Regional Subsystem." In *The New Eastern Mediterranean: Theory, Politics and States in a Volatile Era*, edited by S. N. Litsas, and A. Tziampiris, 1–30. Cham: Springer, 2019.

Ulusoy, K. "Turkey and Israel: Changing Patterns of Alliances in the Eastern Mediterranean." *Journal of Balkan and Near Eastern Studies* 22, no. 3 (2020): 415–430.

UNHCR. "Syria Regional Refugee Response." Accessed June 28, 2020. https://data2.unhcr.org/en/situations/syria.

United Nations. *United Nations Convention on the Law of the Sea (UNCLOS)*. Montego Bay: United Nations, 1982.

Uzer, U. "Glorification of the Past as a Political Tool: Ottoman History in Contemporary Turkish Politics." *The Journal of the Middle East and Africa* 9, no. 4 (2018): 339–357.

Uzer, U. "Conservative Narrative: Contemporary neo-Ottomanist Approaches in Turkish Politics." *Middle East Critique* 29, no. 3 (2020): 275–290.

Yavuz, M. H. *Nostalgia for the Empire: The Politics of neo-Ottomanism*. Oxford: Oxford University Press, 2020.

Yaycı, C. "Doğu Akdeniz'de deniz yetki alanlarının sınırlandırılmasında Libya'nın rolü ve etkisi." *Güvenlik Stratejileri Dergisi* 7, no. 14 (2011): 17–41.

Yaycı, C. "Doğu Akdeniz'de Yetki Alanlarının Paylaşılması Sorunu Ve Türkiye." *Bilge Strateji* 4, no. 6 (2012): 1–70.

Yeşiltaş, M. "Deciphering Turkey's Assertive Military and Defense Strategy." *Insight Turkey* 22, no. 3 (2020): 89–114.

Zileli, Ü. "Türkiye'nin en acil beka sorunu: Suriyeliler!..," *Sözcü*, July 23, 2019.

Index

accession negotiations 99, 101–103, 109
actors 7–8, 42, 59–61, 80–82, 122, 125, 146
Adalet ve Kalkinma Partisi (AKP) 8–10, 15–32, 37–39, 41–48, 50–51, 58–59, 63–67, 69–72, 78–82, 85–86, 88, 92–93, 100, 129–133, 147, 166–169
Aegean Sea 165–166, 168–169
African Expansion Action Plan 69
alliance theory 132
Arab Spring 4, 16–17, 26–27, 42, 69, 78, 88
Arab Uprisings 78, 81, 85, 87–88, 91, 159, 163, 165, 168
al-Assad, Bashar 90
Austria 62, 66–67

Bagdonas, Özlem Demirtas 7
Bahrain 87, 123, 127
Balkans 23, 26, 30, 39, 41, 50, 58–59, 63–65, 67–68, 70–72, 147
Balta, Evren 50
bilateral disputes 159–161, 170
Black Sea 124, 133
Blue Homeland (Mavi Vatan) doctrine 11, 161, 165–167

Caucasus regions 124–125, 133
Cold War 3–4, 19–20, 22, 30–31, 38, 63–64, 71, 83–85, 123, 140–142
conservative populism 39, 45–47, 49
conspiracy thinking 9, 49–50
constructivism 2–3, 7, 9–10, 61, 129, 131–134, 141, 150
constructivist expectations 146
constructivist explanations 11, 129, 134
contemporary Turkey-EU relations 99, 104
Cyprus 4, 8, 10, 20, 25, 99, 101, 103–104, 107, 128–129, 159, 161–165; problem 106–107, 158–159, 161–162, 164

Davutoğlu, Ahmet 8, 23–24, 26
domestic factors 79, 107, 133–134
domestic insecurity 22
duality 17, 22

Eastern Mediterranean crisis 158–170
Eastern Mediterranean system 128
East Med trilateral diplomacy 162–165
Egypt 16, 50, 81–83, 87, 90–91, 123–124, 127–128, 131, 134, 162–164, 167
Erdoğan, Tayyip 5, 16, 18–19, 22–32, 38–39, 49–50, 72, 78–79, 81–83, 89, 91–92, 130–132, 149, 151–152, 167–168
Erşen, Emre 148
Eurasia 59, 71–72, 165
Eurasianism 148–150
Europeanization stage 25
EU-Turkey relationship 100, 102–105, 107–108, 110, 159–160, 162, 166, 170

foreign policy 2–4, 6–9, 15–26, 28–32, 37–40, 42–43, 45–51, 57–61, 63–66, 72–73, 78–80, 85–87, 90–91, 99–101, 104–109, 129–131, 141–150, 152, 159, 165; issues 50, 109; militarization of 22, 28–29; tools 58, 60–61, 86

global politics 11, 42, 57–59, 61
Görmez, Mehmet 62
Government of National Accord (GNA) 167
Greece 46, 102–103, 105–106, 122, 127–128, 131, 158–160, 162–165, 167–170
Greek-Turkish disputes 158, 160–161, 167–168
Greek-Turkish relations 158–160, 162, 167, 170
Gül, Abdullah 22
Gülen, Fethullah 130

INDEX

Gülen Movement 63–67, 69–70, 166
Gulmez, Didem Buhari 132

Ikhwan ideology 80
imaginary reality 63
independent foreign policy 21, 109, 141–142
intermediary actors 59
international relations theory 2, 7, 11, 99
intra-alliance opposition theory 132
Iran 26–27, 31, 82, 84, 87, 122–123, 125–127, 130, 132, 148
irresponsibility 46–50
Islamic civilization 16, 168
Islamic Communities 39, 57
Islamic Council of Eurasia 71–72
Islamism 24, 39, 41, 71, 80–81, 147–148
Islamization 22, 26, 63
Israel 26, 51, 81, 86–87, 123–124, 127–128, 134, 162–164, 167
Ivanov, Mihail 64

Kemalism 7–8, 19, 22, 41–43
Khashoggi, Jamal 27
Khramchikhin, Aleksandr 150
Kisakürek, Necip Fazil 47
Kubicek, Paul 10

Lesser, Ian 24

middle powers 4–6, 123, 141
migration crisis 168
Mukherjee, Rohan 30
multipolarity 5, 10, 125, 141, 143
multipolar system 123–125
Muslim Brotherhood 10, 16, 26–27, 42, 78, 127–131, 144, 161

national identity 16–19, 22–23, 30
nationalism 29, 39–40, 63, 147–148, 150
NATO 20, 24, 30–31, 121–122, 124–125, 128, 131, 133, 141, 143, 148, 152
neoclassical realism 6–7, 10, 15, 19, 79–80, 83, 93, 101, 104–105, 123, 133
neo-colonialism 69–70
neo-Ottomanism 9, 15, 18, 63, 69–70, 145, 147–148
neo-realism 2–4, 6–7, 10, 60, 104–105, 132–134, 142–144, 146
neorealist explanations 123
neo-realist hypothesis 142–143
non-state actors 9, 60–61, 72, 86, 93, 125

Özal, Turgut 41, 142

parochialism 80
populism 37–38, 40–42, 44–45, 51
populist foreign policy 37, 39
post-cold war foreign policy 20–22
post-national identity 18–19
power 3–6, 9, 16, 18, 23–25, 29–30, 43–46, 48–49, 61, 71–73, 82–83, 86–87, 92–93, 125, 141–148; maximization 80, 84
pragmatism 79, 105, 140

Qatar 27, 46, 87–88, 123, 127, 131

Ramadan, Tariq 78
regional sub-systemic factors 104, 107
relative power 91, 105, 108, 142
religion 9, 57–69, 71–73, 80, 150
religious institutions 61, 64, 66–72
religious organizations 58, 62–64, 66, 72–73
religious services 62, 66, 71–72
religious soft power 61, 67, 72
religious structures 62, 67, 70
Russia 2, 5–6, 10–11, 24, 28–31, 83–84, 86, 123–126, 128, 140, 142–152, 159, 163
Russian-Turkish relations 140–152

S-400 system 131–134
Saudi Arabia 27, 51, 82–83, 86–88, 92, 123, 127, 131, 134, 150
security maximization 86
shared grievances 10, 140, 144
sociopolitical origins, Turkish foreign policy 19–20
soft power 6, 8, 61, 73
state bureaucracy 42–44, 49, 82, 92
strategic autonomy 9, 15, 17–18, 22, 28–32, 84, 93, 132, 147, 159, 170
structural dynamics 140
sub-systemic factors 83
Syria 5, 10, 27–29, 31–32, 84, 86–87, 102, 104, 106–107, 122–124, 126–128, 130, 133–134, 143–146, 148–150
systemic factors 79–80, 83, 104
systemic incentives 79, 85–86, 91, 101

Taş, Hakki 44, 49, 167
thin-centered ideology 38, 40
transnational politics 57
Turkey-EU Relations 99–102, 108, 110
Turkey's power projection 88–91
Turkish conservative populist discourse 43–49
Turkish Cypriots 29, 164
Turkish-Islamist ideology 45–46

Turkish-Russian relationship 140–143, 145–146, 148, 150–151

UAE 27, 80, 84, 87, 92, 123, 127, 131, 134
UK 68–69
Ukraine 11, 30–31, 92, 111, 122–124, 149, 151–152, 163, 165
United States (US) 4–5, 10–11, 16, 20, 28–32, 58, 68–69, 80, 83–87, 104–106, 121, 123–130, 132–134, 143, 145–146, 159–160
unit-level variables 80, 91–92, 104

US-Turkish relations/Turkish–US relations 121–134

values 61, 64, 108, 145–147
Verbeek, Bertjan 39–40, 42
victimhood 9, 37, 39, 45, 47, 49

Western Europe 58–59, 65–67, 70–71

Yilmaz, Zafer 45–47

Zaslove, Andrej 39–40, 42
Zhelev, Zhelyu 64

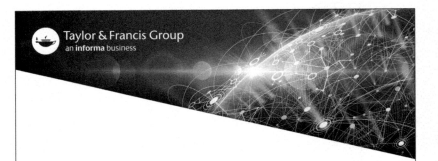